Life in a Muslim Uzbek Village

Cotton Farming After Communism

FIRST EDITION

RUSSELL ZANCA
Northeastern Illinois University

WADSWORTH
CENGAGE Learning

Australia • Brazil • Japan • Korea • Mexico • Singapore • Spain • United Kingdom • United States

WADSWORTH
CENGAGE Learning

Life in a Muslim Uzbek Village: Cotton Farming After Communism, First Edition
Russell Zanca

Acquisitions Editor: Erin Mitchell

Development Editor: Lin Gaylord

Consulting Editor: Janice E. Stockard

Editorial Assistant: Pamela Simon

Marketing Manager: Andrew Keay

Marketing Communications Manager: Tami Strang

Content Project Management: Pre-PressPMG

Print Buyer: Karen Hunt

Permissions Editor: Robyn Young

Production Service: Pre-PressPMG

Cover Image: Russell Zanca

Compositor: Pre-PressPMG

For product information and technology assistance, contact us at **Cengage Learning Customer Sales & Support, 1-800-354-9706**
For permission to use material from this text or product, submit a request online at **cengage.com/permissions**
Further permissions can be emailed to
permissionrequest@cengage.com

Library of Congress Control Number: 2009943655

ISBN-13: 978-0-495-09281-0

ISBN-10: 0-495-09281-9

Wadsworth
20 Davis Drive
Belmont, CA 94002
USA

Cengage Learning is a leading provider of customized learning solutions with office locations around the globe, including Singapore, the United Kingdom, Australia, Mexico, Brazil, and Japan. Locate your local office at:
international.cengage.com/region

Cengage Learning products are represented in Canada by Nelson Education, Ltd.

For your course and learning solutions, visit
academic.cengage.com

Purchase any of our products at your local college store or at our preferred online store **www.CengageBrain.com**

Printed in the United States of America
1 2 3 4 5 6 7 13 12 11 10

For my mother, Barbara Gale Zanca, a truly loving person who always taught me to ask more of myself.

Contents

Foreword

ABOUT THE SERIES

These case studies in cultural anthropology are designed for students in beginning and intermediate courses in the social sciences, to bring them insights into the richness and complexity of human life as it is lived in different ways, in different places. The authors are men and woman who have lived in the societies they write about and who are professionally trained as observers and interpreters of human behavior. Also, the authors are teachers; in their writing, the needs of the student reader remain foremost. It is our belief that when an understanding of ways of life very different from one's own is gained, abstractions and generalizations about the human condition become meaningful.

The scope and character of the series have changed constantly since we published the first case studies in 1960, in keeping with our intention to represent anthropology as it is. We are concerned with the ways in which human groups and communities are coping with the massive changes wrought in their physical and sociopolitical environments in recent decades. We are also concerned with the ways in which established cultures have solved life's problems. Finally, we want to include representation of the various modes of communication and emphasis that are being formed and re-formed as anthropology itself changes.

We think of this series as an instructional series, intended for use in the classroom. We, the editors, have always used case studies in our teaching, whether for beginning students or for advanced graduate students. We start with case studies, whether from our own series or from elsewhere, and weave our way into theory, and then turn again to cases. For us, they are the grounding of our discipline.

ABOUT THE AUTHOR

Russell Zanca received his PhD in anthropology from the University of Illinois at Urbana–Champaign, and is currently Associate Professor of Anthropology at Northeastern Illinois University. His interests in Uzbekistan go back to his first encounters with Soviet immigrants from Uzbekistan in Queens, New York, in the early 1980s. Russell began working in Uzbekistan in 1992 and has since made about 10 research trips there for various lengths of time. His research interests have changed over the years from rural household economies and the Soviet experience to religious practice and activism, oral history of the early Soviet period, cookery, and, most recently, labor migration. Russell's first book, *Everyday Life in Central Asia Past and Present,* was co-edited with Dr. Jeff Sahadeo of Carleton University, Russell's next book project focuses on oral history and the collectivization of agriculture in Uzbekistan during the 1920s and 1930s. He is the proud father of Joseph and Miranda, and loves coaching football in his spare time.

ABOUT THIS CASE STUDY

This newest addition to the CSCA Series is a welcome contribution to the ethnography of Central Asia, a critical world region that is—unfortunately—largely unfamiliar to many American students. Russell Zanca, the anthropologist who brings us *Life in a Muslim Uzbek Village: Cotton Farming After Communism*, set out to live and conduct his anthropological research among the people of one rural village in Uzbekistan. His goal was to learn about village culture and the lives of village residents by focusing his observations and interview questions on people's daily lives and struggles in newly independent Uzbekistan. In his interviews, however, Zanca also sought to tap people's memories and accounts of their earlier lives under communism, before the collapse of the U.S.S.R. in 1991. How do their new lives as villagers in an independent Uzbekistan compare with their past lives under communism? In what ways do those earlier experiences still affect people's outlook today and continue to shape their expectations and aspirations? Throughout his beautifully written ethnography, Zanca skillfully employs an historical lens both to provide fuller context for understanding culture change in Boburkent—and to illuminate the origins of the shared meanings and world of rural villagers in Uzbekistan today.

Zanca began his extended period of residence and ethnographic fieldwork in Boburkent in the mid-1990s and continued to visit and conduct interviews throughout this first decade of the twenty-first century. His prolonged co-residence and sustained fieldwork enable Zanca to bring us a near-insider's perspective on the major political events that have shaped the lives of villagers in Boburkent. One constant across the shifting political terrain of the last two centuries has been villagers' reliance on cotton farming to support their families and cultural life. As the primary economic endeavor, cotton cultivation, along with the agricultural rhythms and work associated with it, became linked to other arenas of village life, including weddings and festivals, Islamic practice, family organization and gender hierarchy, and patterns of consumption within the home and marketplace. Zanca focuses his ethnographic lens on each of these areas in turn, providing engaging accounts of the multiple dimensions of village cultural life. Because politics, economic subsistence strategies, and culture have become intimately intertwined with the cotton industry in Uzbekistan, Zanca is able to explore changes in all of these areas as he maps out changes in the organization and productivity of cotton farming. Along the way, he seeks to answer key questions: What does cotton cultivation mean to people in Boburkent—and how will the changing market and price for cotton affect the villagers and their culture? In this post-Soviet era, what are the repercussions of intensifying globalization and increasing transmigration for the residents of Boburkent?

A major theme emerging across the chapters of *Life in a Muslim Uzbek Village* is the social construction and significance of Uzbek identity. Just *when* the villagers of Boburkent (and other people settled in this region) became first known as "Uzbeks" and began to self-identify as such is a question that Zanca sets out to investigate. He takes students along on this journey of discovery, teasing from villagers' accounts and historical sources the multiple origins and dimensions of Uzbek identity. As students will come to appreciate in *Life in a Muslim Uzbek Village*, identities emerge through complex processes over time. Among the diverse contributions to the formation of Uzbek identity tracked by Zanca are those made, for example, by historical nomadic and pastoral populations, by conquering tribes and empire builders, and by local people's religious practice, Islam. Zanca places particular emphasis on the role played by power and politics in the shaping of Uzbek identity in both historical and contemporary times.

Into his rich ethnographic account of life in a rural Uzbek village, Zanca skillfully weaves discussion and reflection on the practice of fieldwork. These excursions into anthropological method are brief and artfully placed at just the right junctures in his ethnographic narrative. Often highly reflective (and sometimes humorous), these occasional methodological discussions provide students with insight into how ethnographic information is obtained during fieldwork: in answer to interview questions, embedded in stories, pieced together from life histories, based on direct observation, or through a combination of these techniques. In several instances, Zanca provides excerpted portions of conversations between himself and a villager to illustrate the different challenges of doing good fieldwork. Among other things, these conversations enable students to appreciate the way in which an interviewee's situation—shaped by characteristics such as age, gender, and economic and political status—influences that person's perspective, and hence the information provided to the anthropologist. In addition, these conversations virtually take students "into the field," giving them privileged insight into the importance of local relationships and rapport (established by the anthropologist) both for conducting productive interviews and for constructing ethnographic accounts that present diverse points of view.

Students in both introductory and upper-division anthropology classes will find Zanca's case study a compelling ethnography that sheds new light on village life in Central Asia in the twenty-first century. With *Life in a Muslim Uzbek Village: Cotton Farming after Communism*, Zanca opens a window onto a people and a place in an era of intensifying globalization and rapid cultural change. We invite you to join Russell Zanca in the following chapters as he becomes acquainted with the men and women who live in the village of Boburkent and comes to know their everyday struggles to preserve (or re-invent) productive, meaningful lives.

Janice E. Stockard and George Spindler
CSCA Series Editors

Preface

This book contains three maps that should help readers gain something of an idea of where Uzbekistan is in relation to the rest of Asia and Europe as well as where Boburkent lies in relation to Uzbekistan itself. My colleague, Dr. Dennis Grammenos, kindly drew up a general map of Eurasia (including the territory of the former U.S.S.R.), a map of the fertile and historically significant Ferghana Valley (shared by three Central Asian countries), and a map of the Amir Temur collective farm village of Boburkent.

While cotton farming serves as a key part of this ethnography, the real story of this anthropological work is the erosion of the Communist political order and socialist way of life for Uzbek villagers, who had lived as citizens of the Soviet Union since the 1920s. My work here neither endorses one political order over another nor spells out what the solution to the erosion of the old way of life should be. Rather, I have tried to inform readers what these villagers think about the passing of socialism and the turn to an unscripted capitalism. Since 1991 (the year Uzbekistan declared itself an independent republic or nation-state), the post-Communist political leadership has maintained firm and domineering control over the formerly state-administered collective farms (*kolkhozes*), but it does not support rural life with the same kinds of relatively generous welfare benefits as were offered by the Soviet regime.

Most Americans knew relatively little about life in the Soviet Union during the Cold War (1945–1991), and there was a general inclination to think of that vast country as Russia. Russia, indeed, is a vast country—but the Soviet Union also contained large territories whose peoples and cultures were neither Russian nor Slavic, but rather Turkic or Persian, among other ethnicities. California-sized Uzbekistan was one such part of that defunct country. And when I first began working in Uzbekistan in 1992, even fellow anthropologists had little familiarity with the place. In a sense, then, this is really the first ethnographic work that aims to introduce American students to Uzbek culture in a wide and accessible sense.

More than familiarizing readers with an unknown people for its own sake, however, my work provides a more practical understanding of how the processes of economic degradation at the level of this small Uzbek village have international implications—namely, in the form of labor migration. This phenomenon embodies many of the trends associated with globalization today. While labor migration is an important option for poor farming people from Honduras to Uzbekistan, it is also fraught with all kinds of tensions and potentially destabilizing consequences for the global order, mainly because migrants are vulnerable to abuse and because people in the countries receiving migrants sometimes resent and fear them, often on very unfounded but profound bases.

Where the sort of people with whom I lived and who are depicted in this book end up in the coming years remains a huge unknown. Nevertheless, I do hope this work helps students become aware of how people live in Uzbekistan, why they hold the opinions they do, and why the undertake the actions they do.

My research in Central Asia began in the early 1990s and has continued ever since. The completion of this book would not have been possible without substantial grants from the International Relations and Exchanges Board, the Social Science Research Council, the National Council for Eurasian and East European Research, and the American Council for Teachers of Russian. My writing was greatly facilitated by the annual Summer Workshop of the Russian East European and Eurasian Center at the University of Illinois at Urbana–Champaign.

On a personal level, so many people have helped contribute to my research, formulate my ideas, and work at my writing that I hardly know where to begin in thanking them—but I'll try. Wadsworth staff have shown me inspiration and professionalism as they worked patiently and amiably with me throughout this process. George Spindler played an essential mentoring role in helping me craft my material into a readable book for introductory students, and I am very grateful for his vision and suggestions. Janice Stockard furnished much needed encouragement as she helped me to refine ideas and edit content significantly in the final stages of preparation. My mentors, Demitri Shimkin, F. K. Lehman, Mahir Saul, Uli Schamiloglu, and Anatoly Khazanov, gave me intellectual inspiration of the highest caliber. My ex-wife, Monica Eng, helped me pioneer through the first long stretch of fieldwork in 1993–1994. Friends such as Marianne Kamp, Adeeb Khalid, Charles Steinwedel, David Abramson, Hursandali Darmonov, David Tyson, Steve LeVine, Alan Johnston, Najmiddin Nasafi, Eric Sievers, Stephen Hegarty, Saodat Kholmatova, Farkhod Nosirov, Stephen Kercher, Nicholas Kilzer, Richard Hallett, Shahrzad Mahootian, Firuza Nouritova, Elyor Karimov, and Alisher Ilkhomov really helped me understand how to write what I wanted to say.

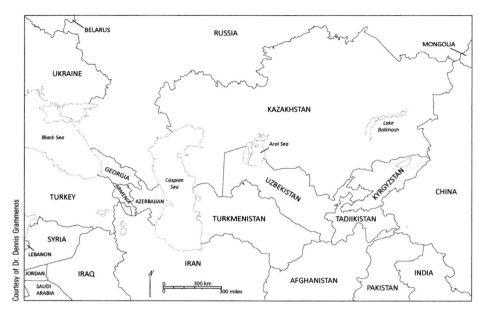

FIGURE 0.1 A general map of contemporary Eurasia with Uzbekistan roughly in the center.

FIGURE 0.2 This map indicates the three countries—Kyrgyzstan, Tadjikistan, and Uzbekistan—that share the Ferghana Valley, an economic and strategic center of Central Asia. The author's research was centered in Namangan in eastern Uzbekistan.

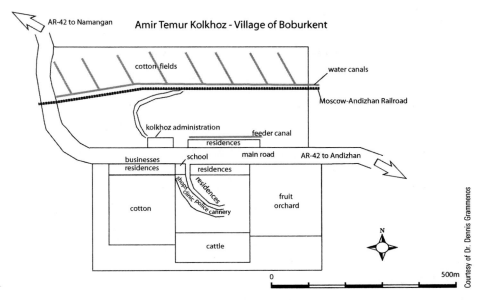

FIGURE 0.3   This map shows the rough dimensions of the author's main site of field research: Boburkent, a part of the Amir Temur Kolkhoz located in Namangan Province, Uzbekistan.

Lastly, my greatest debt goes to the people of Boburkent for putting up with me and making me feel as if I belonged, all the while helping to give me the vital information that forms the heart of this book. I fervently hope that I have represented their views and attitudes justly.

Introduction

In 1990, friends who had learned Uzbek well were asked by a girl in an Uzbek village, "Do all Americans speak Uzbek as well as you do?" If she had only known that at the time fewer than ten U.S. universities provided courses in Uzbek to mere handfuls of students! It is safe to say that less than 20 years ago, Americans and Uzbeks did not know much about one another. To this day, friends, family, and colleagues—all of whom have no particular interest in Uzbekistan—routinely ask me which religion the Uzbeks practice, whether Uzbeks have their own language, and how it is that I get there. They are straightforward questions, testifying to the fact that even after 19 years of political independence from the former U.S.S.R. (Union of Soviet Socialist Republics), Americans barely know anything at all about Uzbekistan. Unlike Afghanistan, Uzbekistan's southern neighbor, where the United States has waged war since 2001, newsworthy events rarely occur there.

Whenever I visit the Uzbek capital city, Tashkent, I remind myself just how "un-central" this Central Asian metropolis is to most Westerners. Nevertheless, it is a modern city of more than 2 million people, including representatives from numerous minority ethnic populations, including Russians, Jews, Kazakhs, Koreans, and Tatars. And like all great cities, there are abundant varieties of dishes to sample—everything from commonplace kabob stands and new hamburger joints to haute cuisine Indian and Turkish restaurants. Furthermore, one can walk along one of the main thoroughfares on a Saturday evening and practically feel as if one is in any European or American city, with thumping rap music, and young men and women dressed in fashionable and risqué attire as they head off to restaurants, taverns, and discotheques. Tashkent represents one kind of Uzbekistan—namely, the kind that wants to retain its cosmopolitanism from the Soviet era as its population strives to live at least partly in a successful, materially oriented world.

Because this book is an account of rural life, I should note that Uzbekistan has its share of prominent cities besides Tashkent. Samarkand, Bukhara, and

Namangan—cities to the south, southwest, and east of Tashkent, respectively—all have populations that exceed 300,000 people; Samarkand, in fact, is home to more than half a million residents.

Samarkand is best known for its stunning turquoise architecture dating from the fourteenth and fifteenth centuries, when it became a civilizational center in the Islamic world under the leadership of Tamerlane (1336–1405) and his successors, known as the Timurids. Bukhara has long been associated with Muslim piety and education, having achieved high status in the Islamic world during the Samanid dynasty of the tenth and eleventh centuries. And there are lesser cities, too, including Andijan (close to the eastern border with Kyrgyzstan), Navoii (in the center), and Urgench (in the country's northwest, close to Turkmenistan). Still, in a country of roughly 27 million people, two-thirds (65 percent) of the people are classified as rural. Compare this to the United States, where approximately 75 percent of our population lives in urban areas. Conditions in cities for millions of people may be dirtier, noisier, more crowded, and unfriendly than the countryside they left, but cities maintain the promise of prosperity. As an anthropologist, I know that studies such as mine will become less typical as more ethnography inevitably becomes urban based.

Even though Uzbeks have been living in Uzbekistan for a long time, they have not always been Uzbeks. This is actually true for many peoples and their eponymous connections, such as Italians, Nigerians, and Indians. We usually like to think of ourselves as being from a given place with old traditions and historical continuity best embodied in our ethnic and national labeling. Most of us also like to think that our cultures are deeply rooted in historical time, which explains why we attach a great deal of importance to our sense of identity; heritages often determine a lot about our pride in ourselves. Governments also play on the notion of heritage to instill strong feelings of unity and belonging as they attempt to develop national coherence. Leaders tend to harp on these notions, especially when they govern emerging nation-states, and even more so when the new nation-states are multi-ethnic in nature, featuring competing arguments about which group of people is oldest and who has been living on a given territory the longest.

Anthropologists refer to these arguments about a group's claim to long development in a single occupied place as *primordialist*. Primordialist arguments in new countries of the former Soviet Union are a part of their historical and anthropological traditions going back to the late nineteenth century. Current variations on primordialist theory in Uzbekistan are motivated by new national ideologies that had to be constructed in a slap-dash manner because of the abrupt end of the U.S.S.R. Uzbeks have had to weld a narrative of national development via historical events onto a place, the Uzbekistan Republic (Boyarin 1994, in Richardson 2005:20). This understanding has been incorporated into the recent story whenever one tries to explain what Uzbekistan is and where it arose. In other words, how long have there been an Uzbek people and an Uzbek nation? Although these questions may be matters of mere curiosity for inquisitive outsiders, they truly matter to Central Asian citizens, especially Uzbeks. Since Uzbeks stopped being Soviet citizens after 1991, it has become important for millions of people to gain a concrete sense of both their ethnic legacy and their national entitlement.

The questions about who Uzbeks are and what Uzbekistan is cannot consider all of the very complicated historical and political arguments that long have occupied scholars. Suffice to say, considerable consensus exists that during the 1500s, on territory that today is Uzbekistan, there lived groups of nomadic and semi-nomadic tribes who called themselves Ozbeks/Uzbeks, and were referred to as such by outsiders. These livestock-raising horsemen presumably descended from a fourteenth-century leader known as Ozbek Khan, who himself was a descendant of the Mongolian conqueror Chingiz Khan, and who became a ruler of the Mongols' northwestern branch of the empire, known as the Golden Horde. Ozbek Khan and his line later became associated with the Kipchaks, associated with the territory of today's northwestern Uzbekistan and Kazakhstan, although they spread throughout many areas of Central Asia (Ilkhamov 2004). Later, many of these groups—and there were dozens of them—were loosely identified as Uzbek tribes, with "Uzbek" becoming something akin to a supra-ethnic label. Interestingly, many Uzbeks in the country's southern and central provinces have retained their tribal identities, which have much to do with their dialects, sense of place, kinship relations, and material culture.

Originally, the Uzbek tribal groups were people whose origins were mainly Turkic, meaning that they probably emerged as migrants several millennia ago from areas that are today partly in Mongolia, China, and southern Siberia, specifically the Altai mountains. Turkic peoples, incidentally, moved from their hearth in eastern Eurasia in a variety of waves, often as pastoralist peoples simply pursuing their endless quest for fodder and water, but also coming as invading armies and empire builders, as was the case of the Turk Qaghanate of the sixth century, the Oghuz Turk of the tenth and eleventh centuries, and the Kipchaks of the thirteenth and fourteenth centuries (Findley 2005). These last peoples are credited as the forebears of today's Kazakh and Uzbek pastoralist populations, and their presence helps to account for the East Asian phenotypes of many Uzbek people (Caroe 1953).

The peoples who coalesced eventually to become contemporary Uzbeks included groups of Persian peoples, such as today's Tajiks, not to mention other east Eurasians, such as Mongols, and Caucasians—peoples from in and around the mountains between the Black and Caspian Seas. Above all, the modern ethno-national term Uzbek is a twentieth-century idea. Into the late nineteenth century, for example, most urban Uzbeks were referred to as Sarts. Academic descriptions of Sarts, including their language and cultural characteristics, show them to be the grandparents and great-grandparents of contemporary urban Uzbeks (Arsen'eva and Petrushevskago 1900:449–451).

The Uzbeks and other Central Asian peoples, such as the Kyrgyz, Tajiks, and Turkmen, experienced colonization after the mid-nineteenth century as the Russian Empire conquered their lands for military and economic purposes, especially with the aim of making Central Asia its hub for cotton cultivation. The historian Adeeb Khalid calls Central Asia under Russian rule "the most colonial possession of the tsarist empire" (2006:866).

While the imperial academic administrators, including geographers and anthropologists, were keen to understand the different ethnic groups and their associated territories, they did not attempt to create national–territorial divisions based on ethnic or linguistic similarities. Rather, the rulers viewed these people mostly as Turkic Muslim subjects for whom they expressed little interest in nation building, although they clearly wanted to "civilize" those whom they considered backward (Brower, 2005).

This attitude changed significantly after the Bolshevik Revolution in 1917. The revolutionaries worked to ensure that ethnicity and nationality would assume less importance to the peoples of the old Russian empire. They intended that ethnic groups should see their most important affiliations as being with the new Communist state and its ideology, which emphasized classlessness and equality between working people and "peasants"—the term revolutionaries used to denote all farming peoples of the empire.

Paradoxically, the Bolsheviks calculated that peoples of the empire would benefit from being grouped into national territories, a move they hoped would rapidly modernize these peoples in part via expressions of their unique ethnicities and languages as they imbibed socialism. New evidence also suggests that the Bolsheviks created the Central Asian republics not so much to divide Muslims from one another, but rather to make it easier for themselves to govern what they considered a volatile environment where there was little unity at the popular level based on either religion or language (Haugen 2003).

These processes led to the formation of countries such as Uzbekistan and Tajikistan. Significantly, Bolshevik thought was not far removed from the views of their tsarist predecessors: Russians overall saw Central Asia as an area of cultural underdevelopment. In creating territorial nations, the Bolsheviks reasoned that the building up of national republics would result in a more rapid advance toward a new understanding of reality as they adapted to a socialist way of life. According to this perspective, individuals' loyalties would now be identified with the nation rather than with the family, tribe, or clan in the manner that characterized the pre-Soviet order in Central Asia (Lubin and Feirman 1994:396). Thus the Uzbek Soviet Socialist Republic was founded in 1925. Today, as we look back upon this era, it makes sense to view that political strategy as having had both successes and failures. On the one hand, Uzbekistan really was well integrated into Soviet society by the late 1980s. On the other hand, many Uzbeks developed a heightened sense of their ethno-national unity just as they saw themselves as distinct from the peoples of other Soviet republics.

In sum, an independent Uzbekistan first appeared only in 1991. Its emergence followed on the heels of Uzbekistan's belated arrival as a nation whose people identified themselves first and foremost as Uzbeks—an event that did not occur until well after the establishment of the Soviet Union, after the middle of the 1930s.

How does this fresh perspective on the past reveal itself in daily life? In cities, the typical pattern consists of erecting new museums and monuments of given personages and eras. In rural areas, the process differs. For example, actions as simple as renaming a street or a collective farm itself (toponymic changes) enable leaders to start removing association with the Soviet past and replacing it with indigenous notions of the reignited sense of nation. These measures aim to convince citizens that they connect to a past peopled by great minds, people who built great cities and who conquered vast territories, even if such cities and empires had nothing to do with the word "Uzbek."

Uzbekistan is an arid, California-sized country. With 27 million people, the country has had one of the most rapidly growing populations among the ex-U.S.S.R. nation-states for several decades now. Most young rural people still intend to raise families with three to four children (or more).

Because Uzbekistan's climate is continental and the country lacks an abundance of water sources, only a little more than 10 percent of its entire territory is suitable for agriculture. What Uzbekistan does have is a complicated and wasteful irrigation network. An elaborate system of canals is ubiquitous wherever people have considered raising crops. The country's best-watered regions and primary growing territories are located around Tashkent (a large oasis in and of itself owing to the Chirchik River), in Samarkand, and in Uzbekistan's east, known as the Ferghana Valley, which Uzbeks proudly call the "Golden Valley" (*Altin Vodii*). The Ferghana Valley plays a prominent role in regional history. It qualifies as the "fruit basket" of Central Asia because of its tasty and productive orchards, which still supply vast quantities of fruit to far-flung areas of the old Soviet Union. The region also produces substantial amounts of wheat and rice. But the valley does not belong to Uzbekistan alone: Both Kyrgyzstan and Tajikistan share parts of this lush, almond-shaped region, some 150 miles from east to west and perhaps 50 miles from north to south, respectively. Nevertheless, most of the valley's farms, towns, and cities lie within the borders of Uzbekistan.

Well watered by the surrounding mountains, which form a part of the towering Tien Shan and Pamir ranges, Uzbekistan's part of the valley has rarely lacked for water. During the past two decades, however, water has become a political weapon: Uzbekistan depends on Kyrgyzstan for the valley's water. In the 1990s, disputes emerged between Uzbekistan and Kyrgyzstan involving the countries' supplies of gas and water. Mutual dependence minus Soviet management partly explains the emerging problems. And this is one issue that bespeaks a common sense of loss that, in a twist of fate, resulted in political independence. The structures and organization of daily life for millions in Central Asia changed after the collapse of the Soviet Union—often for the worse, as evidenced by the imposition of border controls, the proliferation of currencies, and the micro-territorialization of resources. Simply put, the constraints over human movements—people moving through space to visit relatives and friends, conduct business, and use natural resources—have increased in the wake of the U.S.S.R. This is the irony that few politicians, scholars, and citizens foresaw back in the heady days when it seemed perfectly reasonable to urge the collapse of Communist states while rallying to the cause of Western-style political independence and free market economies.

If water problems typify the predicament of post-Soviet life, then surely the fact that water is so intimately bound up with the Uzbeks' ability to raise crops spells trouble for the farming economy for the foreseeable future. Given that Uzbekistan has a low quotient of arable land relative to its territory, what has kept so many people tied to an agrarian lifestyle for so long in Uzbekistan? Cotton. Cotton has long made up the backbone of Uzbekistan's economy and served as the key source of wealth for peasant farmers. Even today cotton remains the premiere cash crop in Uzbekistan, even though significant amounts of territory have been taken out of production to raise food crops such as wheat and rice. The particular nature of cotton farming and the manner in which people live with cotton in rapidly globalizing Uzbekistan is the main topic of this book. My exploration of the nature of farming lives reveals that people have had to be resourceful in their pursuits owing to the post–Soviet path taken.

Cotton has been grown on Uzbekistan's soil for millennia, as attested to by Chinese chroniclers nearly 2000 years ago. It was not until the country's mid-nineteenth-century colonization, however, that Uzbeks began raising cotton on a mass scale. The Russians wanted to achieve self-sufficiency in cotton production rather than being dependent on expensive importation from countries such as the United States. Their efforts spawned the beginnings of a plantation-like system in Central Asia.

While peasants (Uzbeks use the term *dehqon*) were exploited, they were not slaves as was true of African American workers on cotton plantations in the United States during the eighteenth and much of the nineteenth centuries. Yet cotton was to assume a role of ever-increasing dominance in the historic "Land Between the Rivers" (this phrase comes from Arab conquerors of the seventh century, who called the region *Mawar-an-nahr*), a name reflective of the rivers Amu and Syr that bracket much Uzbek territory from south to north today. With the establishment of the Soviet Union, cotton production increased exponentially until after World War II, at which point it expanded astronomically.

By the early 1980s, the Uzbek Soviet republic contributed mightily to the U.S.S.R.'s emergence as a major cotton exporter. During that decade, the country ranked second only to China in total output. The Turkmen and Tajik republics also contributed to the Soviet output, but Uzbekistan remained the center, accounting for approximately 70 percent of all Soviet cotton. Because it devoted so much of its economy to harvesting cotton for the U.S.S.R., Uzbekistan had to acquire most other goods from other regions of the country, giving it something of a socialist-colonialist dependency on the Russian republic. Approximately 40 percent of the Uzbek labor force directly engaged in cotton work during the 1980s.

The rapid expansion of cotton, however, proved deleterious to both the people and the environment. Given the Soviet techniques for cotton production, the industry could not expand quickly enough to employ the growing population as well as provide a rising living standard. By the late 1980s, conditions on the farms had stagnated and begun to decline. The immediate turmoil of independence caused an acceleration of this process. In hindsight, we see that the Soviet emphasis on cotton impeded agricultural diversification, industrialization, and urbanization. As a result, it left Uzbekistan relatively backward compared to Russia and other European areas of the U.S.S.R.

My use of the phrase *cotton plantations* came from my consultants—the people with whom I had the opportunity to live and work during my stints of fieldwork from 1992 to 2004. They half-jokingly compare their situation to those of American slaves of yesteryear. Furthermore, it was the Soviets who introduced the concept and reality of mega-farms, which they called *sovkhozes* and *kolkhozes*. These farms were created in the late 1920s and 1930s with the idea of developing industrialized farming based on a model adapted from factories. The idea was to create massive farms with thousands of people working for the state, which would assume ownership virtually over everything, including land, seed, and machinery. State farming aimed to help modernize peasants and place the Soviet Union on an agrarian footing that would rival the best European and American methods.

In Uzbekistan, the farms achieved many types of successes over the years, but the people who raised cotton did not exactly have the freedom to pursue other ways of life or to grow cotton as they saw fit. Life for most was commanded from above, and this in part accounts for the feeling that people lived on plantations.

Since Uzbekistan became independent, the tendency for people is to identify their working lives more with the plantation concept. Even without the Soviet system, the new state still very much commands their existence. For example, there are harsh consequences for farms that do not fulfill state-mandated plans for production. Thus, while farmers may benefit little materially from raising cotton in comparison to the situation in the late Soviet period, they also face penalties for failing to reach targets, including the cutting off of supplies and possible prison sentences for local leaders. Furthermore, the welfare benefits from Soviet days have been curtailed, so that people have to be more resourceful and cunning than ever before to make ends meet. In essence, it is even tougher to farm cotton today than it was during the Soviet period. And while there are any number of ways people can—and do—remove themselves from these plantations, cotton privatization is just starting. The state's cotton monopolization continues, serving to retard the growth and development of rural society.

While cotton-growing peasants usually know little of the workings of the global market, or even what price a ton of good-quality cotton fetches internationally, such people do understand that they are the force that makes Uzbekistan the world's fourth largest cotton producer, which makes them aware of its overall wealth-generating potential. They understand, too, the role that cotton played for Uzbekistan within the U.S.S.R., and they understand that it plays a vital role in the independence period. Peasants travel to towns and cities, watch television every day, and have children who use computers at school—and most of these children aspire to a life outside of cotton. Furthermore, a given rural town always contains people with higher education, including those who are studying in the capital, or even abroad. And as Uzbekistan breaks away from the insulating sense of economic and political self-sufficiency of the Soviet system, more rural residents are coming into direct contact with imported goods, new institutions, and foreign people, all of which combine to promote diffusion, and hence culture change.

A major task for any anthropologist in his ethnography is to represent the opinions, ideas, attitudes, and outlooks of his consultants as accurately as possible. I take this responsibility seriously. In the pages that follow, I hope readers will feel rewarded by the numerous examples of edited consultants' remarks that I provide to strengthen the major points of this book. Nowhere do I feel a greater challenge than in the job of representing the Uzbek peasants—that is, people's discussions of their own practices and beliefs as they relate them to a world in flux that impinges on their lives with greater frequency daily.

In the decades that were required for rural Uzbeks to move from a peripheral existence within a weak Eurasian empire to their post–World War II status (the conditions that prevailed in Communist countries, such as China and the former Soviet Union, with emphases on state ownership over production and the stated goal of economic equity and the erosion of class society) within the world's only other superpower, the Uzbeks helped construct a society and a way of life that instilled pride and confidence in the populace. This helps explain why the economic downturn associated with post-Soviet life, coupled with a new authoritarian leadership, have caused popular responses reflecting a Third World or developing world condition in light of globalization. In particular, Uzbeks have come to experience yawning gaps in income between the wealthy and the poor, chronic underemployment, a lack of local or national production of consumer goods, people migrating from the countryside to the cities, and migration abroad, mainly as shuttle traders and labor migrants.

In this sense, one can draw parallels between Uzbekistan and Russia and Mexico and the United States. Globalization takes into account many factors of the post–Cold War era, but none more significant than the triumph of capitalism as the dominating organization of all national economies, with rare exceptions. Other factors in Uzbekistan's (de-)evolution, such as transnational labor migration, are discussed where appropriate in following chapters.

The book's organization emphasizes my concern to educate students and laypersons about relatively unknown Uzbekistan, while concentrating on the interrelationships among rural society, its economy, and the farms. To do so, I begin by describing the research project that led me to the idea for this book.

Chapter 1 reflects my goals for carrying out fieldwork from 1993 to 1994. An explanation of this process, with its trials and triumphs, ensues. I discuss what I had to do to get to the site and which kinds of contacts I made in Tashkent, including the kind of institutional affiliations a scholar needs have to get to his site and the role government agencies can play in allowing a foreigner to travel and work as he wishes. From there, the focus becomes the structure and arrangements of collectives (kolkhozes), including their living arrangements, family size, and the anthropologically based type of family found within these organizations. The outlines of family life then merge with discussion of availability of goods and services on the kolkhoz as well as business transacted there, the things that people shop for, and so on. After considering the basic ways in which people earn their living, I examine the nature of local power and the penetration of the state into

Courtesy of Russell Zanca

F I G U R E 0.4 The author enjoys a bowl of beer in Namangan with other thirsty patrons.

daily life. To conclude, I examine villagers' connections to regional centers and provincial cities, including how people connect with one another via transportation and social ties to cities. This latter point is crucial for understanding how people circumvent some of the state's strictures.

Chapter 2 delves into the ethnography of farming. Here readers will consider the outlooks of consultants in discussions that include labor, leisure, household maintenance, and reliance on institutions for education, welfare, repairs, wellness, and even help in financing weddings. I then consider village-level issues of supply and demand affecting people as consumers and producers—needs and wants, and where they find these things. Which recent developments are influencing consumers? Farmers are increasingly being tied into markets as they seek networks between the countryside and towns, enabling them to secure products, materials, and jobs to ensure better health care, higher education for their children, and even ways out of military service.

Next I examine how villagers process and assess their lives in and out of socialism. In mulling the Soviet legacy, they reveal the various methods of acting on and accessing their everyday needs, in addition to the ways that they fulfill aspirations both for themselves and for their relatives and friends. Readers will gain a richer understanding of how people compare the way they live now to their Soviet experiences. We take stock of various age groups and sexes as part of this discussion, because older and younger people as well as men and women cannot all recollect a shared past. These responses tell us something about the Soviet Central Asian legacy, so that we ourselves can make better judgments about the extent to which the Soviet period is now considered a nightmare versus a peaceful and prosperous interlude when measured against the present—or is it somewhere in between? Lastly, do Uzbek cultural practices help villagers adapt to circumstances, or are their methods and approaches based on the very Soviet life to which they grew accustomed?

History is the main subject of Chapter 3, especially that surrounding cotton in first Turkestan (which comprised most of formerly Soviet Central Asia, with the exclusion of much of contemporary Kazakhstan) and then Uzbekistan; emphasis is placed on the history of the Ferghana Valley. Perhaps the most important aspect of the cotton cycle is the annual harvest, which occurs in late summer to fall. The harvest serves as a focal point of communality, so its consideration incorporates the predominance of a cotton-centered life in terms of harvest-derived income, cotton's roles in providing villagers with fuel and food, labor, the pros and cons of cotton in the common imagination, cotton as the primary integrator between villagers and global capital, the key role played by schoolchildren in the harvest, the gendered nature of cotton work, the intricacies of social relations in the fields, and the mass media's reporting of this cycle—which is usually a source of frustration and sarcasm for villagers. Lastly, I look at sources of entertainment as well as the nature of poverty on the farms. These widely disparate issues cannot be disentangled from the success and failure of the harvest.

Few things in Uzbek village life are dearer to people than their culinary and ceremonial festivities. Chapter 4 scrutinizes these issues by considering Uzbeks' daily life and special occasions, such as circumcisions, weddings, and holidays, including the Perso-Turkic New Year, *Navruz*, and the Muslim sacred month of *Ramadan/Ramazan*. All manner of life's individual milestones and unifying events that bring families together reveal careful planning and execution. In part, Uzbeks undertake these events with an eye toward orchestrating their own futures. Furthermore, local and national politics shape celebrations (i.e., the ideology of holidays that might be seen as more ethnic or national, such as Navruz). How then do we assess people's response to the politicization of holidays regarding both attitudes and activities?

Chapter 4 also explores participants' behavior at weddings and the preparations that go into making these events a success. Why, for example, do weddings basically serve to bankrupt families, and why is the entire village invited to the celebration? From this discussion we move into the realm of differences that may be encountered among people of different generations and sexes: What are the different moral positions taken toward celebratory events? Should vodka and champagne be served? How do older adults see the behavior of teenagers and young adults in comparison to themselves? What has gone into the shaping of morality based on pre-Soviet knowledge of social norms? From Soviet norms? Does all this create intra-village conflict or lead to a breakdown of morality?

According to whom? Do these social problems really exist, or are they merely the subjective claims of an outsider?

If a village case study serves to say meaningful things about culture, then the contesting viewpoints expressed by villagers have to coincide with those expressed throughout the rest of the country. I take this position as I concentrate on morality and ethics regarding gender, especially in terms of Soviet thinking and what I will call "new Uzbek thinking"—that is, thinking based on the independence ideology. In Chapter 5, I mediate between the old and the new as I bring to light debates about gender—to wit, what should girls and women achieve in life, and how will they get there? How Uzbeks themselves shape these outcomes will have massive effects on the place and rights of women in society, and they may result in either the kinds of gains or losses for women that will have consequences for Uzbekistan's ability to develop as a prosperous and competitive country. Connected to the aforementioned issues is education. What are the Uzbek perspectives on education? For example, how do ideas about education conform to local notions of right action, including the subordinating of family or group good over the individual's needs, wants, and goals?

Uzbekistan features a long tradition of respect and deference toward elders and people of authority. How are these forms of comportment changing, if at all? What will the implications be for individuals who feel incapable of making any serious decision without approval from those higher in social rank? Given that every culture manifests both idealized and actual notions of right conduct in daily affairs, do we notice new types of family and kin functions along with much of the breakdown of kolkhoz socioeconomic order? We might expect to see the emergence of a new pattern of dependency or reliance on certain family members for help and support, which has much to do with the nature of patrilineal society in Uzbekistan. Serving and relying upon particular relatives and not others is part of the order of a person's life. If these rules break down, or if people stop observing them, what are the consequences for family normalcy? For example, what will happen to long-established patterns of residence rules for marriage, if the approval of parents and other relatives is no longer sought?

Finally, because all states reflect the practices and beliefs of lower-level institutions of social life, how do governing bodies in Uzbekistan function in social life? Specifically, what roles are played by the institutions that regulate and oversee community activities, tax collection, charity for the needy, marital discord, cases of abuse and neglect, and other aspects of village life?

In Chapter 6, I examine consultants' passions about practical and ideological issues that affect their lives. These issues are the subjects of daily conversation, and the topics people address once they solve life's basic needs for the day. Indeed, they sometimes arise when such needs were not satisfied as they should have been. For example, challenges to public health improvement loom large in Uzbekistan now that services and medicines are no longer free. Chapter 6 looks at the levels of health care available to villagers and considers how they appraise their recent experiences with the government-run system. Once a vaunted feature of the Soviet condition and a guaranteed ticket to upward mobility for many a kolkhoznik, education does not seem to enjoy the pride of place as it once did, mainly because there appear not to be enough employment positions that warrant the effort required to obtain a professional degree. At a time when people use much of their productive thought to figure out how they can make more money, going to school often seems like an unjustifiable luxury.

Since the late 1980s, Islam has been playing a bigger role in Uzbek life than was true in almost all of the Soviet period. In trying to distinguish the differences in orientation among Muslims, one basic polarity concerns those who are mainly young and outward looking and those (mainly older) who are insular and adhere to traditional religious conventions. Although other tendencies exist, this polarity does reflect a basic divide in the country separating acceptable from unacceptable orientations to others in society.

These polar differences are diagrammed below. On the left side (A), some younger people tend to identify with international Islamist movements and their politics, including groups as extremist as al Qaeda. On the right side (B), the vast majority of faithful Uzbek Muslims adhere more to the traditions of Sufism, as well as the blending of Muslim orthodoxy with pre-Islamic conventions of faith. Sufism was one of the main vehicles through which Islam spread into Central Asia nearly 1300 years ago. Traditionally, many Central Asians also adhered to the Hanafi school of jurisprudence, which remains one of the more liberal forms in comparison to other Sunni schools. Chapter 6 teases out where most villagers stand on the question of religion's role in society and in their personal lives. This discussion will help readers understand some of the unique features of Islam in Uzbekistan.

Chapter 6 also captures Uzbek opinions on public order, family obligations for individuals, the importance of marriage and procreation, regional mobility and migration, freedom of conscience, and the possibilities for economic diversification and choice, especially pertaining to activities/pursuits.

The last chapter ends by addressing popular outlooks toward the benefits of independence—an especially important issue given so many of the drawbacks already mentioned. These perspectives focus on the opportunities to go abroad for work, education, and other benefits, the chance to become a businessperson, and the country's fitful but gradual opening to the non-Eurasian world. Consultants explain their take on the state leadership, including what it should be doing on behalf of the citizens and how farming might better be restructured, especially regarding land ownership. We then move to discussion of national policies (and nationalistic trends), including the importance of the nation-state ideal to people with its attendant development of borders, armies, currencies, forms of exclusivism,

A. Muslims influenced by international Islamists		B. Muslims who maintain Central Asian Sufi traditions

FIGURE 0.5 Polar ends of Islamic faith.

and its orientation to the world as a new part of the international community—how it connects itself or plugs into this established but changing order. In the end, I consider how the arguments about the Soviet legacy as well as previous incarnations of Uzbek heritage fit into people's conception of their new status. In other words, what effects do abstract debates about the nation have on practical abilities to hamper or move people forward in their daily lives?

A short conclusion sums up the kind of contributions that an anthropological study of this peasant society during a time of upheaval makes. Longitudinal studies in rural Central Asia offer us, as anthropologists, a way of saying something meaningful about a nation even at a remove from national leaders and governmental politics. This perspective helps us to obtain more balanced (or at least nuanced) understandings of societies because the focus is on the area where most of the country's people live—the countryside in this case.

1

Just Getting from Here to There in Uzbekistan

INTRODUCTION

Chapter 1 describes my original goals and the overall purpose of carrying out my long-term fieldwork from 1993 to 1994. An explanation of the fieldwork process, with its attendant trials and triumphs, ensues. I discuss how I got interested in Central Asia and explain my scholarly preparation for conducting overseas research. In this section, I relate the steps I had to take to get to the field site; the necessary contacts that I made in Tashkent, including the kind of institutional affiliations that a scholar needs have to get to his or her field site; and the role that government agencies played in allowing this foreign researcher to travel and work as he wished.

The next section describes what happened once I settled into the village of Boburkent. I discuss the outlines of family life—a topic that merges with a consideration of the availability of goods and services on the kolkhoz as well as business transacted, the things that people shop for, and so on. A look at the structure and arrangements of collective farms (kolkhozes) follows, to include living arrangements, family size, and type of family unit based on standard anthropological classification. After considering the basic ways in which people earn their living, I examine the nature of local political power and the interpenetration of the state and politics into daily peasant life. To conclude the chapter, I explore how villagers are connected to larger entities, such as regional centers and provincial cities, and how people are connected both by transportation services and by family ties to urban settings. This latter point is crucial to understanding how people circumvent some of the socioeconomic strictures of the state itself.

ENCOUNTERING CENTRAL ASIA
IN QUEENS, NEW YORK

I suppose it is a very good thing that I grew up in Queens, New York. In addition to the New York Mets, Queens has a lot of different people from lots of different places in this world. In the early 1980s, I worked for one of my neighbors, who owned a kosher butcher shop. I delivered orders after school, and I helped Artie, the owner, and Sidney, his partner, clean up before closing. Sidney, who had been born in a *shtetel* in western Ukraine, would drive me a few times every week to deliver to the "Russians." I was 16, and I didn't know much at the time, but I knew that the particular Jews to whom we delivered the cheapest and not-the-freshest cuts of meat (in 10- and 12-pound packages!) were not Russians. True, they spoke Russian—even to me, which didn't make much sense—and they had lots of gold- and silver-capped teeth, and they even offered me shots of vodka and something to eat in lieu of tips on cold winter evenings, but they just didn't look or dress Russian. It took me a few months to understand that they were Bukharan Jews—a distinctly indigenous Central Asian Jewish people who had lived in cities, such as Bukhara, Samarkand, Tashkent, and Dushanbe for hundreds of years. The language they spoke, in addition to Russian, is closely related to modern Tajik and Persian.

As a high school student, I developed a passion for Russian literature and a developing interest in all things Soviet. I knew by my senior year that I just had to travel to the Soviet Union. Unfortunately, it would be several years more before I actually visited. My first immersion into Soviet "culture" came via an undergraduate ethnographic project in Queens among the very same Bukharan Jews. Meanwhile, I had started to read the sizable literature on Central Asia in general, and Uzbekistan in particular, as I studied the history and politics of the Soviet Union.

The Bukharan Jews rode a wave of migration to the United States during the late 1970s, the period known as détente, when the Cold War warmed up just a bit during the presidency of Jimmy Carter and the Soviet premiership of Leonid Brezhnev. At this time many Americans were involved in calling for the "freeing" of Soviet Jews, who were seen mainly as an oppressed minority in the Union of Soviet Socialist Republics (U.S.S.R.) and who, among other things, were denied the freedom to worship because the Soviet Union was officially an atheistic state. The Soviet leadership agreed to allow many of the country's citizens to file for emigration visas, mainly Jews. Many of these Soviet Jews— whether European (Ashkenazi) or Bukharan (Sephardic)—ultimately settled in Western Europe, Israel, and the United States. Queens, New York, became a major resettlement hub for the "Bukharans" of Uzbekistan.

I wish I could state unequivocally that my undergraduate thesis project was an unqualified success, but fairness demands that I claim it as an unqualified "experience." The people who had seemed so friendly when I delivered meat now began scorning me routinely when I started asking what must have seemed to them dopey, naive questions, such as "Why did you want to leave the

U.S.S.R.?", in halting, stammering Russian. Donning a Russian-style hat in winter and proudly sporting Soviet lapel pins also did little to endear me to many people in this newly established immigrant community. And it wasn't long before children were turning to one another and muttering "Kay-Geh-Beh" (KGB, the Soviet secret police) whenever I approached or walked by on the street or in their synagogue. Adults, only a tad more subtly, asked me if I wasn't working for the *government*?

This was my first taste of an accusation that dogs me to this day when I am working in Central Asia, and that is a sobriquet commonly applied to many an anthropologist: spy. In a way, we have to expect this appellation, because so many of our questions are a combination of the prying, the irksome, and the probing, put to people in ways that exasperate them to the point where they say, "What possible explanation could there be for a person who wants to live with us and badger us all day with endless questions about the minutiae of life?"

Fortunately, I had a sympathetic undergraduate thesis advisor, who thought my efforts worthwhile, even if the results did not make for the most compelling ethnographic read. He inspired me to try harder and provided much food for thought before I undertook another such project. Many of the things I did learn, which propelled me forward into future work in Central Asia, centered on the strong artistic traditions of the Bukharans and their efforts to set me straight on issues of nationality and ethnicity in the former Soviet Union. While I never researched the arts per se, we are fortunate to have a book by a noted ethnomusicologist on Bukharan Jewish music and culture (Levin 2001). I was drawn to issues of identity in Central Asia because it has always seemed far more complex than the issues of identity in the United States. For example, I couldn't understand why the Bukharans wouldn't assent to being called Uzbeks, given that they hailed from Uzbekistan. Jewish just meant one's religion. Not so in Eurasia! There, even today, "Jewish" means both one's nation and one's ethnic group in addition to being one's faith. In time I would learn that republics such as Uzbekistan and Kyrgyzstan, Tajikistan and Kazakhstan, were peopled with many different ethnic groups, and that very often these ethnic differences were reflected in an individual's documentation, especially passports. This separation really is a foreign concept to Americans, for whom citizenship means everyone's nationality ipso facto is "U.S.A."

THE ACADEMIC PATH TO UZBEKISTAN

As a graduate student preparing a thesis proposal to conduct fieldwork in Uzbekistan, I planned to work on two issues: (1) the everyday life practices and concerns of peasant collective farmers just after the collapse of the U.S.S.R. in a small village, and (2) the more controversial issue of inter-ethnic conflict. At the time (1992), Western scholars still knew virtually nothing about what ordinary life was like for Central Asians, including where they shopped, what their typical meals were, what kinds of jobs they did, how often people traveled between town and country, the kinds of things rural people aspired to do as adults, and so forth. Relative to the second issue, in the final years before the Soviet Union's collapse, a number of violent incidents transpired between Central Asian ethnic and national groups, including Meshkhetian Turks (a Caucasian Turkic people) and Uzbeks, and Kyrgyz and Uzbeks, especially during 1989 and 1990. The latter conflagration most impressed me, and I wanted to know how deep-rooted sources of conflict were in the Ferghana Valley (FV), where inter-ethnic conflict claimed several hundred lives in June 1990.

At the time, a prevalent hypothesis stated that Central Asian peoples would come to blows only if there were fomentation from without, meaning some nefarious organizing force. Naturally, the KGB was suspected of having sown ethnic discord in an attempt to show that maintaining Soviet power throughout Eurasia would be the only way to ensure that national groups harboring deep-seated animosities toward one another could be controlled. That position was certainly a radical argument—but like so many conspiracy-based theories, it proved very hard to corroborate, despite the claims put forth by some conspiracy-minded publications (Razakov 1993). Many people tend to like these kinds of theories because they are straightforward and dramatic. Some Americans, for example, entertain similarly nefarious ideas about the assassination of President John Kennedy and the terrorist attacks of September 11, 2001. While some of these arguments may contain grains of truth, reality usually turns out to be more complicated. Furthermore, in terms of mass participation in violent acts, it is unreasonable to accept the idea that people are marionettes who cannot be seen as responsible for their own actions. With these caveats in mind, I reasoned that if I could find an appropriate village in Uzbekistan that was close to Kyrgyzstan, I could study the inner workings of a collective farm in the new post-Soviet era as well as make my cross-border forays to investigate the "Osh events" (Osh is a large, FV city—with a population of ±500,000—in southern Kyrgyzstan where many of the killings between Uzbeks and Kyrgyz took place).

Curiously, one of my academic mentors at the time—a person of vast experience in Soviet affairs, who was one of the last true anthropological polymaths (he had worked on a vast number of projects in many different parts of the world since the early 1930s)—expressed some skepticism about my inter-ethnic conflict research. He simply thought it would not be an easy project to pull off, especially given the highly secretive nature of issues that pertain to security and large-scale sociopolitical problems in the former U.S.S.R., even taking into account its most recent breakup. He joked that if the granting institutions that provide the funds to anthropological doctoral candidates for their fieldwork projects ever compared what the candidates said they will do in the field as opposed to what they actually end up doing and arguing, then no one would ever get a plugged nickel.

What he expressed—rather correctly, as it turns out—is that it is not so difficult to come up with an interesting hunch or hypothesis that one wants to investigate in the field. However, the reality of being at one's field site can change intentions rapidly because people (the investigator's anthropological subjects) tend to let anthropologists know quickly whether they have chosen an appropriate research topic that the consultants or informants are willing to discuss. Because anthropologists do not work with inert, inorganic, or controllable organic materials or animals, we neither perform controlled experiments in our science nor often have the chance to replicate the research operations (i.e., interviewing) that we have already performed. Human beings will willingly subject themselves to questions and observations only if they think it worth their time, or at least think it will do them no harm.

Another mentor kindly provided me with the address of an Uzbek farm schoolteacher whom he had visited during his own research on education in Central Asia just a year earlier (1991). The address turned out to be a proverbial godsend. Mr. Alijon Ergashev of the small village of Boburkent, a part of the Sverdlov Kolkhoz (today's Amir Temur Kolkhoz), would prove to be an invaluable resource—a primary consultant, facilitator, guide, teacher, and, above all, friend. The two of us initiated a correspondence, which gave me a chance to write semiliterate letters in Uzbek telling Ergashev about my plans. He would then respond graciously, helping to give me an inkling of what village life was like and where I might stay, and making me feel very welcome. I finally felt that I was bridging the chasm between my first student project among the Bukharans and the kind of serious undertaking that would help determine my professional goals.

FROM MOSCOW TO TASHKENT

My bride of a few months and I set out for Moscow shortly after the attempted coup to restore Communism to power in the Soviet Union in the fall of 1993. At the time, this route through Moscow was one of the only ways to get to Uzbekistan from the United States—the way it had long been. We spent a few lazy and unproductive weeks kicking around Moscow while waiting for the documents allowing us to spend a prolonged period in Uzbekistan to be approved. Monica, my wife, hoped to freelance for both print and radio media, so she was able to use the time getting pointers from the National Public Radio person of the time in Moscow.

Winter came early that year, and we left for Tashkent not a moment too soon, as the snow and ice were already piling up in Moscow. We arrived in Tashkent on a beautiful fall morning amidst the yellow glows of sunshine and turned leaves. A friend I knew from the previous summer met us, and I tried to settle down as quickly as I could to get to the FV village some 250 miles east of the capital. At that time, a few other American expatriate scholars were also working on various doctoral projects or studying Uzbek, so we had a terrific community of like-minded academic colleagues. In addition, we had access to people who could turn us on to finding the necessary things that we needed both for daily living and for our long stay in the countryside.

As mentioned earlier, Tashkent is a major Eurasian metropolis. The city is sprawling, but with the exception of the Old City or Asian Tashkent (the area that

Courtesy of Russell Zanca

F I G U R E 1.1   One of Tashkent's most famous modern monuments: a commemoration of the devastating earthquake that destroyed much of the city on April 26, 1966. This monument shows a family pushing back nature to build anew.

retains the basic pre-European design begun by the Russians in the 1870s), Tashkent is laid out on an easily navigable grid pattern. In fact, its very broad and straight avenues were in part modeled on the urban planning of St. Petersburg (Sahadeo 2007:36). Dated but fully functional trams, trolley buses, buses, and a gorgeously constructed subway nicely serve Tashkent; getting around was never a problem, and locals were almost always very willing to provide directions. The only problems occurred because of so much renaming and the replacement of Soviet monuments and statues with those more in line with the new nationalist Uzbek ideology that the state was developing. Hence, a street such as Gorky (a renowned Russian Communist writer) might be renamed *Buyuk Ipak Yoli* (The Great Silk Road). Locals, however, would continue to call the street by its old name or, as sometimes happened, simply had no idea where a place was if I used the new street name.

Even given its large size and cosmopolitan feel, Tashkent in the early 1990s was a very sociable and homey sort of city, and Americans truly were well-treated guests. People whom we had only just met in a cab, on a bus, or in the market would no sooner establish contact with us than they would invite us to their homes for dinner. Had we accepted all of these offers, we probably wouldn't have had to worry too much about grocery shopping.

Speaking of shopping, this period coincided with a very interesting development in Uzbekistan, and in many of the other former Soviet republics. Even into late 1993, most of the former Soviet republics remained within the *ruble* zone, meaning they used the old Soviet currency and still nominally remained within

Courtesy of Russell Zanca

F I G U R E 1.2 A main thoroughfare in Tashkent, Uzbekistan's capital. The signboard reads: "Uzbekistan is free and equal in the world."

the Russian currency system. This made Uzbekistan eminently affordable for graduate students used to a penny-pinching way of life. Sadly, this situation changed with the introduction of the *sum-kupon*, the new temporary Uzbek currency. Prices skyrocketed overnight, and we could not keep up with the rate of inflation. But our difficulties were miniscule in comparison to those of the local people. Their old currency, even if they had saved a lot of it, soon became totally valueless, and the explosive inflation cast many people even to even worse financial hardship than they had experienced during the perestroika years (the final Soviet years). During Thanksgiving, matters became especially bad, and many of us who considered making an elaborate dinner (Uzbeks have almost all of the necessary products and ingredients to prepare a great Thanksgiving meal) had to tighten our belts. This system gradually stabilized for foreigners with hard currencies such as American dollars, but something on the order of an American Depression-lite would continue plaguing Uzbeks until well after their own currency, the *sum*, was introduced in the summer of 1994.

AMONG FELLOW SCHOLARS AT THE UZBEKISTAN ACADEMY OF SCIENCES

Meanwhile, I established myself as a researcher at the History Institute of the Uzbek Academy of Sciences. This new status allowed me library access privileges. Because I was told it would probably be some three weeks—it turned out to be closer to five—before I received approval to do my fieldwork in the FV province of Namangan, I tried to spend my time usefully by doing as much background reading and note taking at the libraries as I could in preparation for my sojourn on the farm. Having an official affiliation with the Academy of Sciences of the Republic of Uzbekistan formed a crucial part of the necessary connections and relations a foreign scholar needs to then be cleared for scholarly research in other facilities throughout the country, such as archives and government statistical bureaus, and to obtain the necessary Ministry of Foreign Affairs stamps within one's passport just to get on a plane or train and travel some distance.

Relations at the History Institute were cordial, but not always warm. The Uzbek scholars treated the foreign researchers not so much as colleagues, but rather as guests of limited understanding (and that perception was not exactly false). As such, not all were willing to help us because we were unproven as scholars. For example, I was assigned a couple of mentors, including the person who was supposed to oversee my work. I found certain aspects of his personality pleasant and others useless for engaging me as I had hoped. In time, I managed to work with other people at the History Institute who gave me the guidance that I really required.

Basically, the Soviet system had academic traditions partly based on the German model. If a foreigner did not show good familiarity with the prominent writings by Soviet scholars, then Uzbek scholars didn't want much to do with him or her. Generally, Tashkent anthropology colleagues expressed support for my project, but couldn't understand why I was doing it by myself: Soviet scholars traditionally employ a team ethnography approach, where a whole group goes off together to cover various aspects of cultural life in a community study. Furthermore, they looked down on the idea that I would be stationed for many months rather than a few weeks at a time, a venture that they considered wasteful, full of deprivations, and boring.

The strangest gulf in understanding, however, related to my Uzbek colleagues' opinion that one really doesn't learn all that much from peasants because they are not educated people! I recall spending some time during one desultory afternoon with local graduate students after yet another failed, wheel-spinning attempt to secure my internal visa from the responsible ministry, where I always seemed to arrive at the wrong time. For a while talk concerned the prospects for learning about seminal events in Soviet history from collective farmers. One of the students just could not understand why I thought this undertaking would prove valuable among "uneducated" people.

> Well, go ahead and interview them, but don't forget to do your work
> in the archives and libraries after you get back. That's where you'll really
> find out about *that* [emphasis added] history. Kolkhozniks can't tell you
> very much.

I can't say that all of the others shared her viewpoint—certainly not a couple of young anthropologists who had already worked in Samarkand and Andijan provinces. They had begun to focus on the personal stories of peasants' lives, of which almost all Soviet ethnography is bereft.

I benefited from hearing this opinion because it stimulated debate that I found very productive. In the end, I realized that what my host colleagues were really saying is that the emic perspective (the perspective of people being studied ethnographically), especially on matters of history or explanations for the development of practices, beliefs, and other aspects of life, might be of limited value in comparison to the scholarship already published on said topics.

It is worth devoting space here to discussion of relations between host colleagues and me, because if a visiting scholar does not assert himself in cultivating good and respectful relations with his academic hosts, he potentially opens himself up to major hindrances in doing his work. Frankly, whenever a young anthropologist undertakes fieldwork in a foreign setting, he should be conscious of representing his own country as best he can. Scholars receive grant monies to buy necessary equipment, obtain transportation, and pay general living expenses for the period of research requested. Generally, the granting institutions are funded through U.S. government agencies, such as the Department of State. Ultimately, American taxpayers support much scholarly research—and scholars may want to take this point to heart. Naturally, the vast majority of us want to maintain good working relations with our colleagues, even if we don't see eye-to-eye on many intellectual or political issues.

Another key point is that government bodies work hard to negotiate agreements with their own counterparts from other countries so that scholars will enjoy the rights to conduct their research in a way that is supposed to be unobstructed. The more we work on our personal relationships as anthropologists, the further we increase our chances not only for guaranteeing access to the people, places, and materials we wish to access, but also in paving the way for others to follow in our stead. It also makes it easier for us to return and do additional research and projects in future.

One of the key dilemmas American scholars may face in foreign settings while working with their local counterparts in materially poor countries with dictatorial governing situations is jealousy. Graduate students especially may be resented because they are thought to be unworthy of funding by host colleagues. After all, what we consider a small amount of grant money by the standards of ordinary American salaries may be perceived as a small fortune by our host colleagues, who may be paid poorly and infrequently by everybody's standards. Foreign-based anthropologists may take dressing well, eating well, having technological ownership (e.g., laptops), and enjoying unfettered access to multiple sources of information for granted, but host colleagues often cannot.

This is exactly how it was for me in Uzbekistan. Part of the way that this jealousy manifested itself was through an expectation of material or other reciprocity that could go behind a simple token of appreciation. For example, I was often asked for technology (e.g., computers, printers) in exchange for the approval of documentation or the perceived help extended to me. Some Uzbek colleagues also wanted me to help procure visas, so that they or someone in their family could travel to the United States. At times, I found these requests off-putting and even morally repugnant, but I used my training in anthropology to help me understand why these requests usually seemed perfectly appropriate to the person making them.

I came to the conclusion that this is how the Uzbek scholars had learned to survive and succeed in their own professional system, especially when times became trying. They provided me with a concrete understanding of unequal power relations, expressing on an individual level something of what the unequal relations may be about at higher levels, such as between governments. Anthropologists need to be able to develop the ability to serve host colleagues, be honest with them, and be discerning all at the same time, in ways that steer clear from judgment, shaming, and moralizing within limits of course. At the risk of sounding trite, one has to proceed anthropologically in every phase of professional involvement once getting to the fieldwork site and its environs.

WHAT COULD BE SO BAD ABOUT THE COUNTRYSIDE?

We wanted to be settled in the *qishloq* (Uzbek village, meaning "winter place") before winter set in, and it was now December. In Tashkent again, friends and fellow scholars just couldn't see us making it in the conservatively religious city of Namangan (possibly the most conservative in all of Central Asia), let alone then taking off for the qishloq and the kolkhoz. They eventually just chuckled good-naturedly and shook their heads. People rarely were very specific about what was so bad or wrong with life out there, but they continually implied or stated that the countryside was primitive, dirty, and cold. It also makes sense to think that people had ulterior motives in decrying village life's unseemliness as they tried in vain to dissuade me from laying down any research roots there. Combining the Soviet position that outsiders should not get too well acquainted with the harsh reality of rural life, and the Uzbek cultural preoccupation with being thought ill of, it didn't take long to realize that many of these people simply were mortified by the idea that a young American couple would return to the United States to report that the qishloq was indeed hellish, and that Uzbeks in general lived a lousy life.

Another of my most important consultants, who has since emigrated to Australia, was raised in the village where I was headed (he was best friends with Ergashev). Pulat Nazarov kept saying, "Things there are really very bad there now, very bad. Nobody can afford to buy coal. There isn't much to eat." That warning was about as concrete as it got. This notion and the admonishment to make sure where my money was at all times at least had the effect of not raising my expectations.

Given my earlier description of the friendliness of Tashkenters, I must point out that our arrival in Uzbekistan coincided with generally bad relations between the United States and Uzbekistan. As a consequence, in official capacities Americans were not always treated so well. One practical manifestation of the bad international relations came in the form of differential rates that Americans were expected to pay as part of the recently reformed visa regime. Depending how long one would be staying in the country, one was expected to pay a certain rate for the visa; when its term ran out, one was supposed to get a new visa and pay another fee. In time I figured out how to talk my way out of these periodic charges: I learned that many laws in Uzbekistan pertaining to foreigners seemed to be established for the gullible, and that there was almost always a way to talk one's way out of these situations or make a counter-offer to responsible officials that couldn't exactly be construed as a bribe. Put simply, it was important to turn stand-offs into moments of good, local-level diplomacy.

Similarly, local police often stopped Americans for a variety of reasons to accost them. First, they wanted to make sure the visitors' papers were in order. Second, they checked whether Americans had authorization to be living in a particular place, such as an apartment; one also had to clear this with the Ministry of Foreign Affairs (MFA) and the local police station, known by its old Soviet acronym *OVIR* (the department responsible for the regulation of passports and visas). Third, the less upstanding officers hoped to intimidate Americans into paying them money rather than face a worse roughing-up and interrogation if the person were taken into custody on any number of invented charges. Occasional fistfights ensued over these harassments.

GETTING CLOSER TO THE VILLAGE

We boarded an overnight train to Namangan once we finally had our paperwork in order. Train travel, while not a luxury affair in Uzbekistan, has its high points, not the least of which are camaraderie with other passengers, the sharing of food, and the swapping of stories about one's own life and interests. To be sure, there are drunks to endure, thieves to be alert for, extremely poor lighting, and ramshackle sleeper cars.

We received a welcome on the platform at dawn once we departed the train. Who should it be but an MFA-related, uniformed official who smiled a lot as he asked to see our documents, and then practiced his English on us: "Do you like Uzbekistan? America is a very big country." We smiled, and learned not to show displeasure or anxiety. In time and after countless security encounters like this, one realizes that everyone is a part of or caught up in the system, and that even the security representatives can be decent people, too. Naturally, it is the corrupt ones one has to guard against. At any rate, all of the paperwork trials were beginning to make sense. If nothing else, we didn't really have to worry about getting lost or going missing in Uzbekistan for too long a time. By the end of my stay, I became quite friendly with some of my "security detail," and actually looked forward to seeing them at airports, train stations, and bus terminals. I sometimes had the feeling that I was in Mayberry RFD-Police State.

As we were settling temporarily into Namangan life, we relied on the help of a good friend and consultant, Ominahon Hamraeva, a bank accountant, who helped us negotiate the local officialdom of the OVIR office. Although the MFA folk in Tashkent had certified us for fieldwork in the Ferghana Valley, we still had to get more approvals—and hence stamps in our passports from the provincial official. Colonel Tursunov, a man as wide as he was tall, gave the impression that he would burst his smart but faded uniform at any minute. He was not a man given to small talk, much as other officials were, and he never seemed particularly interested in our citizenship, our families, and other aspects of our lives. Even Ominahon could not charm him or get him to warm up, which meant we were in for a rough ride. The colonel wanted two things from us: evidence that we were HIV negative and a fixed amount of dollars. According to the law, both American businesspeople and tourists were expected to pay for the designated periods of their visas. For reasons that have now grown a little hazy, we had several meetings with the colonel.

Over filling lunches of spicy, vinegared mutton kabobs, out-of-this-world Namangan *obi-non* (tandir-baked bread), and pots of weak green tea, we and Ominahon strategized about what to do with "Comrade Colonel Tursunov," as we addressed him in fawning attempts to win points. I summoned up my theatrical abilities—modest at best—in an effort to appear earnest and distressed, telling Colonel Tursunov that the AIDS-test stuff couldn't possibly apply to people like us, but to businesspeople, those inveterate risk takers. As for the money, surely that requirement couldn't apply to us either, because the law stated that it applied to tourists and businesspeople. Even though there was no academic visa, we were not here for profit making; therefore, to charge us would be a matter of unfairness. Colonel Tursunov listened with his stony demeanor, and pointed to his documents. Our next tack—a desperate one to be sure—was to tell him that in Tashkent, we were told we wouldn't have to be concerned about these matters. His reply: "That's Tashkent; this is Namangan." The colonel said that if we wanted to go back to Tashkent and get official, supporting documents, that decision would be up to us. We threatened to do just that, and intimated that this issue was going to be scandalous for him. Comrade Colonel Tursunov acted less than ruffled.

During our last encounter, and at Ominahon's suggestion, we presented him with pens and postcards from Chicago, our hometown. Ominahon thought this gesture might just soften him up. She was right. The colonel looked exasperated to see us again, but greeted us professionally. He smiled when he looked at the postcards and ballpoints, and then the questions began:

- "What is Chicago like?"
- "How were the Bulls?" (These were the Michael Jordan years!)
- "Why did we want to live on a kolkhoz?"

This line of questioning went on for 15 minutes or so. In the end, Colonel Tursunov asked us to pay a standard processing fee, something on the order of $0.25, and gave us our stamps, telling us to stop by whenever we were in town, and reminding us that we should not forget to renew our residency status in another three months time.

It took some time to process these events. In the end, the colonel wasn't necessarily looking for something big, but rather something from us that would show we recognized his office and respected the risk he may have taken on our behalf. It is highly unlikely that many American businesspeople or tourists were appearing with any frequency in Namangan then, so he knew we were exceptional. Colonel Tursunov also could identify with our difficulties as students. Above all, we all figured out a graceful way to handle a bureaucratically designed snare together. Yes, many bureaucrats enjoy the proverbial power trip, but they also have to answer to people in even higher offices, and they have to be aware of which sorts of independent actions can get them into trouble. This issue often tends to be overlooked when dealing with bureaucrats working in authoritarian countries. Finally, the colonel's remark about this being Namangan and not Tashkent probably was meant to emphasize his higher status: He wanted to clarify that he was calling the shots, and that I had better not try to act arrogantly by demeaning the province in favor of the capital. At the time, I still didn't fully appreciate significant regional differences among Uzbek people.

Once we were in Namangan, people said it was crazy to think of living in the Chorbozor district where we were headed, and then to a village with no natural gas and no running water, out there where all the people worked hard but had nothing. These sterling recommendations convinced me that renting an apartment in Namangan might not be such a bad idea. So, for $40 per month, we took a three-bedroom flat where we could find privacy, fix meals the way we wanted, wash our own clothes, and bathe on our short monthly visits back to Namangan. The only problem that we occasionally met with there was that a friend and business partner of our landlord had a spare key and used the living room area for trysts with his mistress. After a few complaints, however, Botir (the landlord) forced his partner to seek his afternoon delights elsewhere.

Many days of limbo ensued. Impatience grew, and then the phone finally rang. It was finally time to meet Alijon, the man whom I would come to call *Aliaka* (Big Brother Ali; Uzbek men often refer to other men as older or younger brother, *aka* or *uka*). We set sail that day in the only type of car that ever seemed to be available whenever there were loads of luggage to stow—a Moskvich. This car is slightly larger than a Cooper Mini, and seems to have the pickup of a couple of asthmatic horses. The four of us, including the driver, who seemed larger than the car itself, took off into the fog enshrouded countryside. The road seemed endless, forever twisting and winding. I couldn't see a thing, and not just because of the fog; I was basically buried under three pieces of luggage. This ride gave me one of my only instances of existential angst: What was I doing with my life, and why did I drag my poor newlywed wife along? Such questions are all part of the crucible of becoming an anthropologist. After an hour or so, we arrived at Chorbozor.

THE ROAD TO THE KOLKHOZ

Pahlavan Mahmud (*Pahlavan* means "athlete" or "hero," and ours was just so—a former circus strongman), the driver, was ready for lunch. We pulled off a main thoroughfare and entered a restaurant that looked like a courthouse. After mounting a flight of stairs, we entered a cavernous and dimly lit dining room. As if on cue, nearly all of the patrons looked up from their plates or fell silent, gluing their

eyes on the four of us as vapor billowed upward from their food, mouths, and
nostrils. After the novelty wore off, we sat down to enormous bowls of soup and
rice with meat. Sensing that the large portions stretched my credulity, one of our
hosts announced, "It's cold now, so you've got to eat a lot to stay warm." This
phrase or a variation of it would be repeated frequently over the ensuing days,
weeks, and months. He was right, too: In that restaurant where everyone sat fully
dressed in winter coats, hats, and boots, it was only the food that really took the
chill from us. Central heating cannot be overrated.

Once we had finished eating, a few of the nearby patrons inquired about our
identities. When they heard that we were not planning on staying in Chorbozor,
but rather moving on to the Sverdlov kolkhoz some 15 miles to the east for
about a year's time, they expressed near-disbelief and empathy. This was beginning to seem comical: Uzbeks drew the gradations and implications from urban
to rural life much more sharply than I had imagined possible. Now it became
apparent that many of the warnings and disparaging comments about kolkhoz
life stemmed not just from metropolitan parochialism or from concern about
our comfort and well-being, though such reasons factored into the remarks.
Rather, these admonitions may well be rooted in Soviet-wide, ideologically
tinged conceptions about how foreigners perceive Soviet/post-Soviet reality. In
other words, if ordinary people play up the lowliness and backwardness of the

FIGURE 1.3 An
overly crowded village bus.
All manner of industrial
shortages caused unreli-
ability in rural transportation networks for most
people.

Courtesy of Russell Zanca

hinterlands, the foreigners themselves will understand that you, too, think life "out there" is underdeveloped.

VILLAGE ECONOMIC BASICS

At the time of our arrival, the village of Boburkent made up one-third of the kolkhoz settlement. All of the villages are connected to the central part of the farm, the administrative buildings by roads that themselves connect the villages to the district centers, and that lead in turn to the provincial capitals. Given this arrangement, the transportation and communication links should be very good. It really is a matter of technological efficiency and the availability of fuels and spare parts for machines that sometimes make relatively short distances seem so much farther away.

The Sverdlov Collective Farm, located slightly closer to Andijan (to the southeast) than Namangan (to the northwest), contained nearly 1200 housing units and a population numbering close to 7000. Most of the population engaged in some form of agriculture or agriculturally related work on nearly 1300 hectares of arable land. (The name of the farm changed some months after we settled there, becoming Amir Temur/Tamerlane Kolkhoz.) Boburkent, with more than 400 housing units, housed the administrative center of the farm as well as its post office, police department, tire and auto mechanic shop, canning factory, machine repair station, farm social services committee office, and a health clinic/hospital. In addition, a number of formerly kolkhoz-owned shops were apparent, and some newly opened private kiosks. The kolkhoz's layout did not follow any traditional pattern, but rather was more typical of Soviet collective farm villages overall. Roads that cut through and across the village were wide and graded with appropriate road signs, if not always paved.

Some key features of settled Central Asian culture, however, were retained even with the Soviet spatial alterations. For example, houses' windows might face the streets and the public, but they were not used for much in the way of exposure or openness. In the same respect, people did not practice much in the way of landscaping outside of their homes in the areas that faced the public world. Rather, Central Asians reserved their best decorating and landscaping for their internal courtyards, which remained very private worlds. In these areas, people created their own type of sanctuary from the public domains. One would find similarities here to many housing arrangements in parts of the Middle East and South Asia. To some degree, privacy in domestic living reflects larger values about the protection of personal and family honor.

The commercial life of the kolkhoz town center did not serve consumers' needs well, an issue that I often asked my consultants about. While some of the shops performed essential services, such as auto or appliance repairs, the dry goods stores offered eclectic and erratically supplied goods. The inventory also changed frequently, with little explanation for some of the received stock. Some stores, for example, might stock fruit preserves, boxes of tea, and rice—all useful foodstuffs. Alongside these items, however, one might find a heap of flimsy, plastic toilet seats, oddly bent flatware, and hospital-style slippers. Another store might be stocked full with mineral water, fortified wine (*portvain*), vodka, thermoses, plastic buckets, large bars of all-purpose lye soap, and carry-all bags. While almost all of these items had their uses, they hardly made for one-stop shopping sorts of arrangements. The toilet seats were hardest to fathom given that Uzbek villagers have outhouses and do not sit to urinate or defecate!

Although the state retail system was ending, the state in the form of district-level government or the kolkhoz enterprise itself continued to own the real estate. New private real estate auctions were beginning at the time of my fieldwork, but the highest bidders invariably turned out to be entrenched bureaucrats with power or well-connected people with significant financial backing. Other, less established entrepreneurial folk pooled resources to rent the space, and it was then up to them to stock the shelves. The government relied on shopkeepers to pay taxes as well as rent. Because there was no longer a central command administration for securing supplies, the items for sale became a matter of trying to secure basic Soviet-type items that people might buy at affordable prices. Informants told me that the need for these shops persisted because they sometimes carried things that people needed or requested, but that they would never rely on them for the wide variety of provisioning any household needs.

The kiosks, in contrast, were a different story. These venues were truly private shops that individuals had paid a considerable sum to open and maintain. Once the small overhead and wholesale prices were covered, all of the profits went to the salespeople. These shops were crammed with a large variety of goods, few of which were vital consumer goods. Large supplies of booze, soft drinks, cigarettes, sweet candies and cookies, imported shampoos, combs, chewing gum, recorded cassette tapes, disposable razors, cheap batteries, "disposable" electronics, toys, school supplies, and pulp fiction or "scientific" pamphlets made up most of the available goods.

The introduction of the kiosks heralded a new era of petty import substitution. Most of the goods sold at these shops came from China, Iran, and Turkey, and adult villagers rarely had a high opinion of the products' quality. The distrust toward foreign products might not always be a matter of actual good or bad quality, but rather evidence that people dislike change from tastes, shapes, and styles to which they have long been accustomed. More troubling was the fact that most customers had to be informed about usage of the products they were purchasing because they couldn't read the foreign-language labels. For example, women had to be convinced that sunflower oil was good for cooking because the oil was very light and clear, unlike their everyday cottonseed oil, and because the label's photo didn't depict the use of oil in or on foodstuffs as Uzbeks would prepare them. Despite these challenges, the kiosks added variety and color next to the decidedly drearier state shops, and people found them useful in a pinch when they were having guests, going visiting, or looking for a gift.

Kiosks became part of an entirely new network of village entrepreneurship that went well beyond the typical kolkhoz peasant business-minded outlet of selling surplus produce in nearby marketplaces. To be sure, plenty of men and women whom I got to know did just that. They might, in fact, stop cultivating a diversified garden plot and instead grow just strawberries, black-eyed peas, cabbage, melons, or tomatoes. Oftentimes, the growers would simply give the produce to a younger family member to sell, usually to young men. Kiosks, however, provided a gateway to the acquisition of somewhat prestigious imported items, and they imparted to young men—and, less frequently, young women—a kind of energy and purposefulness that barely remunerated kolkhoz work couldn't. A sense of both adventure and illicitness accompanied the village youths who set off for the large cities of Uzbekistan, or even abroad, to bring back goods that they hoped they could sell for serious money.

Officially, the Uzbek government supported private enterprise as a part of its liberalizing orientation. In reality, it erected many roadblocks to unfettered entrepreneurship through practices such as tight regional border controls, high taxation and duties on goods people either brought from farming areas to sell or transported back from the cities to sell at places such as kiosks and small bazaars, and virtually unregulated police corruption that enabled many in the security forces to shake down or seize would-be merchants' monies and supplies, albeit at a petty level. Even so, these challenges could not dissuade the petty business actors who felt that the risks were worth taking because it was just about the only alternative to the kolkhoz lifestyle.

Informants stressed that merchandising and entrepreneurship went hand-in-hand with their strong handicrafts and artisanal traditions, especially in the FV, where the reputation for woodworking, tool making, cutlery, copper working, and textile manufacture was high. People also liked to poke fun at their own commercial proclivities by telling jokes about the legendary Uzbek reputation for selling fruits and vegetables whenever possible:

> You know it's not true that the Americans were the first country
> to reach the moon. We Uzbeks actually were the first there. The
> Americans reported that no sooner had they landed on the moon than
> they heard a knock–knock–knock on the spacecraft door. When they
> looked out the window, there was a guy with a big sack and a *duppi*
> [the Uzbek skullcap], and he said, "Well, are you going to buy these
> cucumbers or not?"

Of course, villagers had a wide range of jobs and professions, even if upward of 80 percent at least seasonally took part in one or another aspect of the cotton, wheat, and rice harvesting in addition to more private development, such as grape or apricot harvesting. Villagers also worked full-time as schoolteachers, various medical professionals, butchers, shoemakers, electrical workers, bookkeepers and accountants, auto mechanics, police, and shopkeepers. Nevertheless, many of these people also had cotton-harvesting duties, including the schoolteachers and children older than the age of ten. Practically

FIGURE 1.4 An ornately carved door—one marker of relative wealth and high status for a village resident. The words at the top are a Qur'anic blessing.

no able-bodied adult failed to engage in some part of the seasonal agricultural routines. The difference today from the Soviet past is that people try very hard to avoid the kolkhoz administration's requirements regarding cotton work, if they feel they will receive too little compensation for their efforts. The mid-1990s witnessed much of this behavior owing to a serious decline in the international price for cotton, which continued through 1999 (Pomfret 2006:29).

A newer strategy (and a theme discussed in depth in Chapter 6) was simply leaving the village—and, therefore, the kolkhoz—altogether. Urban migration is a very recent phenomenon in Central Asia, which was a clear indicator that Uzbekistan had not been a typical developing country under Soviet rule. It is certainly true that the Soviet system tightly regulated the movements of peasants from the countryside to the cities throughout its 70-year history. It is also the case, however, that village life provided a modicum of material comfort and well-being that took away the edge of desperation more typical in countries of South Asia, Southeast Asia, and Latin America. An Uzbek historian has told me that people in Tashkent refer to this factor as the *kishlakizatsiia* of the capital, which is a Russian-language rendering of *qishloq*, meaning the "villagization" of the capital. This trends can be discerned in a number of ways, including more livestock grazing on traffic islands downtown, or boys riding horseback or donkeyback next to late-model Mercedes Benzes. Furthermore, the concept extends to Tashkent residents who have adopted rural ways, such as rearing a few livestock, to supplement their primary income sources.

Rural residents do more than just take up a rural way of life in the city; most actually want to get far away from it in terms of the urban labor practices they adopt. Villagers in Uzbekistan try to work as bakers, street food vendors, construction workers, market salespeople, and day laborers in the cities in ways similar to what Mexicans try to achieve in the United States. Rural Uzbeks in Tashkent and other cities also often live without official residence permits, and they can be fined (or worse) if they are caught and are unable to bribe their way out of these less-than-strictly enforced rules.

A little more than a decade after the collapse of the Soviet Union, Tashkent's population had soared to roughly 3.5 million owing to this wave of country-to-city immigration. In 2004, the city finally took action against the new residents by throwing out many laborers who lacked *propiski*, the necessary residence permit. The government justified the sweep against the "illegals" on the basis of recent terrorist attacks.

Courtesy of Russell Zanca

FIGURE 1.5 Typical Boburkent home of mud, straw, and wood. Note the high walls and absence of windows facing the street. Windows face the inner courtyard. The log outside is a resting or chatting spot.

BUYING AND SELLING

When it comes to consumption or shopping practices, people in rural Uzbekistan are concerned about finding a large variety of goods where they can compete to find the best prices. In this sense, they are similar to consumers on a universal level. What they wish to buy and what they do buy naturally reflect their cultural practices, beliefs, and tastes. Simply put, Uzbeks don't usually buy pork, because they are Muslims, and Muslims are prohibited from eating pork. Uzbeks look for the same basic things that most Americans do—food, clothing, tools, auto parts, bicycles, furniture, shoes, and so on. Given that people on kolkhozes often have to travel considerable distances—sometimes 5, 20, or 50 kilometers—to reach centers where they can find what they want, it seemed pertinent to know where they liked to do their shopping and why.

Mechanized transportation only became more of a headache in the first years of Uzbek independence because of the high cost of fuel and the frequent shortages of spare parts. People crammed into buses, minivans, and sedans in an effort to get from here to there. Sometimes one might see a family of four on a motorcycle, especially with a sidecar, and bicycles and donkeys became more common than anyone could remember in recent times, according to many informants. Once products or commodities (e.g., livestock) were purchased, however, it could be an even more difficult matter to find transport home. One of the strangest transporting innovations I encountered occurred at a busy Sunday bazaar some 8 kilometers from Boburkent, where a man needed to pay someone to help him transport five or so head of sheep back to his home. After making an arrangement, he and the driver hopped in the cab and drove the sheep back to his house in the hinged and forked bucket of an excavator! (See Figure 5.3 on page 132 for a photograph.)

During my interviews with nearly 20 adult villagers about their consumption patterns (slightly more women than men), I asked these individuals where they preferred to shop, and for which kinds of things in particular. As a testament to villagers' non-isolation, interviewees noted that they enjoyed going on trips to nearby cities (not just to the capital) whenever the opportunity arose. As a break from unremitting kolkhoz labor, especially for women, a town or city visit entailed a chance to dress up, see a wider variety of life, eat luxury foods such as ice cream or kabobs with bread from refined flour, and shop for all kinds of things that they rarely if ever encountered in nearby markets. People were happy to obtain ordinary food items, seed, paper products, basic liquors, tools, secondhand goods, certain types of everyday clothing, basic soaps, and many handmade textiles at many local markets within an 8- to 10-kilometer radius. However, people would head out to district or provincial centers, such as the Chorbozor market or Namangan's and Andijon's numerous markets, to find items such as furniture, including woodworked bassinets, chests, and wardrobes; luxury foods, such as candies and white breads; winter wear; stylish boots and shoes; cutlery; new auto parts; electronics and machines; high-quality liquors; jewelry; a large quantity of sugar; and fine clothing or regional wear, such as quilted robes (*chopon*). Usually, the closer the market is to a big urban center, the cheaper the prices will be because of the increased urban competition and the shorter transportation distances for imported products.

One curious note: Almost all of the women from Boburkent did not partic-ularly like shopping in Namangan (a city located the province in which their farm was located), because they felt the city was too religious and conservative. Most women there wear loose-fitting lavender-colored or white headscarves, which they keep partly secured by holding one end in their mouths. Village women did not like the idea of having to wear a head covering; they simply felt Namangan was a little too religious, and they didn't want to conform to local practices.

Both men and women said that they preferred Andijan for goods and prices, but that Andijan people were less kind than Namangan folk. They also saw the former group as more apt to swindle consumers. In regional terms, they felt that their own FV character and outlook were closer to those of Andijanis, and peo-ple from a town very close to this city originally settled their own kolkhoz.

Why people might feel particularly close to a marketplace in one city or an-other also has much to do with their previous experiences in such places. For ex-ample, some of the villagers studied at technical or teaching colleges in either Andijan or Namangan, a factor that had positive effects on their shopping desires. If nothing else, they felt comfortable and knowledgeable about negotiating partic-ular urban places. Increasingly, people from Boburkent and nearby villages, such as Iangi Hayot, have begun move to the cities, at least temporarily, and this wave of immigration makes it much more conducive to visit and shop with relatives or for-mer neighbors who now are connected directly to urban worlds.

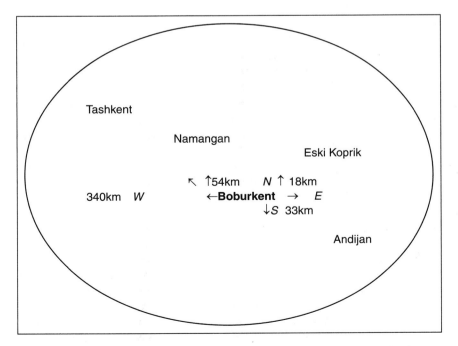

FIGURE 1.6 Shopping locations/marketplaces within the radius of Boburkent.

Villagers do some marketing at least once a week, and they have to be mindful of market days. Some markets may be open a few days of the week or every day, but they will have big market days perhaps once or twice during each week. Sunday has long functioned as one of the main market days, especially for the biggest markets; this is the one true day off for nearly all working people in the former U.S.S.R. The informal Uzbek word for Sunday is *Bozorkuni*, meaning "Marketday." In the kolkhoz villages and smallest towns, major market days are just as likely to occur on weekdays as on weekends. The obvious advantage of these midweek dates in rural areas is that the markets have a chance to compete with their larger brethren, because most people use their Sundays to travel to the previously mentioned marketing locales.

As much as villagers occasionally enjoy a relatively far-off shopping excursion, they do not undertake these marketing trips lightly. Besides going for needful things from time to time, what are the other reasons to make these considerable trips? Special occasions, including holidays and weddings, are primary times to head off to Andijan or Namangan. In these cities, people can buy Coca-Cola, beer, bread, salads, dresses, furniture, and other items in bulk or as gifts. They may visit the larger markets in late August with children to buy all sorts of supplies and new clothes for school. Similarly, they may be more likely to travel to cities on holidays to shop and to take in the public spectacles and artistic performances to commemorate the day or time.

WHEN DOES THE BUS COME?

The pitfalls awaiting traveling villagers during the era in which I did my research included overcrowded boneshaker buses and unreliable, infrequent travel schedules, which had worsened by the early 1990s and continued to decline into the new millennium. Thankfully, transportation has improved in many parts of the republic since 2000. The truth is that the Uzbek villages have good infrastructure relative to neighboring countries, including Afghanistan and Iran, when it comes to roads and highways. Boburkent itself is separated by a main road that basically runs from Namangan to Andijan. Thus, if one can pay a makeshift cabbie what he asks for, then the traveler can probably reach a major city from the village within an hour. Most people, however, have to wait and then crowd on to buses. My wife and I relied on this mode of transportation because it was cheap and because I was determined to travel as the locals do. We certainly had our share of bus riding experiences, a few of which are summarized here to illustrate how it is that people go from place to place in Uzbekistan.

Waiting for buses outside central terminals in the district or provincial or capital towns and cities frequently became a very frustrating game because the scheduling was so imprecise. Whenever we saw a sizable number of people, our expectations were raised. We figured the would-be passengers must have been there for some time, or that their numbers alone signified a bus was on the way. Early in these experiences we would ask, "When do you think the bus will come?" The response to this query most of the time was "*khozir*"—the Uzbek word for "now." In terms of the bus's arrival, however, it really meant "at some time." People who were as annoyed or frustrated as we were might look askance and click their tongues off of the roof of their mouths, an utterance that meant "Who knows?" This utterance often means "No," albeit in a softer or informal way.

When the bus finally did arrive, it might be an old, lumbering Hungarian Ikarus coach, or yellow vehicle that looked half 1950s school bus, half battle tank. And a battle was usually what we were in for: The buses were almost always fully packed when they passed through Boburkent in any direction. An orderly queue to board was not an Uzbek convention. Instead, the locals preferred the no-holds-barred-I'm-getting-on-that-bus-if-it's-the-last-thing-I-ever-do approach. Elderly women who appeared sweet and grandmotherly only a few moments previously whipped themselves into fullback mode in a fourth down and goal-to-go situation. Eventually, all of the passengers got on, perhaps a bit sweatier and bruised for the experience, but happy to be on our way.

Speaking of sweat, Uzbeks typically do not like open windows in moving vehicles. Like many people around the world, they believe that blowing wind on some part of their body will give them a cold, and they are especially fearful for young children in these conditions, even when outdoor temperatures are close to 100 degrees. I do recall one very funny experience I had returning from Namangan to Boburkent on a blistering summer day in 1996. We passengers had bought tickets and boarded the bus at the terminal. We rushed on to make sure we at least had a good place to stand, and then proceeded to pour sweat. This hellish situation proved too much for most riders, and the men began to open windows and push open the ventilation flaps. The driver finally came out of the dispatcher's office and took his seat behind the wheel. Then a man from the back of the bus shouted out: "Hey, Owner of this Sauna, let's get going!" Everybody laughed, and the first breeze felt magnificent as we drove off near sunset through a sea of cotton fields.

Once my wife fainted on the bus due to overcrowding. I was also pick pocketed, though the thief got away with the equivalent of only $0.27, money I gladly would have given him had he asked. On long-distance trips, we became the center of attention once people knew our identities, and these turned out to be jovial times. People would offer food, and we shared reading materials, mainly dated American magazines, such as *Newsweek* or *People*. The passengers loved these publications and would ask us all sorts of questions about the photos. While crowded bus travel has little charm appeal, there were a few aspects of human kindness or consideration that I found impressive on these journeys and that bespoke communal relations in trying situations. People who had the coveted seats almost always gave them up for a mother and child, or for the aged. In circumstances where a mother might be younger than the seated female passengers, she would simply hand her young child off to a granny. Children never seemed to fuss much about this transfer, which probably has much to do with being socialized in such a way that many adults of a type are able to care for children in a variety of circumstances. Finally, people who boarded with heavy packages often could rely on a seated passenger to hold at least some of their belongings, making the trade-off seem a basic matter of fairness.

KOLKHOZ LIVING ARRANGEMENTS AND
FAMILY HOUSEHOLDS

Once we reached the village, we needed to decide where to live, or have someone resolve the matter for us. Originally, we were to stay with Alijon, his wife, and four of their six children. They lived in a typical Uzbek village housing compound, which contained two separate small houses bordering an average garden plot, about 0.1 hectare (a hectare is a bit less than half an acre) where the family raised corn in addition to a variety of fruits, nuts, vegetables, and herbs—exclusively for themselves. Within the compound was an area for a cow and her calf, a pen for several sheep, and a chicken coop with about ten chickens. Alijon's house contains four rooms, plus a kitchen/hearth room, and a basement and flat roof for storage. Most houses have mansard-style roofs of corrugated metal, as did Alijon's.

Alijon's father and mother lived on the other side of the enclosed compound. Uzbeks typically follow a residence pattern known as patrilineal ultimogeniture, which means that married sons usually bring their brides to their parents' house to live or else live close by, depending on housing conditions, wealth, and other factors. The youngest son is supposed to stay in his father's house the longest with his bride and offspring; the idea is that the youngest son should take care of his parents in their final years.

Contrary to our expectations, Alijon initially placed us with his divorced sister on the other side of the village. She had two young boys, and her home had a large extra room to spare. We stayed there for several months through the winter and into the spring, but our relations with his sister, Firuzahon ("hon" is an honorific title meaning "Lady"), were never very good. In addition, I occasionally became the source of malicious gossip because many people thought it was poor form for me to be staying in the home of a single mother, even though my own wife was with me, save for a few occasions when she pursued her own work in other places. We eventually moved in with Alijon, which proved a far better arrangement.

While every house in Boburkent has its minor differences in layout, size, and decorations, most are uniform, and few standing today were built before the 1960s. House building requires a major effort in the Uzbek countryside, mainly because ready-made materials aren't generally available, nor are professional contracting outfits. The homes are modest wattle-and-daub affairs. All bricks are made from local mud, and the wood comes mainly from local poplar trees. Hay is another supporting material; it is mixed with mud for use as a construction material. Floors generally are earthen, but many people also manage to include a layer of concrete when available.

Overall, the advantage of mud brick homes is that they stay thermoregulated throughout most of the year, or at least until extremely hot or cold temperatures have been sustained for a week or more. People in this area of Uzbekistan tend to whitewash the walls of their homes and the walls that separate neighboring compounds, and they prefer a light blue paint or green paint for metal entrance gates and wooden doors. The disadvantage of mud brick walls is

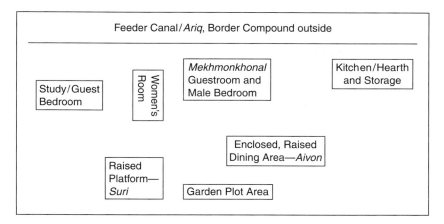

F I G U R E 1.7   Diagram of a typical house/compound layout in Boburkent. (Proportions are not to scale.)

that they may weather and buckle very easily, especially when an elaborate network of reinforcement is absent; villagers ordinarily do not employ this kind of infrastructure. For this reason, it is a ubiquitous sight in summer in villages to see people digging for soft, moist earth and mixing it with water to make more mud bricks. Because rain tends to wear away at the whitewashing quickly, paint is in high demand during the summer, too.

For wealthier people, house doors should be of ornately carved hardwoods. Three or four Boburkent households had such carved doors during my stay, which according to consultants reflected the development of increased income differences among families. Decorative woodcarving has a long tradition in Central Asia.

Rural Uzbek houses rarely have more than four rooms, unless additions have been built to accommodate married children. Three or four rooms generally are the norm. The house's featured and largest space is the *mehmonkhona*—the guestroom or living room. Here people keep their best quilts and pillows (the main furniture), and often a television or a music system. This space is called the guestroom not necessarily because it is where a visitor might stay overnight, but rather because it is where Uzbeks always entertain their guests. Its large size reflects the need to accommodate many guests, especially for weddings and other celebrations and social rituals. The other rooms all tend to be reserved for sleeping. It would be rare to find the concept of a master bedroom, although a father may have a room or build an additional room just for himself once he reaches middle age. The reason that bedrooms are quite similar in size has to do with the absence of concepts such as children's rooms and parents' rooms. The normal state is for men and women to not sleep in the same room, save for Wednesday nights ("making love nights"). Ordinarily, mothers sleep with young children in one room, and fathers sleep in another room. As children mature, boys will sleep in the same room as their fathers and girls will stay in the same room as their mothers.

The kitchen or hearth area usually is built into the house, but forms a separate room with its own entrance. It may lead the way to the cellar, which villagers use mainly for food storage. We will take up the household theme again in Chapters 4 and 5 to explore in more detail family dynamics, division of labor by sex and age, meal preparations, and celebrations within the home.

The villages and farms of the Chorbozor district are spread out over an area of some 200 square kilometers in the central FV. All had electrical utility service, although some villages didn't receive electric power until the early 1960s. Boburkent became electrified in 1960. Unfortunately, the power supply could be fickle, and temporary blackouts were a common occurrence.

Over the years, people had come to rely on electricity to power their lighting, their central water tap, and radio and television. Radio and television service ensured that those who were interested could keep informed about world and local events, though the Uzbek media's reporting seemed not so much investigative in nature as inclined to serve up press releases from the president's office.

Locally, people concerned themselves with news of the national economy and the harvests in particular. According to the television news program anchors, the news was good. The country produced more and more, cotton and wheat were abundant, and people were living well. This was fine, except that almost no one agreed with the information. Alijon would listen and say, with a dismissive wave of his hand, "It's all for [President Islom] Karimov." Like most Uzbek village men of middle age, Alijon spent considerable time socializing in his own home or the home of others—eating, drinking, playing cards, reminiscing, and talking at length on any number of topical issues. As long as the electricity worked, the television always blared away. The men frequently reacted to the news in ways similar to Alijon, at least when it came to the national conditions of the economy, especially cotton farming and agriculture. The media usually managed to skirt the issue of bad weather, even if one could look through a window and watch the raindrops fall. It wasn't just the way the farm functioned that showed experienced peasants a new form of the Soviet system remained intact; they also had modern communication with which to measure the treatment their agricultural conditions received from the authorities.

THE DEMANDING, SELFISH STATE AND ITS RELATIONSHIP TO THE KOLKHOZ

A common conceit about Soviet socialism is that it made people unambitious and uncompetitive because they depended so heavily on government to provide for them. The problem with this argument is that it often neglects just how punishing the state bodies could be when production quotas weren't fulfilled. The punishments themselves were collective, and included reduced salaries, lower amounts of in kind payments (e.g., wheat, cooking oil, rice), and fewer outlays for the farm's infrastructure, including electricity, heating fuel, and so forth. While collective farm peasants were dependent on the state, ambition and competition not only raised their standards of living, but could also bring individual notoriety in the forms of awards and commendations for labor and service; even cash bonuses formed a part of this mix.

After independence, the Soviet Uzbek Communist Party leadership, which suddenly morphed into the People's Democratic Party of Uzbekistan, declared that they would pursue an inevitable approach toward capitalism and private ownership, but that they would proceed slowly. That has, indeed, been the case. Kolkhoz peasants—that large majority of people on the farms who are directly involved in agricultural work and who draw their salaries almost exclusively from farm labor—immediately faced a quandary. The state could not simply privatize all of the land because it would have meant selling relatively small parcels, such as lots of 0.5 hectare per family. In addition, this practice would not have been sustainable, given the lack of institutions to support individual farmers and all of their overhead and equipment requirements—not to mention that three generations of people had not experienced this kind of individualist orientation during their lifetimes. Alternatively, the state could have sold larger parcels to wealthier people, but that course of action might have rendered many people "peasants" in the classic sense—that is, people making their livings by the grace of a class of landlords.

More importantly, the new state leadership most definitely did not want to lose monopolistic control over this sector's supply of raw cotton, given that this material is one of the most important sources of revenue for the Uzbek government. The cotton system, as controlled by the state for many decades now, remains one of the most potent sources of government control and power. The state buys cotton from the farms after setting production targets that the farms must meet. It allocates outlays ahead of time—before the harvest is in—but will pay for only what the farm actually produces. Essentially, the state cuts the farms in for a small share of the profits it makes based on international market prices for cotton and bankrolls the rest among various ministries or branches of the government.

Peasant informants understand that this system wasn't going to change overnight, but they expected to see reforms coupled with an ability for themselves to pursue alternative types of work where they could diversify what they raised (several case examples are provided in Chapter 2). What turned out to be less than a welcome strategy was the state's abnegation, at least in practice, of many of its former welfare responsibilities to the farms, including health subsidies; free public education, specifically with regard to school supplies; pensions for the elderly, disabled, and single mothers; and price supports for basic foodstuffs. I use the phrase "in practice" because officially laws did not always change, and pensions certainly were not taken away. In reality, they just weren't paid on time, and the amounts allocated did not keep pace with the high levels of inflation that occurred in the mid-1990s. For the villagers, however, the bottom line was that a new phase of life had begun where the worst aspects of the Soviet system persisted and the best were dispensed with, at least temporarily.

Uzbeks, like almost all other Soviet peoples, began to farm collectively in the early 1930s, following more than a decade of Bolshevik experiments in socialist agricultural organization, including small farmer groups working together on cooperatives. In other parts of Eurasia, and especially in Russia, the notion of private, individual farming was an alien concept. This isn't to say that private, small-scale or large-scale farming is somehow impossible in Eurasia—far from it. Rather, the point being made here is that people cannot simply innovate in just a few years time to adopt a pattern of production with which they have virtually no prior experience.

I asked no fewer than 50 kolkhoz peasants and villagers what they would want if they had their druthers about farming. Almost everyone liked the idea of having their own farm, and many were familiar with the rudiments of farming in the United States. They knew, for example, that some farmers had huge farms, easily the size of their kolkhoz, and that the government didn't tell farmers what to grow, when to grow it, and how much to grow. While many romanticized American farming, they could also be quite realistic about their own conditions, their high population density (between 350 and 400 persons per square kilometer), and the issue of multigenerational patterns of collective labor. Overall, informants thought that given their conditions and the continued importance that cotton would play in the local economy, some form of collectivized agriculture should be retained for the foreseeable future.

Similar vantage points have emerged on the question of collectives in research conducted in other parts of the former Soviet Union. One example comes from one of the few Western anthropologists who researched and wrote about collective farming during the Soviet period. Caroline Humphrey found a similar attitude to farming on a return trip she made to a Bashkir (a Mongolian ethnic group) collective farm in Siberia in the aftermath of the disassociation of the Soviet republics. In questioning whether the role of collectivism is dead throughout ex-Soviet Eurasia, Humphrey opines as follows:

> … it will be argued here that collective enterprises of one form or another are still highly relevant to our times. Why so? First, and very simply, large numbers of collectivities still exist in Russia, and in many regions they and many other forms of joint agricultural enterprise are indispensable to the way farming is now organized and the way people imagine their lives (1998:ix).

In 1998, I had the opportunity to carry out baseline socioeconomic research among pastoralist Uzbeks of a sheep collective in central Uzbekistan, Navoii, province. Among the many questions on our survey about their economic lifestyle and intentions for the future was one about the type of agricultural arrangement or enterprise that they would like to have. Among the 76 respondents, a little more than 70 percent favored retaining the kolkhoz not only because it was the system to which they had grown accustomed, but also because many considered that they had fared well enough under this system. Perhaps the one consideration they are not factoring in is the notion that the entire Soviet way of life has been undone.

While we cannot say with any assurance that all of the Uzbeks grouped on collective farms feel similarly to the relative handfuls of people discussed here, a considerable number of studies appear to confirm the continued saliency of collective farming at least in the minds of peasants. One of the troubling issues that farm residents somewhat grudgingly recognize is that the large rural populations make it well nigh impossible to find employment for all: There are simply too many hands for the agricultural work that needs to be done, even during the harvest periods when the idea is to pick as much cotton as possible, as fast as possible. This is not an example of gainful employment in any case because it is temporary work, and very badly paid work at that.

According to my calculations, given the fluctuating inflation in the mid-1990s, and the fact that currency was given an official higher value than a floated currency would have demonstrated, cotton pickers earned approximately $0.02 for every kilogram of cotton picked. Even the very best and toughest cotton pickers can earn no more than a few dollars per day at this rate. Uzbekistan has sacrificed quality and yield to the sheer amount of territory used to grow cotton, which explains why much of its cotton does not bring in the value per kilogram that Egyptian or American cotton does. Recent economic analysis also indicates that 20 percent or more of the labor devoted to agriculture is unnecessary, and the new state will not subsidize this work as generously as the Soviet Union did (Horsman 2003:53). The question that must be solved is this: How can people in Uzbekistan develop an agricultural way of life that provides long-term sustainability and satisfactory income to the farming population? If large-scale farming based on collectivism is doomed to failure, then how will small-scale, more privatized farming achieve financial independence from the state and keep the Uzbek people fed and productive?

State intervention into the affairs of citizens dominates the rural employment arena in a most confounding way because people remain tied to jobs that provide salaries only in principle. An older consultant, a man of about 60 years, struck me as someone who either had an unswerving faith in the state to follow through on its commitments to people or was simply optimistic. He told me that he was owed two years' worth of wages. When I expressed exasperation that anyone should have to wait that long to get a salary and suggested that perhaps he would never see his money, he nonchalantly replied, "No, they will pay us. A lot of people are in the same situation. It just takes time, but we'll get our money." For him, having experienced several of these wage arrears throughout the course of his adulthood, the delay in payment simply didn't seem worth panicking about. In truth, kolkhoz life was replete with feast or famine, wages or no-wages periods in Soviet history, and only really began stabilizing and improving for the peasantry in the period 1960–1987. This factor partly explains what enables a person to take a prolonged period of nonpayment of wages in stride.

While coercion definitely plays a role in getting people to prepare the cotton fields, weed them, irrigate them, sow the seeds, and use pesticides when necessary, there is always something about their long tenure as cotton-raising peasants that keeps Uzbek workers in the fields when there is little material incentive to continue this practice. This partly has to do with how important cotton is in the course of daily life; it also reflects an attitude of resignation. People do not necessarily do something new just because they can; instead, they stick with what they know how to do and are used to doing. I will return to the topic of the pervasiveness and attractiveness of cotton in Chapter 3.

Insofar as the kolkhoz system essentially remains a huge state fiefdom, the state must keep some percentage of the population employed in the cotton and wheat sectors. Some of the most recent reporting at the time of this writing (from the years 2006 and 2007) shows that the state can act punitively toward people who do not plant or harvest cotton, and may also force them to harvest wheat early to meet production quotas as well as to retain control over mechanization in the form of tractors and combines. People may actually go to jail for not doing exactly as the state dictates. The control over both cotton harvesting and the tractors and combines follows Soviet practices from the late 1920s. Even so, a growing number of people from the villages are trying to detach themselves from dependency on the state's demands by pursuing informal, but often legal commercial activities, or by opting to work outside Uzbekistan (e.g., in Kazakhstan, in Russia, and increasingly in the West). Fearing the state's backlash for failing to participate in kolkhoz work brigades as demanded is one thing; the fact that the state repeatedly fails to provide adequate compensation for labor, either in the form of monies or subsidies, is another consideration entirely. The latter concern makes people worry more about not having enough of the basics for themselves and their own families. Chapter 2 explores the history of the current agricultural situation in Uzbekistan, including the makings of the plantations. This discussion is then extended to include information about villagers' relationship to their understanding of local history, and an investigation of whether the past or aspects of the past provide them with any sort of cultural models for behavior or work in future. It should help us to understand how people are beginning to process and evaluate the Soviet past.

CONCLUSION

This chapter has given readers a sense of how I became interested in Uzbekistan, how I pursued my academic interests to get there, and what sorts of difficulties I encountered and advice I received in attempting to work on an Uzbek collective farm before and after arriving in Uzbekistan. Once reaching the collective farm village, I formed impressions of the environment and life there, describing how residents saw themselves in relation to me and their understanding of my fieldwork. In addition to providing a sense of what constitutes a farm in rural Uzbekistan, my work—as explored throughout this book—sought to clarify the relationship between the state and national governments and their agrarian constituents, here the people of Boburkent.

QUESTIONS

1. Which challenges does an anthropologist face in getting to a chosen field site in Uzbekistan?

2. According to local residents, how was village life on the collective farm changing after the Soviet collapse?

3. Given that the Uzbek state maintained control over the collective farms after the Soviet collapse, which elements of the old system began changing after the formation of the new republic?

2

Historical Connections and Today's Kolkhoz

While several changes to rural land ownership have occurred over the last century, the tillers of the Uzbek soil remain in a position similar to the one occupied by their ancestors, part of a line extending back nearly 120 years vis-à-vis their relationship to their overlords. Today landowning prospects for the majority of peasants remain slim. This chapter explains why it still makes sense to talk about Uzbek farm laborers as "peasants," a term that warrants a flexible understanding. This knowledge helps to place today's villagers in an historical context. Their history inevitably shapes people's understanding of their surroundings and place in their society, even when they do not necessarily know their modern history all that well, or at least to the extent that academics write about it.

Of course, no analyst of the historical conditions of the peasants seriously could argue that this group's economic status has not improved, along with their social positions and chances to increase their status. Even class mobility has become possible. For example, any child of a kolkhoznik will go to school, and some may succeed in attending a university or technical college; these individuals may become members of the professional class or academic cadre. Such a change in status would have been exceedingly rare in the pre-revolutionary period (before 1917).

The best reason to show that "peasant" cannot be considered a static category, and that peasants change according to their own actions as well as those of states, comes from the collectivization process that began in 1929. Under this policy of bringing farming people fully under the umbrellas of the socialist system, often at the costs of both freedom and lives, rural people truly were transformed (Berdichewsky 1973:28). In a nutshell, collectivization led to the peasant class category in the Soviet Union becoming the flip side of the industrial working class. The latter had been tasked with the duty of leading the peasants toward socialist construction and consciousness. Indeed, by the late 1930s, it was no longer possible to see the peasantry in the U.S.S.R. as a class in itself that retained its characteristic of being a legion of small holders or a typical peasantry where family farming predominated (Shanin 1984:184).

That anthropologists and historians do not regard the peasant idea in precisely the same way comes through in our scholarly writings. Historians tend not to get too worked up about the notion of treating people as isolated, outside the state, or denigrated—issues that anthropologists often seem to be concerned about to the exclusion of analytical specificity. Clearly, historians recognize these possibilities and objections, but they remain focused on seeing peasants as an appropriate group of producers within society who are definitely incorporated within state systems, even if marginalized and unequally so.

In examining what has happened to Mexican peasants who have migrated to California and have taken up a new way of life (socially, economically, and so on), Michael Kearney (1996) argues that the category of "peasant" is no longer academically useful. He goes even further to identify dates in time when peasants existed—and stopped existing—as a social scientific category of persons. His conceptualization may make sense in a certain sociocultural or national context, but may not be helpful in all situations. Even so, Kearney has made a valuable contribution to anthropology in taking one of our most discussed research objects and making us rethink why we accept certain notions and reject others. This is what good scholarship does.

For my own part, I am inclined to use the historical and social science literature on Russia to help me contextualize and explain the peasant notion in Uzbekistan. Teodor Shanin, a renowned historian of agrarian Russia and Soviet power, writes of meaningfulness in regard to peasantry in part because it stems from analytical terms that he claims originated in the "socio-legal structure of the Russian empire." He goes further to note that one is correct to speak of peasants as a "real" entity, regionally and nationally, because peasants acted "coherent[ly] and ... self-consciously" (1985:81). Another historian of Russia, Vinogradoff, says that the way Russians used land and partitioned their communes reveals that they acted as a social class on their own behalf and confounded the authorities by their "rationality" (1975:6–19).

My own goal here is to discuss just a few features of the Russian peasants so as to make a comparison to the Uzbeks; clearly, not everything that characterized the Russian peasants applies equally well to the Uzbek villagers. Nevertheless, Russian colonialism (post-1865) and later Soviet domination influenced and affected Uzbek village life to the extent that discussion of the Russian peasantry and the Russian empire has relevance. After all, Russian and Soviet authorities targeted the Uzbeks when they embarked on their civilizing missions. In response to this Russian Soviet cultural engineering, kolkhozes from Estonia to Uzbekistan became alike in many ways.

In Russia until 1861, the peasants were virtual slaves, known as serfs. They lived in a system rather different, but with some similarities, from that holding sway throughout most of Europe from AD 1000 onward. Russian serfs more or less belonged to the Russian gentry and titled nobility whose lands they worked.

The serf peasants lived in communitarian villages, known as *mir*, and organized production through their own households, known as *dvor*. Just as one could inherit land, so one could inherit the serf peasants who worked that land, along with their children—hence the slavery-like aspect of this order. The major difference from other slave systems is that Russian serfs paid taxes through their landlords and, therefore, were ultimately "enserfed to the state" (Pipes 1974:105). The period harshest for Russian serf peasants (a system begun in earnest early in the sixteenth century) occurred when a similar serfdom began ending in Western Europe—specifically, during the eighteenth century (Taylor 1995:303).

Russian peasants had next to no political representation and little inkling as to how rights they desired could be gained other than through haphazard, violent outbursts directed at those ruling elements closest to them. The anthropologist Eric Wolf (1969) wrote a book where he discussed the overall ineffectiveness of peasant rebellions and wars to achieve a fundamentally new society. As pointed out by Wolf, even the great peasant rebellions in Russian or Central Asian history rarely enabled the peasants to achieve more than the state's wrath. However, at least in Russian history it was the savage violence of peasant rebellions that sometimes led the tsarist authorities to consider enacting reforms.

Leading progressive and leftist revolutionary thinkers, such as Antonio Gramsci, depicted Russian peasants before the 1917 revolution distastefully, claiming that the peasant's universe was one of shadows:

> The peasant has always lived outside the rule of law—he has never had a juridical personality, nor a moral individuality. He lives on as an anarchic element, an independent atom in a chaotic tumult, constrained by his fear of the police and the devil. He had no understanding of organization, of the state of discipline (1988:114).

Even though the prejudices toward the food producers of the Russian empire seemed to have been shared equally by rightist and leftist political forces in society, the Bolsheviks believed that the only way to transform the peasants into a class of acceptable Soviet citizens was to "proletarianize" them—that is, make the ways they worked and their working conditions as similar as possible to those of their industrial counterparts.

Following the Soviet collapse, a major problem of political or organizational life for peasants has not been that they cannot understand the nature of political representation or that they are ignorant about how they are governed. For the most part, peasants are aware of such matters. Rather, in the ensuing authoritarian environment, they have been afraid to press for reforms and improvements—physical or abstract—that would outpace the reforms the national leadership has set. To be seen as contrary to the state's positions is to invite legal trouble, the irony naturally being that repression of political action rarely is legal. Prerevolutionary peasants suffered from a lack of locally interested and invested bureaucratic organizations. Today little trust exists with regard to those who have positions of power, even if they themselves are rural; bureaucrats achieve their positions by closing off any path that might lead to the airing of common grievances. They pretend that the state still cares the most for people's welfare and problems—so why would anyone need to take independent action or work outside the state's most local channels?

Returning to the Russian empire and the eventual freeing of the serfs in 1861, one must bear in mind that the grip of the landed gentry was not truly loosened until 1917. For the majority of cases of freed serfs who became landowners in the tsarist period, these events mainly took place under the state's auspices. Many freed serfs settled on lands beyond European Russia. Until the middle of the first decade of the twentieth century, the influx of landless Russians, mainly from Russia's central and southern areas, into Central Asia, including the steppes of Kazakhstan, did not result in a situation of crisis proportions between the Central Asians and the settlers—unlike the events that would occur ten years later. The great Stolypin Reform (1906), however, opened the way for many poor Russians to resettle in the Ferghana Valley (FV) as well as in other parts of Central Asia (Brower 2003:143–144).

The effects of this wave of resettlement included a severe strain on available resources, especially on the irrigation systems. Those investments made by the empire to alleviate this specific situation were geared mainly toward the resettling Russians and focused almost exclusively on benefits related to cotton growing (Ginzburg 1991:37–46). By 1909, the results of land confiscations from Central Asians and the resettlement by Russians on those confiscated lands had begun to alarm the Turkestan Governor-General (the tsar's ruler over much of what is today's Central Asian republics, excluding northern Kazakhstan), P. I. Mischenko. As a representative of sovereign Russian power, Mischenko was part of the internal debate among other members of the leadership regarding both the resettlement of Russians in Central Asia and the various positions then taken about how best to appease Central Asians, which entailed the control over movements such as pan-Islamism or pan-Turkism. Recognizing the uneasy conditions, Mischenko spoke of a "most serious turnabout" in the mood of Central Asians toward Russians and those representing tsarist agrarian policies (Diakin 1996:49). Just before the Central Asian Uprising of 1916 (a protest against peasants being drafted into the tsarist empire's military during World War I), for example, the income of Russian settlers into the FV on average was twice that of the indigenous inhabitants.

Until the revolution, peasants of the Russian empire had essentially two choices open to them if they chose to leave the villages behind and give up farming: They could join the military on a 25-year tour of duty (few actually served the entire period; Ransel 1992:125), or they could be among the coveted few who received state passports to work in the new urban factories. Nevertheless, many of those who did leave their natal villages for extended periods maintained membership in their respective mir (a communal organization based on kin ties and holding resources and labor in common), and the expatriates often returned to their home villages from time to time. Rather than specific policies or decrees, few factors had as much to do with changes in peasant culture and the introduction of peasants to the Russian state as their own willful moves away from the villages. This was the process that eventually began shifting Russia as a whole away from a peasant way of life.

One may find it reasonable to think that the drive to collectivize peasants in the late 1920s to mid-1930s would have started the final phase of transforming the Eurasian peasantry. Even though the exponents of this plan tried to "take care of rural barbarians," a peasant life nevertheless persisted (Slezkine 1994:436). Political and economic changes tell us less about culture change than we often realize. This fact explains why fieldwork is crucial: It introduces another body of evidence to help balance the weights of historical writings and ideological positions so characteristic of Soviet and Cold War scholarship.

In Russia and the European lands of the empire, the Bolsheviks would have enjoyed even less success in transforming the peasantry and winning partial support had they relied solely on the party's rank and file; the forces most influential in altering peasant consciousness were none other than the sons of peasants who had seen the world beyond their villages. No event shattered the relative stability of the peasant worldview and politicized the peasants as dramatically as World War I did. As Gramsci noted of the war's impact:

> The change occurred especially in Russia, and was one of the essential
> factors in the revolution. What industrialism had not brought about in
> its normal process of development was produced by the war (1988:115).

Keep in mind that close to 80 percent of those who participated in this war and died on Russia's behalf were peasant soldiers. Unlike the Bolsheviks who utilized the blood and sweat of millions of peasants to industrialize the Soviet Union, the tsarist regime simply squandered peasant lives in a war that only helped dissolve the empire itself.

Given this reading of events, the fact is undeniable that culture change had been in the offing for peasants throughout Russia from the middle of the nineteenth century, especially with increased urbanization. Later, after the Bolsheviks came to power, a period of relative economic liberalization ensued for peasants. Known as the New Economic Policy (NEP), this period lasted roughly from 1921 to 1929. The collectivization that began in earnest in 1929 was launched partly to crush whatever independent farming had arisen among peasants during the NEP. Of course, just because the Bolsheviks planned to make the state recognize the value of agricultural workers, it does not mean that they succeeded in transforming all past practices and outlooks, even 70-plus years into the future.

After World War II, Soviet sociologists believed that one group of farm workers clearly had broken free of their peasant status, becoming full-fledged state workers. These were the people who farmed the *sovkhozes* (Soviet farms) as opposed to *kolkhozes* (the type of farm that we have discussed exclusively up to this point). The two types of Soviet farms existed throughout the U.S.S.R. As factory-type farmers, *sovkhozniks* were viewed as members of the working class. In contrast, *kolkhoznik* field laborers remained peasants.

Although one would be hard pressed to show that the kolkhozniks had much say over the kinds of crops they raised or what their farm might need in terms of investments, at least the presumption was that the kolkhoz farm leadership did. The central idea here in distinguishing these two types of farm workers is that the kolkhoznik depended less on a state wage and more on the overall produce that his farm sold. Soviet sociological opinion held that kolkhoz members retained part of "the more traditional peasant mode of production." The term "mode of production" comes from the writings of Karl Marx and means everything about a particular economic way of life, especially how people produce the things that they need, utilizing their labor, tools, and materials. The term also subsumes the idea of the "relations of production," meaning how people are organized and managed with regard to their work. Soviet academics once thought that the peasants would be altogether integrated completely into the working class by the 1980s (Lane 1971:55–58), but according to their own criteria this seems not to have happened.

While discussion so far has centered on peasants in Eurasia, especially during Russian and Soviet history, the fact is that we should not over-generalize about the similarities between peasants in Russia and Central Asia. Serfdom, for example, is not characteristic of landlord–tenant relationships in Central Asia.

In the nineteenth century, the forebears of today's Uzbeks never clamored to join the Russian empire's army, and there were very few industrial cities for them to resettle in. By the late nineteenth century, however, the beginnings of Russian-controlled and -operated cities arose close to the fields of cotton production. Textile industries quickly arose in FV cities, such as Kokand, Andijan, and Skobelev (Margilan after the colonial era) after 1875. As a rule, Uzbeks did not migrate to these cities. Instead, and most interestingly, the trend among Central Asians who lived in crowded towns and small cities during the eighteenth and nineteenth centuries was to create new farming settlements—a sort of ruralization.

The new settlements of that time may encompass many contemporary Uzbek kolkhoz villages. We see these roots reflected in the suffixes of many village names, such as Sherazem*chek* and Buston*chek*. "Chek" endings highlight a couple of important land-related notions. The most common usage relates to the strips or parcels of land that peasants worked by hand, usually a piece worked on by an individual (Sukhareva and Bikjanova 1955:35). "Chek" also signifies a territory granted to an individual or group who wanted to settle noncultivated land. Those who were to settle and farm the territory arranged to pay tribute or taxes for their housing and usufruct rights, and the land was chartered as a distinct settlement on a permanent basis. After the new settlers worked out an exchange agreement, people vied among themselves for local leadership roles as well as for rights over parcels of land and the regulation of water. Although many of these chek settlements strike visitors as the embodiment of old traditions and long-preserved settlement styles, in fact they are often no more than 150 to 200 years old.

Worldview—a way of thinking and an outlook on one's own life—is the term that best defines the peasant category in twenty-first-century Uzbekistan. The Uzbeks' worldviews indicate their peasantness in an existential sense through the ways in which they talk about the state, their livelihoods, their social events, the goods and services important to them, and their very distinctiveness from town or urban life. It is not simply a matter of being rural, but rather of living an agricultural life. Furthermore, the official texts and political discourse over more than 50 years reinforce people's own identity as peasants. The post-Soviet experience, with its rhetoric of emerging ideologies of national pride and independence, recognizes the farming population as a distinct social category (Karimov 1994). To demonstrate this kind of a worldview, the voice of Bobur-kenters may best express its presence.

The socioeconomic history of many FV villages, especially in the Namangan–Andijan area, close to Namangan's craggy, tortuous 60-kilometer border with Kyrgyzstan, predates the Russian imperial advance by more than a century. In some cases, villages were established considerably earlier, especially those close to the Norin River (which joins the Syr River north of the FV) (Bernshtam 1951:33). Unfortunately, local records, when available, lack precision. As a consequence, it is often possible to write about these villages' histories only in barest outline. Boburkent's history, written by a village school principal, states that its founding dates back "long, long ago some 200–300 years" (Tursunbaev 1974:1). Using this work, it becomes possible to localize history and describe general conditions among FV peasants from the beginning of Russian colonial expansion into the area.

From the nineteenth century onward, FV history shows changes that tie together ethnic groups and their economic pursuits—changes that even brought on transformations of ethnicity and corresponding work regimes. Many people who say that they are Uzbeks today also claim other identities for themselves, such as Kipchak or Sart, that have a basis in historical self-designation as well as in Russian ethnography, regional and linguistic differences, physical appearance, and past economies.

Generally, people who today say that they are Sart (occasionally encountered among senior citizens) represent themselves as descendants of FV farmers or town dwellers who have led settled existences for centuries. They assert that their language is rooted in the Old Uzbek/Chaghatai language, which in turn is the basis for modern literary Uzbek. FV Sarts, known to Russian anthropologists as those Uzbeks who had lost a sense of clan or tribal distinctions (relating to kinship ties as a primary criterion of group inclusiveness), may be distinguished from many other Uzbeks from southern, central, and western areas, who retained kinship affiliations of identity long after 1917 (Inogamov 1955:8).

Qipchoqs claim herdsmen and nomads as ancestors. They represent themselves as part of the original Uzbek nation of nomadic warriors who began systematic conquest of Central Asia's oases in the fourteenth and fifteenth centuries. Their agrarian past is not long, and many claim that they lived among or even as Kyrgyz just a few generations ago.

Namangan province's Kipchaks, who seem to retain a kind of demonstrated descent (meaning that people know who their actual ancestors were going back at least four generations), along with a more pastoralist lifestyle, are found (at least as late as the mid-1950s) in the foothills areas of the province—parts of today's Qosonsoi region (Inogamov 1959:21). Boburkent's residents mainly claimed to be of Kipchak origin, but there is no radical departure among residents having a better sense of their "clan" affiliations or descent reckoning based on these sub-ethnic labels. Rather, several older Sarts who were able to cite paternal ancestors (descent is reckoned patrilineally) could identify ancestors back four to five generations.

Following is part of a conversation I had with a village carpenter (C) concerning the settlement of Boburkent:

RZ: What were you saying about fighting that took place here? Who fought?

  C: What I was saying was that Boburkent was a Sart village. I mean the people all were Namanganers.

RZ: So they all came from the city?

  C: No, not necessarily. A lot of them were village people, too. But then Kipchaks moved in; they were also called *Qizil Chopon*.

RZ: Qizil Chopon [Red Robes]! What does that mean?

  C: That's what they were called. They also called them *Qizil Tol* [Red Willows] and *Qora Tol* [Black Willows]. Anyway, they fought here to take the land for themselves, and they fought against the Kokand Khanate, too.

RZ: And who won?

  C: Well, nobody really won. Eventually, more Kipchak settlement occurred. They were known because they couldn't say "wheat" properly. They would say "*bodoi*" instead of "*bughdoi*."

Settlement for the Kipchaks also resulted partly from later policies adopted by the Russians and partly because European peasants settled their pastures with imperial expansion in the nineteenth century. This description provides a synopsis of Sart and Kipchak differences among the people of a FV village. The historical literature for both groups is vast. The distinction made between the two shows us that significant shifts have taken place among the ethnic populations of today's kolkhozes, further undermining the idea of static communities. To be sure, the distances that people moved into and out of were not vast, but the immigration nevertheless upset the notion of traditionalism and the timeless endurance of customs, rituals, and economy that sometimes appear in the literature (Poliakov 1991).

Overall, the settlements' patterns reflecting the historical record from the 1700s in the FV show patterns of cultivation and a peasant lifestyle. In the last quarter of the nineteenth century, when large-scale commodity production in agriculture begins with Russian colonization and cotton farms, we do not see corresponding mass migration or even significant migration of rural Uzbeks to the nearby cities. Local labor and craft talents were utilized from among the urban populace themselves. What applied to population movements among the Russian peasantry—namely, mass urban migration and participation in imperial institutions bringing the Russians out of the countryside—did not apply to Central Asians. The commodification of Central Asian agriculture (or what we could suggest was its "cottonization") resulted merely in the temporary improvement of sharecropping conditions. Simply put, it made working the fields a more viable option than had previously been true, especially in the FV's eastern part, the Andizhan *uezd* (district; known today as *raion* in Russian and *tuman* in Uzbek) (Sukhareva & Bikjanova 1955:47).

Courtesy of Russell Zanca

FIGURE 2.1 Boburkent elders who provided much local history.

When the imperial leadership attempted to wrench the rural inhabitants of Central Asia away from their localities, the people of Central Asia rebelled violently. The significance of this settlement and livelihood pattern has to be recognized. During the 1970s, when it became clear that the FV Uzbeks had an excess of labor (due to increases in the sizes of their extended families), urban migration was not looked upon as a favorable option for youth. In 1985, for example, nearly half of all married Uzbek women between the ages of 18 and 44 either wanted or thought it was acceptable to have six children. Most rural people preferred extended family life with high unemployment on the farm to a more anonymous urban existence (Patnaik 1995:159).

REINTERPRETING THE SOVIET-CONSTRUCTED
PAST, REFLECTING ON CONTINUITY

Today, what kinds of things do people discuss when asked about society, social organization, and the way in which workers made a living before there was a Soviet life? Here we can compare popular views with the extant documents and scholarship on such topics. One of the benefits of national independence is increased freedom for scholars, journalists, and other publicists to explore subjects that were either maligned or belittled during much of the Soviet period, such as the armed conflict waged by some Central Asians against Soviet power after the Civil War (1918–1921), or the nature of religious practice in Uzbek society before the Bolsheviks tried to crush it. Most of the interviewees with whom I spoke expressed confidence that the pre-October (1917) past was far better— rural life—than that depicted by the Soviets. Numerous features related to that period were portrayed so positively that I often wondered to what extent some of my informants really knew anything about the earlier time.

This section includes three excerpts from conversations I had with informants about their understandings of life before Soviet power; overall these understandings contradict the views expressed in books from the Soviet period. In the first excerpt, I talk to two men (M1 and M2) about their own views related to ordinary peasants who farmed for the local *boi/bek* (landowner and/or wealthy man). Soviet texts usually speak of the landlessness of the average FV peasant before and during colonization, the fact that he was grossly exploited by the landlord, that he was forever in debt, and that he had to give the landlord one-fifth or more of the crop he harvested for himself as tax. Sources also describe the peasants' unfulfilled needs that were the landlord's responsibilities, such as proper clothing and food.

RZ: Do you think peasants lived better before the Revolution?

M1: Not really, not when you compare our technology and lifestyles. We're poor, but the population gained a lot, especially in terms of education.

M2: In some ways they did live better because no one kept forcing them into the fields. They had more choices.

RZ: What choices? Wouldn't they go hungry if they didn't work all day for the landlord?

M2: Look, there were good and bad landlords, but in our culture the person who hired you had responsibilities to you. If a person were treated badly, he could leave and go elsewhere.

M1: That's true. It wouldn't make much sense to treat people so that you were hated. We were told everyone who was rich was bad, but that wasn't always the case.

RZ: Yes, but how could you just move a whole family, or leave your own village because the landlord exploited you?

M2: You know that we always have relatives nearby. People can help each other out of difficult problems.

RZ: But what about having to give over most of what you reaped to the landowner and eating *palov* [pilaf] only on special occasions?

M2: Sure, *they* tell you everything was bad. People didn't have to give up a fifth, but more like a tenth of their crop. If the boi wanted you to work well, how could he get away with just feeding people bread? Those people ate well. There was food in abundance then and plenty of meat because of all the grass.

M1: At harvest time so many hands were needed, they had to hire *mardikor* [seasonal or day workers]. If those people were mistreated, they could leave and find other work pretty quickly. No, they had to be treated well and fed properly. So ask yourself now if the old world was all that bad.

M2: Water was an even bigger problem than land. It always will be. Back then you had to pay for the rights to use it, to water the crops. The canals were not as big or extensive as they are today, so you always had disputes and people trying to cheat the system. It was best always to live closest to the source.

The second excerpt comes from a discussion with a married couple in their early 50s, who are designated as "husband" (H) and "wife" (W) below. I asked them questions about household work during their grandparents' youth—shortly before the Revolution. Talk turned to other matters of social history.

RZ: Who did most of the work around the house?

W: The women, of course, just like today. But then it was different because the women didn't work in the fields picking cotton or anything else. They stayed at home.

H: They weren't supposed to be seen doing work in public. People considered it shameful for a woman to do agricultural labor as they do today. She tended vegetable gardens near the house and did everything else at home.

RZ: Do you think most women like the opportunity to work in the fields?

W: No way. It's terrible work and they hardly make any money. Besides, a woman has to do all the work at home. It would be better just to have that work. In the fields, just look what happens to women! The sun makes them black and wrinkled, and their hands become large and rough like men's. We lose our beauty and get old fast.

H: Kolkhoz work is like slavery. Women do it because men don't want to. They don't forbid their wives to work; on the contrary, they say go and join with a brigade [cotton picking and farming labor group]. Before independence, families had to have some members working in the fields at harvest time. You might get into trouble if someone from your family didn't show up. Men sometimes did, but women always did. So many people are needed for the harvest. When cotton became so intensively farmed, they had to bring the women and children into the labor force.

RZ: Since so many people talk of the dangers of cotton because of the pesticides and defoliants, don't you worry about all of the cottonseed oil you consume? Why do Uzbeks like this oil so much?

H: "Like it so much?!" It's all we have. You're probably right about it being dangerous, but that's what we eat. People are just used to it, and they begin to miss the flavor and the texture of foods if they don't eat it for a while.

W: My grandfather told me about flaxseed oil. That's what Uzbeks used to eat, and it was delicious and good for you. Back then people were robust and had bright complexions. People were more beautiful.

H: Cotton has been bad for us in so many ways. Just look at all the children we have. That's a result of the Soviet system, too.

RZ: I'm afraid I don't understand that. Isn't it the Soviets who always said the Uzbeks, or the Muslims generally, have too many kids? "Why don't they practice birth control?" And in Uzbek you have all of these proverbs about the joy of many children. In fact, Uzbeks always ask a person right away how many children do you have, even if they have just learned your name.

 H: To a certain extent, that's all true. We do think it's extremely important to have children and that people cannot be fulfilled without children in their lives. But the Soviets made it so that we would have only more and more children through the cotton economy. A family needs lots of extra hands for all of the work. And with socialism helping to take care of all of the people, it became like a cycle that kept increasing. It's as if our cultural tendencies became exaggerated. Instead of four children, people thought six, seven or more is better; it will make you "richer." And now ... it's no good.

The third excerpt stems from discussions that I had on several occasions with a schoolteacher about authority figures and the respect due them in times predating Soviet political offices. In the village today, schoolteachers are accorded a kind of de facto authority because of their role as educators, as learned people, and as people who have some role to play in the ethical instruction of children. The teacher (T) is also a man in his early 50s, and he gained most of his awareness about how people of local authority and leadership once were treated from older people, including his own father, a man who also had been a teacher.

RZ: Everybody in Uzbekistan, whether they're Uzbek or not, talks about the fact that Uzbeks revere older people so much and that for this reason you don't find the dissolution of the family, or simply older people living alone, going hungry, and feeling like a burden on their children. Russians always say that this is a great feature of your culture. Would you say it's as true of the village today as it ever was?

 T: It's an obvious point about our family life, and, indeed, we wouldn't think of moving away from our parents if we knew that they would be alone; that's just unthinkable. But you see, before older people, well, older men ... they played a much bigger role in the community, but with the Communists the titles of leadership conferred on older people, such as *mahalla bosh* or *oqsoqol* [community leader and senior leader, literally "white beard"], were changed. They became political positions for the Communists, yet they preserved the traditional titles.

RZ: So are you suggesting people stopped respecting older people as authority figures decades ago?

 T: Yes, but not in the sense of the scorn or contempt people were encouraged to have for the *mullo* [local religious guide and leader, maligned by Communists as a local agent of oppression]. It was different. Younger people will always listen to what older people say, pretending like they're going to follow what an older person says, but then the older person heads off, and the younger person just does what he wants. He doesn't have to heed that kind of person.

Courtesy of Russell Zanca

F I G U R E   2.2   The man in the foreground facing the camera is an assistant school principal and local historian—and a major consultant for the author.

In the old days, elders watched out for things going wrong in the community [neighborhood/street] or in the village. They would try to settle problems. If they so much as saw you spitting into the *ariq* [feeder canal and major source of any particular household's water], they would say, "Hey! What do you think you're doing polluting the water!" Our water was much cleaner then. They would also visit the weddings and make sure everything was alright, checking up on behavior and all. They didn't need any weapons to make their words stick.

Coming home one night from a men's wedding preparation party (*sabzi qirish*—"the carrot peeling") and walking along the village's main road, the teacher and I encounter drunken male teenagers and young men sitting in the road. They greet us, but don't move much and are brazen about their activity by doing nothing to hide their empty liquor bottles. We walk on:

T: That behavior is not right.

RZ: You mean the boys and their drinking?

T: Of course. They're not supposed to be out there, lying all over the road. Nowadays, with little work, this is what they do. In the past they would never have acted so shamelessly; they wouldn't have been outside sitting and drinking. And what kind of greeting was that!

RZ: So you didn't do that as teenager? This is new?

T: Absolutely not. We wouldn't have even thought to do that without at least some pretext, like a wedding or an army send-off party. They are our sons, but we act as if that's acceptable behavior. I think it's bad for our village. We're losing good values that we've had for a long time.

In each of the preceding dialogues, the overarching tone is one of approval for past socioeconomic and authoritative structures within the village. Rather than reflecting or affirming the positions expressed in Soviet scholarship through the 1980s, villagers whom I interviewed tended to express opposing viewpoints. Part of their willingness to speak openly to a visiting American anthropologist reflects political changes that began in the late 1980s. Some of it also comes from "counter-Soviet" publications these informants had recently read, and from their sense of the local past as related to them by older relatives. My fieldwork corresponded to a time when the West and America did not represent a threat to local people, unlike in the earlier Soviet period. In this sense, I was really fortunate.

Naturally, some informants' statements seem overly rosy when discussing this remote past that they themselves never experienced. Still, one can appreciate their efforts to see positive attributes and the seeming desire to reclaim those attributes in the face of Soviet hegemony, which controlled their ability to see their past as they may have wished to know it. They try to mend a tear in cultural continuity that was ripped by Soviet efforts to separate their history into periods of darkness and light.

My Uzbek interviewees also want to endorse a peasant society of yesteryear that they idealize, though they admit problems with irrigation management and the infrequent, abusive boi (landlord). Soviet propagandists usually contrasted the Communist accomplishments with the backwardness of old Central Asian peasant society. Villagers have an understanding of the philosophy underlying this practice, and independence has instilled in them a kind of skepticism toward Soviet writings about their old ways; they would just as soon deny most aspects of history that bespeak their inferiority to Russia and Soviet Russians. While praising many aspects of their lives under socialism, they would not countenance the idea that they needed the Soviet system under Russian dominance to make them a "better" and "happier" people.

One term anthropologists use to refer to this idealized way of seeing the past, specifically in the face of a dominating state that is not exactly seen as an organic political development (where local people would have exercised a lot of control), is "traditionalism." The French anthropologist and Central Asian specialist Olivier Roy captures this sense in writing about wealthy Afghans in the 1960s:

> By traditionalism we mean the desire to freeze society so that it conforms to the memory of what it once was; it is society as described by our grandfathers. In this vision history and tradition are merged; the historical development of society is effaced in favour of an imaginary timeless realm under attack from pernicious modernity (1986:3).

Maybe these people always held such positions about their pre-Soviet past, but now more than ever they seem to think the present and the future will benefit from the incorporation of past values and practices. Although no overt nationalism or ethnic exclusivism are suggested by informants, they do assert that Uzbek ways and conduct are superior to Soviet/Russian or European/colonial practices. This view is not necessarily a rejection of modernism (already a part of their lives and the lives of past generations), but rather a rejection of the historicism long characteristic of the Soviet method for interpreting the historically progressive developments among "backward" peoples—interpretive historical materialism (Petrova-Averkieva 1980:19–27).

Since the fall of the U.S.S.R., many people have become willing to articulate a different past than what they learned. In the Soviet era, even if they doubted aspects of the Soviet telling of their past, and especially of their nineteenth-century history, they often trod lightly over the counterintuitive ideology. With certain new freedoms regarding the critique of Soviet history, one almost has to expect an exaggeration about practices and society that long have been maligned. People want to make it known how they would prefer to see their past now that they feel more in charge of it.

When it comes to the official changing of ideologies, nationalist state for Communist polity, and socioeconomic conditions accompanying the severing of so many Soviet-wide connections and commitments, it is natural to see the emergence of a generation gap. It may be easy to shrug off the difference between the teacher and the drunken youth as a kind of timeless jousting between the conservatism of middle age and the insouciance of youth, but that is not the entire story. Why? Because the possibilities and opportunities, not to mention the aspirations for and of those generations, are of distinct worlds—in the simplest terms owing to the Cold War (1946–1991) and post–Cold War (1991 and beyond) eras. During the Cold War, life could be characterized as having concerned promises of quixotic, contained socialism. The universe wrought by World War II and the unsettling excitement of opening up to an overwhelming world were most visually characterized by the unlimited consumer goods and a new optimism: If I can just get a great job and make lots of money, I can afford it all. This new powerful grip is that of global capitalism.

PARADOXES OF COLONIALIST OBSERVERS: SAVAGES IGNOBLE AND NOBLE YESTERDAY AND TODAY

Remarks about the decency and wholesomeness of the pre-Soviet era may reflect a degree of wishful thinking, but it is just as likely that they serve consciousness in a way that is scornful not of Russia per se, but rather scornful toward the Soviet-instituted agricultural system that arose as a particular Western type that denigrated many aspects of the indigenous system. This is no classical anti-colonialism, although the revisionary take on late Russian imperial and Soviet history certainly has its anti-domination aspects. For independence to become something more meaningful in a village setting other than abstract political statements and new institutions, people want to show that their fore-fathers inhabited a Central Asia that was replete with positive elements and its own variants of humanism—points often unexpressed in Soviet historical narra-tives that inscribed peasant life as primitive.

Initial, chance encounters between Russians—as settlers, military personnel, scholars, and even travelers—had untoward consequences for the developing colonizer–colonized relationship. Certain accounts cast so loathsome a shadow on the Uzbek personality that the same prejudices of the Russians toward the "Asiatics," which were indicative of the early accounts, continue to this day among non-Uzbek urbanites. While particular descriptions contain truths that point out contrasts between, for example, how Kazakhs and Uzbeks treat sojour-ners, the narratives overall do not include emic (indigenous) perspectives, nor do they betray long-term investigations into the relatively unknown cultural groups. Not all of these nineteenth-century encounters read contemptuously of the "na-tives," especially when we examine some of the well-crafted ethnographic and geographic accounts left by nineteenth-century scholars such as V. P. Nalivkin (an ethnographer and statesman who lived in Central Asia for a decade) and A. G. Middendorf (a geographer and agronomist with the Imperial Russian Geographical Society). Nevertheless, throughout history the prevailing Russian viewpoint favors Slavic supremacy over the "benighted" and "untrustworthy" Uzbeks (Nalivkin 1880:51–52; Middendorf 1882:329–342).

Middendorf presents an interesting case of a somewhat bewildered official trying to make sense of a culture he understands poorly upon first encounter. This caused him to make rash judgments: "Where one fellow works, ten or fifteen stand around him idling or gaping" (1882:330). Later in his research, he was able to attribute this laziness to his reckoning that in Asia "there are more hands available than needed." In his work, Middendorf admits that he was angry with the Uzbeks at first because they seemed so indolent, but that in time he learned that the nature of their farming was quite different from what he knew in Russia. In time he was to consider that Uzbeks were very good natured and tireless in their field labor, but he continued to muse about how their overall potential compared, whether they were of a lower order of human beings, and so on, relative to Russians.

One more example of a more sensitive imperialist perspective comes from the pen of Ostroumov, who believed one could not hope to understand the lifestyle of the "Sart" (Uzbek) without understanding his religion. Ostroumov spent considerable time during the 1890s studying Uzbeks both in their homes and in society, and writing about the roles and responsibilities of people at great length; he was keenly interested in public legality and morality matters, which he observed on city streets (Tashkent) and in marketplaces. Bucking the received imperial wisdom of the day, Ostroumov disagreed that Uzbeks were lazy and that their culture was static. To the contrary, he saw these people as well man-nered and suave, and bright and capable. He also devoted obligatory pages to their unsurpassed hospitality, respect for the elderly, and fine music. With adequate European education, he thought, they could be assimilated quickly to European ways and integrated into Russia (1896:58–660). In the end, sensitive or not, these nineteenth-century Russian scholars and investigative travelers were incapable of positing an enriching future for Central Asians without *Russification*—that is, the process of becoming more and more Russian-like.

During my fieldwork, villagers often impressed upon me how Russians (either those whom they had encountered or perceived felt thusly), despite changing ideologies and political and economic policies, never really veered from their stereotypical views about Uzbeks laid down in the late nineteenth century. One informant told me that the few Russians who had lived in Uzbek villages changed, becoming more Uzbek over time, but that most Russians in Uzbekistan saw Uzbeks "the way you treat blacks in America"—basically as people glad to pick cotton and dance.

By the same token, people were often wont to tell me that they did not dislike or hate Russians, but that they hated the way in which the superior cultural forms of the country—Soviet Union—were supposed to be embodied in Russianness. Issues of discrimination, racism, ethnic chauvinism, and interethnic relations in the U.S.S.R. are parts of a unique literature. In the remainder of this section, I provide two ethnographic examples that brought home the tense or strained nature of Russian–Uzbek interactions.

While accompanying a friend to the nearby town of Q., where he taught Uzbek in a Russian-language school, we crossed paths with a grief-stricken woman whose husband had just died. The woman, a Russian, had been married to an Uzbek who died suddenly. This town, which had once been home to approximately 30 ethnic groups, now contained only a handful of that pageant of humanity that had reached its peak in the mid-1970s (Russians, Tatars, Ukrainians, Ossetians, Greeks, and Koreans continue living in Q. today). Although the grieving widow looked Uzbek from her clothing, boots, and large white kerchief (*rumol*) that covered her head, when she looked up at me through bloodshot, tear-stained blue eyes, there was no doubt that her physiognomy was atypical for the region. My friend and I expressed condolences, and my friend explained to her who I was and what I had come to do. The she began to tell me about Uzbeks:

> You should know that the Uzbeks are the most wonderful, comforting people. I have so many friends, so many people I can rely on now when I need them most. Their culture is so good, so close. I will never leave this country; the Uzbeks are really like my family. I would never feel such close relations with people anywhere else. But you can't understand this; you're American. I don't think Americans care about each other like we do.

It struck me that she used the term *kul'tura* ("culture"), which the Russians usually apply self-referentially as they point out its absence in the other's ethnic repertoire. Here she was elevating the Uzbeks' customs and way of dealing with death as an ultimate mark of their humanity, and I continued being struck how her statements came out sounding so provocative and political in this odd, yet ordinary context of her husband's death. It almost seems that one would not even really have thought in these terms had the interaction between the various ethnic groups, however workable and accommodating over time, not been fraught with such misperceptions and unexpressed thoughts.

In another situation, I became friendly with the village police officer, whom I had grown to like despite various people telling me that he was keeping tabs on me. Some of his coevals even teased him in front of me about this surveillance, and he would just shake his head. Often, it seemed to me the officer tried to prove that such was not his design. On occasion, we discussed the nature of police work, the old U.S.S.R., and his family life.

One day we sat drinking and literally chewing the fat (we shared a can of marbled corned beef). After weighing the pros and cons of the Soviet Union, the police officer began to relate why one of the favorite Soviet political slogans, "friendship of the peoples"—a reference to the multi-ethnic Soviet state—had been a fiction. He felt this way because his experiences with Russians always gave him the sense that they viewed Central Asians with contempt. The officer went on to relate that in 1991 he had attended a national police conference just outside Moscow, one of his only visits outside Uzbekistan since his years of military service. Unfortunately, the trip did not go well because there was little air of fraternity or collegiality with Russian colleagues. The officer described how some of the Russian police started talking about the violent and rash nature of the Central Asians based on the previous year's inter-ethnic violence in Osh, Kyrgyzstan. He complained that even though the Russians knew Central Asian people were present at the conference, they showed little discretion:

> I was surprised, really. I mean, how could they just talk that way in front of me as if I would think it's normal or right? I would never try to make *them* feel ashamed in the same way. It made me upset because I was thinking that nationality didn't or shouldn't really matter much until that point. Then I knew that they would never trust us as equals, and that's what the U.S.S.R. was all about.

Here was a man who came to a realization or rude awakening about the country he served. The "friendship of the peoples" slogan stopped making sense, even though he told me he felt like a "Soviet person." In the end, the police officer came to see those Russian colleagues not as a few rogues, but rather as representatives of a widespread Russian prejudice toward Central Asians and Caucasians (members of the latter group—ironically in our American context—are referred to as "blacks"). He also pointed out a fact about Central Asian Russians that I had heard scores of times, and that bespeaks a colonial arrogance that Uzbeks find as distasteful as any other facet of the former's superiority complex. Uzbeks resent the fact that Russians usually make little to no effort to speak Uzbek competently: "Yeah, we must be the dumb ones," the officer said. "We have to learn Russian, but for some reason they're incapable of learning Uzbek after two or three generations of having lived among us."

SOCIETY AND LAND DURING THE KOKAND
KHANATE: PRE-RUSSIAN IMPERIAL
UZBEK VILLAGES

The Kokand Khanate (Kokand Kingdom) dominated most of the FV as well as mountainous areas north, east, and south of the valley's center until the Russian conquest (Troitskaia 1969; Bababekov 1990). In other words, most of the territory where I conducted my long-term fieldwork during the mid-1990s had been a part of the Kokand Khanate. People who would be considered Uzbeks today dominated its leadership. If Russian transformation of the rural economy was far-reaching and negative for most of the indigenous peasants, the relationship between state and peasantry that had existed in the Kokand Khanate from the late eighteenth century through the last third of the nineteenth century also cannot be seen as harmonious and prosperous for most of the *dehqon* who tilled the soil at that time.

The historical constant of FV life for the peasants always revolved around access to land and water. Most peasants rarely had secure and steady access to either resource. The Soviet state solved this problem only to the extent that it stripped farming people of any ownership rights to these natural resources and nearly all of the means of production, decided who would work which land and produce which crop, and worked out an elaborately controlled, yet grossly unregulated system of irrigation and water distribution.

Boburkent and the rest of the Amir Temur Collective Farm, founded on inter-riverine swampy lowlands close to the source of the Noryn and Qora Rivers, have never really lacked for adequate water supplies. The region has managed to avoid many of the water disputes that arose in other FV areas. Much of the peopling of this specific area took place at the behest of the khanate; injunctions provided for the forcible resettling of surrounding villagers owing to overcrowding and the strain on resources as far back as the eighteenth century (Akramov 1955:40). On the land question, however, how would a population of 6000-plus today achieve balance if only some 1300 hectares of available land were to be privatized? This question perplexes informants, just as farm officials often are at a loss to explain why kolkhozniks do not receive wages on time. With rising populations of younger people, steadily high birth rates of about 2 percent in some areas, and a population density of less than 400 per square kilometer, the future of land privatization and increasingly available arable land remain the issues foremost in local people's minds.

This section summarizes the historical context of the nature of land ownership before the Revolution. It is not intended to link the older forms to the present relationships, as it is unlikely that the old categories will be reestablished. Conversely, if Islamic organizations gain monetary and political influence or power, the reemergence of *waqf* lands might occur.

The state recognized *amliak*, *mulk*, and *waqf* as three types of property holding in Central Asia prior to Russian domination and the later establishment of the U.S.S.R. These types of ownership were not unique to Central Asia, but have existed in countries where Islam was the majority religion. Consequently, land ownership and use were regulated significantly by *sharia*, which in Muslim societies provides the basis for law and order based on God's word, as codified by scholars; it should serve to govern humanity (Nasr 1989:76). Historically, sharia forms the basis for Islamic jurisprudence, and is a vast subject of discourse and dispute in learned circles—specifically, among the theological body known as the *ulema*. As such, it has often been molded to fit particular political and cultural conditions, reflecting the political interests of dynastic rulers and statesmen (Levy 1971; Hodgson 1974).

Amliak lands were considered state lands, but individual khans (rulers) considered that state lands belonged to them; such lands also were called *padshahlyk* (i.e., something of the *padishah's* [ruler's]). Not surprisingly, most of the territory considered as private lands in the Kokand Khanate were amliak/padshahlyk lands. Peasants cultivated these lands through a kind of hereditary usufruct (use of things produced by the land and its sources, but not ownership of those sources) that required rent. Payments to the treasury were personified in the sense that these became the khan's personal payments. A separate tax was then levied on the actual product of the land—say, wheat—and a part of that product was taken from the peasants as part of the harvest income (see Table 2.1).

Those lands that were earmarked for sale to the local lords, or that were seen as private in the sense closest to what we consider as generally available for real estate sale, were called *mulk*. Occasionally, the mulk lands were held in common by communities, including such territories as pastures, cemeteries, and roads (Valiev 1958:26). Peasants rented and worked plots of mulk land. Separate taxes were levied on the harvests derived from the actual amount of land a given party worked and rented.

Because dry-land farming (where irrigation was not the main water source) accounted for little of FV cultivation, the land itself had—and retains today—little value without sufficient irrigation. Securing the rights to water and receiving adequate amounts were as important a part of agriculture as any other factor. Historically, irrigation management and organization in Uzbekistan have emphasized that control over water's movement often was key in maintaining power and privilege.

T A B L E 2.1   Types of Taxation Levied on Subjects of Kokand Khanate

Name	Significance	Subjects
Somonpuli	Hay tax	Peasants and nomads
Dalali	Brokerage dues, real estate sales	peasants
Ziakat	Cattle and merchandise tax	Peasants and nomads
Otinpuli	Firewood, dry grass tax (fuel)	peasants
Mirob duty	Official taxes from irrigation	peasants
Ghazavat	Military campaign/ defense tax	Peasants and nomads
Qamishpuli	Swamp reed tax, used in building, textile designs, and housewares	Peasants and nomads

The Kokand khan administered water rights indirectly. Actually, the office of the *Kok-bashi* regulated the distribution of waters from the largest canals, and the office of the *Mirob-bashi* or *Oqsoqol* had the duties of overseeing feeder channel (*ariq*) construction, which involved distributing water as well as collecting taxes from both peasants and lords who received water. This office was the closest to the commoners, such that the khanate's smallest administrative unit was spread throughout the principalities (*viloyats*) (Valiev 1958:36).

Today the modern state has replicated some of these patterns and old titles, although they have been hybridized with the system inherited from the Soviets. For example, the states or provinces of Uzbekistan are called *viloyats* again, and each viloyat is headed by a *hokim*, which corresponds to the old title of the leader of a principality. Similarities in title and function can only be drawn so far, however, as the following brief illustration of the old system of political administration of the Kokand Khanate shows. (Note its relevance to the farming population.)

Corruption long has been rife among irrigation administrators, and bribery played a key role in giving certain landowners preferential treatment to water diversion. The effect of such underhanded dealings could be devastating to the poorest peasants, as it could delay and lessen their supplies of water. In addition, water taxes were a huge source of revenue.

Furthermore, natural sources or springs of water tended to be regarded as the property of the owner of the land containing them. These additional water resources became increasingly important to the landless as the population density of the FV steadily increased in the nineteenth century. By established traditions first laid down during the Arab occupation of these territories in the 700s and 800s AD, the poorest peasants had to entreat landlords with gifts requesting the use of "their" springs, further encumbering the poor peasants (Sukhareva & Bikjanova 1955:37). In the Kokand Khanate, *waqf* lands occupied an enormous territory (100,000 *desiatins* ≈ 110,000 hectares) over which religious institutions had legal rights in perpetuity; the lands practically belonged to religious officials. These officials maintained a given region's mosques and, if present, *madrasah* (religious school). In terms of schooling, Quranic instruction was usually the only type available (Holdsworth 1959:13). Records of waqf revenues and fiscal apportioning are not always easy to find, but based on Namangan data, it appears that waqf endowments also supported the religious leaders—or, rather, the peasants' work supported the endowments themselves.

Many peasants who worked waqf lands did so on the basis of their rights as debtors. Accordingly, their tax burdens for their products were heavy, especially the burden known as the *kheraj*. This fee was collected each year and fluctuated from harvest to harvest, but could be as much as one-third or as little as one-fifth of the harvest holdings (Note the contrast from the previous section in terms of what today's people think about this percentage!) The kheraj was applied only to grains and cotton. All properties were subject to this tax, and peasants could pay the tax in money or with the natural product; the latter was the much more likely method of payment. Money was demanded for the tax known as *tanap* (also an old unit of land measurement subject to fluctuating dimensions, ranging

FIGURE 2.3 Harvesting clover on today's state-owned land (kolkhoz), which once was part of the Kokand Khanate.

from one-half to one-sixth hectare), subject to areas raising vineyards, fruit orchards, and clover.

For peasants, it was better to work either waqf or mulk lands because the rents were less than those charged on amliak lands; special privileges were extended to the lords and the religious endowments. Of course, this description focuses on the ideal situation: The reality was that between the sheer amount of taxes levied by individual khans and the cheating of peasants based on accountants' sleight of hand, many peasants were fortunate to get away with "seeds" from an entire harvest (Valiev 1958:31). Table 2.1 shows the types of taxation levied on Kokand peasants and nomads for a variety of items during the reigns of one Khudoiar-Khan, who ruled Kokand at various times from 1845 to 1875. Part of the reason he lost the throne on various occasions has to do with his enacting crushing taxation that caused uprisings.

RUSSIAN IMPERIAL APPROACH TO LANDLESSNESS AND PEASANTRY

Those who came to conquer Central Asia conjectured that they could increase their own popularity and win the peasants over to their vision by changing the notion of ownership and access to land. Accessibility would come through dismantling the khanate's tripartite separation of land ownership. Early on, officials of the Turkestan Governor-Generalship (tsardom's incarnation in Central Asia) recognized peasant poverty as a direct outgrowth of the tenure system and the harsh chain of taxation.

In the mid-1870s, cotton growing made up a minor enterprise in Central Asia. Cotton served domestic needs, including household bedding, pillows, and clothing. Less frequently, people sold it locally to merchants and nomads, who bought FV cotton in rural and urban marketplaces. Before the mid-nineteenth century, no Central Asians raised cotton exclusively, although peasants understood its potential fiscal benefits (Abduraimov 1966:235). The textile that was important and a key source of seasonal revenue was silk, and cocoon production long formed an economic mainstay in Margilan and Namangan. Ferghana Valley lands also produced many foods, especially grains such as wheat, barley, and corn. The region's melons and grapes were also historically esteemed for their qualities and varieties.

Although most acknowledge that the Russian conquest of Central Asia aimed both at boosting the supply of raw materials to Russia proper and heading off any possible British incursions north of the Amu Darya (a natural border that today separates Afghanistan from Turkmenistan and Uzbekistan), the Russian attempt to transform the political economy of the Kokand Khanate that it replaced in 1876 was half-hearted. The Russian method of rule involved its Ministry of War. Through the "Popular–Military" system, power was distributed to the military governors and regional heads. One important result of this new administrative system was the cessation of internecine conflicts between the forces of minor khans, peasant rebellions against the Khanate, and the nomadic Kyrgyz uprisings against Kokand, which had often caused significant damage to crops (Valiev 1958:41–42).

Overall, the Russian approach could be characterized as "hands-off." Because the Europeans had a poor understanding of Central Asian sociopolitical life, they chose not to tamper with economies and social institutions. During the 1880s, they made changes to lighten the tax burdens, and they endeavored to simplify many legal codes concerned with land and water usage and rights. Even through the late 1880s, however, big landlords continued to rule the roost, and little alleviation of the tax burden was noted among peasants.

One of the most energetic tsarist officials who became directly involved with agricultural issues in an effort to increase the income of the newly colonized territory was Governor-General Von Kaufman. In his *Instruction on Organizational Measures in the Ferghana Valley Province*, several articles codify provisions to make the formerly tripartite category of khanate lands available to increasing numbers of landless peasants (Valiev 1958:46). The provisions of this document were worded carefully so as not to disturb the relations on the religious lands. Such colonialism took a far more cautious approach toward local culture and the peasants' sense of social inviolability—the waqf domains—than would be true of the "anti-colonialists" (Bolsheviks) some 40 years later.

Ultimately, the most transformational act of Russian imperialism in the FV occurred with the wide-scale introduction of cotton, though it did not really begin its exponential growth until the mid-1890s. Only the development of this cash crop industry may have completely changed the old mode of production between the *boi* and the *dehqon*, although World War I and the overthrow of Nicholas II intervened to render any proposition about the development of a prosperous middle peasantry a distinct counterfactual—a thing that never was to occur.

The slight benefits experienced by the landless peasants in agricultural areas, such as the FV, began to wane with the cash crop emphasis, as richer landowners bought out the emerging layers of the newly "landed." Ambitions to improve the quality of life for the dehqon, however modest, were stillborn due to the key role and place occupied by this major commodity crop that the rapidly industrializing Russia demanded. Exponential rates of increase in cotton production occurred from the 1880s until 1914; this very period set the trend for the cotton explosion that erupted after the firm establishment of Soviet power in Central Asia by the early 1930s.

This excursus into land ownership indicates that a history of prosperous small-holders seems not to have existed in Uzbekistan, or at least not for any significant period.

Next we examine certain aspects of kinship relations, especially those relevant to household social structure in the past and their modern-day counterparts. Rather than simply describing past social structure, I juxtapose it to the present structure, and then explain its relationship to today's population.

ESSENTIAL ASPECTS OF SOCIAL RELATIONS AND STRUCTURE PAST AND PRESENT

Where I worked, the extended family household structure and residence pattern had long predominated. In relatively recent times, however, the nature of the extended family had changed markedly. The pre-colonial extended family consisted in joint living arrangements, which would necessarily entail all the sons of a married couple living at home with their wives and children. Furthermore, in more remote areas of the FV, it was not uncommon for married brothers' sons to stay at home with their married wives and their paternal grandparents.

The largest extended families generally were the wealthiest, and included polygynous arrangements, later outlawed by the Soviets. Polygyny implies that in extended family household arrangements, a man has to provide separate homes for each wife and her family, even if it means creating subdivisions of the man's own home. Usually, the wealthier households featured extensive housing arrangements resulting in something like a small apartment building. Records and informants' statements from Namangan demonstrate that some extended families included 130 or more people living within an enormous household compound. Richer families tended to favor multistory dwellings with apartments, an arrangement that one still sees today in Namangan.

While some polygyny is practiced covertly today and its frequency has increased since the mid-1990s, informants told me that the practice never really died out even when it was made illegal during the Soviet period (it is illegal today in Uzbekistan). Now men are becoming bolder, especially those men who point to their faith, Islam, which permits up to four wives per husband.

Courtesy of Russell Zanca

FIGURE 2.4 An extended family household with representatives of three generations shown; the paternal grandmother holds a teacup in the right corner.

Law enforcement is lax in regard to polygyny. I learned of several cases of polygynous unions, but the reasons for plural marriage showed little coherence. One case,
for example, involved a middle-age man who wanted a younger wife partly out of
a sense of religious entitlement and partly out of a need, perhaps, to increase his
own status. In another case, a younger, professional man I knew simply fell in love
with a woman he could not bear to be away from, and he managed to convince
his wife that this second marriage would be for the best. He is not particularly
religious. In a third instance, a man who did not want to divorce his wife wanted
a new and more meaningful marriage with additional children.

As was true in the past, a man's decision to take a second wife is rarely decided
on the basis of carnal whims; rather, it is frequently a drawn-out process in which
economic considerations are paramount. By customary and religious law, men are
obligated to take care of their families. Men simply would not be respected within
their own families or communities if they fail to take care of one wife and family,
let alone two. This understanding explained why a particular man joked, "I don't
have enough problems taking care of my children as it is—I need another wife?!"

In certain cases, a man may maintain separate residences, keeping a house or
apartment for his second wife in another town or city. If his first wife is amen-
able to the change, then he might construct separate quarters near his regular
home, which usually was the case in the past as well.

For middle-income and poorer families, historically the pattern has not been
the joint extended family, but rather the stem extended family, which typically
means only the youngest son stays at the familial home with his wife and children. Two reasons predominantly account for this arrangement. First, the

youngest son honored his parents in this way; he was there for them in his old age to take care of them materially and to bury them when they died. Second, in areas where land tenure arrangements were so tight for most families, it would have been impractical for patriarchs to apportion what were already miniscule tracts of land to a number of sons. Thus the Uzbeks of this part of Central Asia practiced a type of *ultimogeniture* (inheritance for the youngest son in this patrilineal setting) regarding the family's arable land and the house itself; this is the inheritance (Bikjanova 1959:25). Rural Uzbeks still prefer the joint extended family, although increasing poverty is working to alter the social structure as more children continue to stay at home for three main reasons:

- They are often unemployed and cannot afford to build new homes. Having no steady income, they could not maintain separate households if they moved into them.
- There has been a chronic shortage of building materials, especially wood. Bricks are not a problem, as they are made from mud. Other materials, including iron, steel, metal roofing, and wiring, are expensive in addition to being in short supply.
- The land shortage is serious in this intensively farmed region.

What applies historically and today is that all those persons living within the same household are subject to the authority and rules of the family patriarch. Where money or other items of material wealth are at stake, traditionally they are pooled and given to the patriarch; he doles them out as he sees fit. Today, however, conflicts may arise when the children make better money or bring in more wealth than their fathers. In such cases, power struggles may erupt because those with higher earning power want to keep some share for themselves. However, as a middle-aged informant declared:

> If my children want to remain in my house, then they have to share what they bring in, and I have to know what they're taking in. Well, I can't force them completely, but if they do not share equally, then they cannot stay at home.

With increasing financial difficulties, the pooling of resources becomes that much more crucial, but it hardly brings out the best in all family members. As one might expect, it is not the matter of wealth or earnings (or lack thereof) that necessarily causes rifts. Generally, families whose members get on well and treat one another respectfully tend to have fewer problems mediating problems and interfamily relationships. Such a truism hardly is unique to Uzbeks.

Young informants by and large wished to have separate homes from their parents, but also wished to live in close proximity to them. Overall, families have to consider cost-efficiency first and foremost, and most are hopeful that local economic fortunes will pick up so that their children will succeed in establishing independent homes of their own in near future.

In Boburkent, during the past two generations (roughly 50 to 60 years), it increasingly became common for household structure to reflect typical European nuclear patterns. In surveying households, I noticed that most people who were married by the mid-1980s were able to establish new residences, and that right through the mid-1990s new homes were being established in a more or less un-used section of the farm. What I found in the "new district" of Boburkent is that the families moving into new homes were not necessarily couples just starting out, however, but rather young families who were able to move away from their parents after four to six years of having lived at home (and often longer) after the birth of a first or second child.

What was historically true and what remains more or less true now is that sons moving away from their fathers' homes often do not live far away, and of-ten want to live as close to their fathers as possible. Ideally, father–son bonds are not only lifelong, but also imply that fathers and sons should always depend on each other, and that sons should seek out their fathers' advice on crucial issues, whether personal or professional. Under the notion that "everybody eats from the same cauldron" or the "divided cauldron" (*qozon buliak qilnar edi*), fathers always try to provide for sons who live at a remove, which betokens cooperation in housing construction, farm work, and investments in livestock, among other issues.

CONTESTING HISTORY

"Until I left this country I really believed it was a great place. What else could I have thought from what we were told and from the books I read in school and at home?"

A VILLAGER WHO EMIGRATED TO THE WEST AND RETURNED, ONLY TO EMIGRATE AGAIN

How do peasants and elites understand the importance and relevance of history following the demise of the U.S.S.R.? In this final section of the chapter, I return to the Russo-Soviet legacy of colonialism and revolution, probing the cultural aspects in terms of how popular receptions of history have been medi-ated. Do modern-day Uzbeks accept or reject official versions of history? This section illustrates how the colonial system furthered its power base by convincing its lowliest subjects that its own mission had the hopes of the collective society uppermost in mind. Colonialist rule often has its softer and disguised aspects of conquest and rule, as "rulers align themselves with the inexorable and universal forces of science, progress, rationality, and modernity," and "[displace] many of the disruptions and excesses of rule into institutions and cultures that were labeled as tradition" (Dirks 1992:7–8).

As mentioned in Chapter 1, I found it frustrating that a number of my Uzbek academic colleagues—even people as young as I was—still had kind of an idea about history from above; that is, they believed that only scholars and intellectuals have informed ideas about history, not ordinary people, and espe-cially not semi-literate peasants. Of course, it is true that as academics we do specialize in learning all of the minutiae that we can in terms of past events, and we work hard to ascertain patterns and trends in people's behavior over time as well as in response to the imposition of power. Nevertheless, it is more than just elitist to ignore the opinions of people who may not have a higher education; it goes against the grain of wanting to understand historical perspectives from as many angles as possible. Needless to say, anthropologists think that it is worthwhile in and of itself to learn and understand how people process and explain their lived experiences.

Nevertheless, it is not my intention to indict many of the talented, earnest, and energetic Tashkent academics with whom I was lucky enough to work and whom I also came to admire. It simply struck me as unfortunate that the prevailing outlook of history from above, which was inherited from the Soviet past, still rules in present-day Uzbekistan.

If it is possible to say that one component of a colonial legacy is the ability of a dominating system to erase from common memory any history that does not correspond to imperial memory, then surely the Soviets can count themselves successful in many instances vis-à-vis Central Asia. However, exceptional is the dominating system that succeeds in making people forget that they have forgotten, although a totally new kind of life never completely replaces the old (Watson 1994:14). For example, some people in Boburkent know that anti-religious policies prevented them from practicing religion as they thought to (the U.S.S.R. officially was an atheistic state). Also, because the stages of economic history prior to socialism were vilified as inhumane forms of economy, according to Soviet ideology, the pre-Soviet period was marked only by dire poverty and exploitation, according to the only texts people read. Nevertheless, people are sure that they may relearn forms of knowledge.

What interested me about popular expressions of a will toward acquiring knowledge was how a person really might go about the process, or attunes himself to issues related to national or local history. While almost all of the middle-aged adults I worked were literate, few people spent much time reading.

The kolkhoz library still functioned, receiving six periodicals sporadically, including three somewhat daily newspapers. Unfortunately, the library was rarely open, and when it was, it often served as a chat and snack area for schoolgirls and the librarians. The main librarian offered the following explanation for the low level of readership:

> Times are difficult now and people work too much and are too tired to come here whenever they have a chance to rest. I don't want this job myself; there's so much to do at home.

I later learned through her that the village school's assistant principal had a written an essay on the history of Boburkent. Even though it took a few weeks, my persistent begging for a copy paid off. After copying the essay out by hand, I read through it carefully, but that turned out to be something of a letdown. It wasn't a greatly detailed piece on local events. The writer spent more time on the local flora and fauna than what I perceived as more exciting issues, such as ownership, local institutions, and social life. Even so, this document helped me confirm oral claims that the area long had been famous for its melons before King Cotton supplanted them.

Answering the question of how people disinter their past today points us toward television and radio as well as popular pamphlets and books dealing with medical, heroic, or cultural themes—literature that is available both in bookstores and at marketplaces. The prominent street texts include a publication on nutrition-based medicine by Avicenna, a biographical rendering of Tamerlane's martial exploits, and a slim selection or writings by Ismail Gaspirali (an educator and pan-Turkist—one who sought to unite all Turkic peoples—of the nineteenth century).

Avicenna's popular tract, *Tabobat Durdonalari* ("Medicinal Pearls"), made the rounds of households. Villagers perused these pamphlets avidly and read them aloud partly for enjoyment and partly in hopes that some of the dietary/medical advice offered by the eleventh-century physician and Bukharan native might still apply to the healthcare-deprived Uzbekistan of the post-Soviet era. Concern with Avicenna's numerous essays devoted to the curative powers of certain foods for particular ailments was very much in vogue. Such beliefs, which also centered on foods judged hot and dry versus cold and wet and hence seen as compatible with particular organismic fluids, such as phlegm or bile, have enjoyed a lengthy genesis in European societies (the concept of the "four humors," for example, may be found in many medical writings of antiquity, including Hippocrates' medical works (Farb & Armelagos 1980:99–100). These self-medicating-via-food notions have became increasingly common in the United States of late, especially with health food aficionados who think that the best health care stems from proper eating.

The Uzbek national state and the mass media that it controls manipulate history in a way that would be familiar to citizens of many other nations. They see history as a way to affirm their nation's triumphs as well as a way to trump the achievements of particular figures with whom they think they share an ethnic heritage. Ordinary people usually do not become so concerned with these matters, which have more to do with nation building and instilling a kind of confidence. As much as this kind of effort can serve a worthy antidote to decades of Soviet history, the new Uzbek government has employed some of the worst features of Soviet propaganda in trying to craft a historical outlook for its citizens. Its strident messages even become ridiculous in the eyes of kolkhozniks and others when everything about the Uzbeks' past is made to seem glorious. They are even barraged by images of history in popular culture, especially through pop songs. According to web-based journalist Bobur Mirzoyev, pop stars play a crucial role in advancing the government's efforts to instill in Uzbek people a sense of the nation with the following theses:

> Uzbekistan is the best country in the world, its leader, Islam Karimov, being the wisest contemporary politician blessed with long-term vision [sic]. All news related to everything from culture to literature to athletics and even to political events abroad are presented from one inevitable angle: thank all gods that are for the happiness of having been born in

this beautiful country—and be happy in such a manner that all enemies of Uzbekistan will feel envy (2007).

The anthropologist Nazif Shahrani wrote about a similar case from his own youth in Afghanistan. In his work, he discussed how one of the pitfalls of nation-states that engage in trying to uplift their citizens through manipulation of the glories of the now national past is that the propagandists neglect to see how deeply mired in everyday problems most citizens are. This type of propaganda simply detracts from the prestige the national state could have in the eyes of its own citizens if it favored more humility over hubris (Shahrani 1994:27).

The personal and the experiential characterize most people's concerns with history in Boburkent. For example, people would like to see the restoration of honor to their relatives who were criminalized during the Soviet period either for political positions taken or for actions deemed contrary to kolkhoz construction. They also share an interest in agrarian life prior to the October Revolution. People see this period as directly relevant to the present when they argue, for example, about the proper role for women in cotton work. Furthermore, informants show curiosity about the nature of village political power and leadership as well as the potential for economic prosperity that might result from an understanding of the previous social intercourse between landowners and peasants.

Of the myriad complaints connected to cotton's legacy, peasants typically exercise themselves most about the crucial role of women in nearly all facets of the harvest. While men complain about this practice a good deal, they do little to shoulder the women's burden themselves. Many argue that Soviet power demanded such work of women both as part of the effort to make them equal to men (concretely by taking them outside the walls of the household) and because the intensification of cotton necessitated it. Today, along with issues as disparate as excessive drinking and immoral behavior, the Soviet system (or, sometimes, the Russians) is blamed for undermining supposed traditional community structures and family order. The renowned radical writer against late French colonialism in North Africa, Frantz Fanon, referred to this issue as the "cultural destruction undertaken by the occupier" (1965:38). Women's complaints focus on their inability to devote themselves to the household. Many are displeased that only Uzbek women do cotton work. As one woman told me, "Russian women never did this work." Such negative outlooks toward both the U.S.S.R. and its main national group betray the perceived colonial characteristic of forced cultural change at the expense of a subordinate national group. At the same time, Soviet power and its executors never sought to turn Uzbeks into Europeans.

Toward the end of the Soviet era, the titles of various political offices were changed in an effort to make them reflect more long-standing notions of vested authority. One such name was that of the village councilman, formerly known as the *qihsloq sovet/shuro;* it is now *oqsoqol. Oqsoqol* traditionally was a term of respect reserved for elderly men whose intelligence and leadership abilities conferred popular honor. These individuals were village elders who served as moderators within and between settlements. Currently the term is applied to bureaucrats, not necessarily senior citizens.

The failure of the national state to change the existing, Soviet-type political structure—save perhaps in terms of the titles used—inspires little confidence in creating an independent way of operating. Upon first hearing men discuss *the* oqsoqol, I became confused and asked for clarification. One man interrupted another who tried to explain the new terminology, saying, "He's not a real oqsoqol—just a party hack whom you should beware of." This case is one of many where governmental attempts to redress the effacement of local institutions during the Soviet period have failed to consider the populace's desires based on traditions and the history of local constituencies. It probably will take more time before the current Uzbek government (or a newer government) transcends various Soviet methods of rule regardless of the idiom it selects to reject the Soviet system. Unlike some other populations facing post-imperial situations, today's Uzbek leaders did little to fight Soviet rule; they, in fact, were staunch defenders of the old regime.

A widely shared redressing of the Soviet period centers on the rehabilitation of one's family members who were disgraced, arrested, deported, or killed. Most of these abuses took place from the 1930s through the early 1950s (especially during the reign of the notorious Soviet dictator, Josef Stalin). In Uzbekistan, admissions of wrongdoing on the part of the state have come about more slowly than in other Central Asian republics, such as Kyrgyzstan.

One kiosk owner in Boburkent always struck me as a particularly freewheeling character. Whenever we saw each other, he wanted to sit and have a drink— the bottomless shot of vodka! He sold pricy items and *nasvoi* (a mild, snuff-like narcotic). When he heard that I had an interest in personal or life histories, he approached me and proceeded to talk about the fate of his grandfather, whose name had been cleared only two years earlier. His grandfather had been a religious man who insisted on maintaining religious practices within the village, and the man actually spoke out against Communism's denial of God in public settings. According to this informant, the grandfather's anti-Soviet activities led to long-lived repercussions:

> You can't understand what it was like to grow up here with that family background behind you. When our government cleared his name, gave us the letter, and apologized on behalf of the country, they gave respect back to my grandfather's name. Since you're here, you should know about these things; you should understand how we lived. It's really nothing at all like the lies you've read. We didn't make sacrifices for the Soviet Union because we always wanted to; we just never saw any other way out, and we never knew anything about the rest of the world.

For the Uzbeks as well as for the visiting anthropologist, understanding how they lived in the past became every bit as important as understanding how people live now. It was an important realization that it was also possible to learn directly about political, economic and sociocultural events and processes, such as the Revolution, the collectivization of agriculture, World War II, and the Khrushchev years (1956–1965), from a mass perspective, given that the majority of Uzbeks are rural, farming people.

Thinking back to that young historian's comment about needing to do my scholarly work mainly in the libraries and the archives, in retrospect she made a good point: Villagers' memories are not the same as narrative history. However, there are village histories to be written, and scholars can make this happen only when they listen to and work with villagers by employing both oral memories and existing texts to forge histories anew. Such projects begin to fulfill the hopes of rural people to gain a more accurate rendering of the modern local past and our desires as Western scholars to gain a deeper understanding of the post-socialist world. The peasant populations of the formerly Soviet territory have been neglected in this sense.

CONCLUSION

This chapter focused on historical connections to today's Boburkent. Following a discussion of the peasant concept in the social sciences, I described how Ferghana Valley villages have changed through time, how scholars of the Russian empire described these villages, and what modern Uzbeks understand of their local history extending back more than a century. These varying accounts of what the past was all about and how outsiders have characterized Uzbeks also have contributed to contemporary ideas about sense of self and the meaning attached to an Uzbek identity. For example, in instances where people believe outsiders have disparaged the society of their ancestors, the local population may have the tendency to romanticize that past. Understanding one's past is always a key consideration in anthropological studies—especially the notion that what is important to villagers about what happened may not be the same concerns of professional historians, to say nothing of the importance of personal histories as opposed to national ones, especially to an individual.

QUESTIONS

1. How do villagers in Boburkent evaluate their pre-Soviet history, and how do their accounts differ from those of Soviet writings?
2. Which salient aspects of historical continuity characterize this Uzbek village and family life today?

3

The Kolkhoz as Plantation

WHO SAYS YOU CAN'T EAT COTTON?
COTTON IN SOCIAL LIFE

In California-sized Uzbekistan, only about 10 percent of territory allows for cultivation through the massive and often wasteful use of irrigation. Most of the water feeds the country's vast cotton farms. For better or worse, cotton represents the past, present, and future of Uzbekistan. Nevertheless, the kolkhozniks as cotton workers would prefer a change from the path of Soviet-style planning and bureaucracy that characterize all phases of the growing cycle. After all, farming cotton as a primary cash crop has fueled economic growth in many a nation, including China, the United States, Egypt, Mali, and Mexico. Historically, those who plant and pick cotton rarely receive many of the profits generated by cotton. Only time will tell if Uzbekistan can break this inequitable pattern, although so far the independence experience gives observers little cause for hope.

Since 1990, Uzbekistan has reduced the amount of territory sown in cotton. Critics allege that this shift in usage is partly a political game or a wrongheaded policy of the state as it has attempted to replace more than 300,000 hectares of cotton with grain, mainly wheat. But reductions aside, the former Soviet farms—or "plantations" as informants call them—have experienced few changes in the way people work, and especially in their dedication to the all-consuming cotton planting and harvesting cycles.

On the Amir Temur Kolkhoz, the people in charge remain dyed-in-the-wool bureaucrats of the *ancien regime*. Most were born and reared in the kolkhoz villages. The knowledge and relationships they have of and to other villagers are extensive and intimate, and their professional lives have been determined by the demands of cotton.

The kolkhoz leadership lords it over its co-villagers. It decides who can and cannot work, who will receive payments in kind and money and wages in a timely fashion, and which village-wide projects will be undertaken or ignored (based on the source of the demands, the relationships to those doing the demanding, and so on). Some of these people work conscientiously, but the general perception among villagers is that all of the kolkhoz leaders are corrupt and use their positions to capitalize on every privilege that they have. In the worst cases, this means directly pocketing kolkhoz income—either the farm's budget or profits.

While bureaucrats do not always hamper reforms, they do little to advance them. They execute orders from the hokimiiat (the regional, provincial, or municipal mayor's or governor's office); they themselves occupy the lowest rungs of power in the state's political system. The kolkhoz leaders work as part of a chain of command that constantly reinforces gradations of power and bounded domains of privilege. They routinely ignore the complaints and grievances of peasants. As an example, consider the blunt response of the rais (farm leader or chairman) to my question about why so many workers complained about not getting paid by the farm for months on end: "They're lying." Those who try to be helpful do so only if there are sympathetic ears at the hokimiiat.

Uzbeks themselves have a love–hate relationship with cotton, as do scholars who have written about this crop's legacy. Both groups love it for the wealth it has provided: Cotton has been the source of comfortable lives and respected professional careers. And both groups hate it: The cotton monoculture has led to productivity retardation, very low living standards, and environmental damage. This last point has ramifications for the Uzbek public health sector, given that tons of chemical fertilizers, defoliants, and pesticides have run off from the fields into the region's network of canals, which provide the people and the land with the most precious resource, water (Lipovsky 1995:540–541).

Cotton as a way of life may have harmed and hurt the Uzbeks in equal measure. The underdevelopment of the countryside is actually a classic case of the overdevelopment of a farming economy based on external economic needs (Wallerstein 1979:53). To speak of backwardness in the Ferghana Valley (FV) is impossible without speaking of the highly specialized, half-mechanized cotton sector. The resulting backwardness has, paradoxically, coincided with colossal-scale modernization and mechanization in Central Asian farming. In earlier decades, Soviet textile needs demanded the overdevelopment of the cotton plantations. Today, although diminished, the needs of the state continue to come first. Given that the world market demand for cotton is virtually insatiable, one can readily understand why the state's needs are guided by this rationale. Relative to greater export commodities, such as gold and oil, cotton requires little capital investment, to say nothing of not having to share profits with foreign concerns.

Likewise, the state depends on its agrarian labor force, but whether these people feel satisfied or dissatisfied is not the state's central concern; popular quiescence is. As long as the workers are willing to endure the demands fostered by current system, the state will continue to mete them out. Such modes of operation are not unique to socialist states, but what appears to take place in rural Uzbekistan is the extension of this particular brand of socialism that David Kideckel describes as "socialism's social contract" (1993:55).

Although nearly all collective farms in the FV are cotton farms, I began my research with little intention of focusing on cotton. However, almost as soon as I set foot in a village attached to a farm, talk of this "white gold" (*oltin pakhta*) simply couldn't be avoided. The ubiquity of cotton in daily talk and in the things of daily life—from pillows and quilts to animal feed—soon overwhelmed me. In fact, making the anti-Soviet statement that "One cannot eat cotton" isn't really true: Uzbeks consume cottonseed oil prodigiously, and the meat they eat comes from animals raised in large part on cotton plant diets. Cotton became the farms' proverbial lifeblood.

This point was made graphically clear to me during *Navruz*, the Central Asian (Afghan–Persian–Turkic) New Year celebrated during the vernal equinox—on or about March 21. An older man, by whom I had been seated for a school celebration, had just finished his *palov* (pilaf), which had been served from the cafeteria to all the teachers and guests who had dropped by. In a gustatory display of oleaginous affection, the senior poured tea from his cup into his bowl, in which only a thick layer of oil remained. After swirling it around for a few seconds, he swallowed it all. Noticing my astonishment, he said, "When you've known hunger, it's always nice to feel full," with a smile that belied the grave way of making his point. No ethnography of a FV village would or could be credible without cotton permeating it.

What little industry exists in villages and the small towns surrounding them is connected mainly to the cleaning, processing, and packing of cotton, or to the extraction of oil from the plant. Trains rumble through villages transporting cotton, and tractors lumber down the narrow asphalt roads carrying a few metric tons of raw cotton bouncing in their trailers. In addition, the inputs and investment for proper cotton ginning, production, and manufacturing of *quality* cotton cloth and fabrics are different from the minimal requirements for successfully raising a crop. Uzbeks have found this process more or less elusive in terms of their own industries, mainly because they had comparatively few finished products industries for textile manufacture in the Soviet Union.

People in the region store bundles of cotton stalks outside their homes as household fuel. They talk incessantly of the previous harvest, its quality, the income they earned from it, the amount the state says it will pay them in the following year (usually the equivalent of a few pennies per kilogram), the amount of money they are still owed (sometimes six months in back pay, or debts mixed in with pensions totaling hundreds of dollars), the prospects for next year's crop, the number of hectares of cotton their family has been assigned to maintain (usually 1 to 2 hectares depending on need, family size, and available working hands), the kolkhoz target plan for the coming season, the uncertainty about whether the tractors will have sufficient fuel for plowing, and the farm's supply of adequate (or inadequate) seed, fertilizers, pesticides, and defoliants. These and many other cotton-related topics form an incalculable list of the specialized, hybridized, even esoteric language of a cotton kolkhoz. Cotton and the life that is a part of it forms part of the focal vocabulary for farming Uzbeks.

SPEAKING OF THINGS BETTER LEFT UNSAID

"You know, we Uzbeks always say, 'Everything's fine,' even when things might really be awful. We only want people closest to us to know our problems," a local *mullo* (religious leader) once remarked to me while reminiscing about his years in the navy during the late 1950s.

Initially, I just couldn't understand why members of the families with whom I was working—specifically parents and adults—were so reluctant to tell me about the awful side of life. At dinners and teas, whenever and wherever we had been invited, the various hosts always kept conversational topics light-hearted and up-beat, which would seem to fit the pattern of dinner parties the world over. They wanted me to feel as comfortable as possible, whereas I wanted them to answer directly about troubling topics. In the words of Olivier Roy, this is hospitality as "a form of defensive screen" (1986:22). In regard to his fieldwork in Afghanistan, Roy refers to people's suspicions about outsiders who appear in villages to gather information. He continues on to say that invitations to a meal and a stay in a home "enmesh guests in a formalism in which the ceremony of greetings and the ritual of the meal leaves little place for the exercise of authority or even *simple investigation* [emphasis added]" (p. 22). Furthermore, to introduce the more probing questions is to break the trappings of light-heartedness.

At first, I did not want to disturb what I saw as the order of things. I was unwilling to sacrifice politeness in the name of science; I did not want to be disliked. Upon realizing that a question had been ducked once or twice, I did not dare to ask a third time.

Of course, I acted as cautiously as I could, trying to sense when I had overstepped a boundary, when I had thought up an inappropriate question in a mirthful setting, and so on. An anthropologist needs to learn how and when to ask the "tough" questions. In my own work, I found that such questions could become appropriate and receive sincere responses only when a great deal of familiarity and affection had been established between informants and me.

Much as in other societies of the Middle East and Central Asia, Uzbek village culture and family dynamics feature a type of insularity toward those who are unknown. This is why pan-Soviet comparisons—thinking Uzbeks are just like Russians—may turn out to be tenuous at best: Even though Russians, for example, and Uzbeks were collectively a "Soviet people," one must exercise caution in comparing behavioral practices on the basis of their shared Soviet status. Their responses in regard to how readily and deeply they would be inclined to complain to strangers about life's bitter pills serve as a study in contrasts. Similarities among neighboring peoples and other Muslim cultural areas prove more meaningful. The intimacy that would allow outsiders to be in the know about family problems or disputes comes rarely, for as Jamous writes of the Rif Berbers, this constitutes a domain of the forbidden (1992:169). Applying this notion in even more explicit terms to Central Asian communities on the whole, Nazif Shahrani says the following:

> Central Asian Muslim communities abide by a particularly strong injunction against divulging information about oneself, one's relatives, friends,

or community to strangers. Guarding such information often is considered a matter of personal and collective security in that it creates a zone of control and exclusivity for the sake of community welfare (1994:21).

Accessing opinions, the past, someone's actual salary, and other "private" information rarely happens until people think the risks to their personal sense of self and membership within the larger collectivity will be neither jeopardized nor violated in the telling process. Cotton turned out to be a point of departure for all manner of questions bound to the Soviet system, village history, personal and family histories, and the disgruntlement of the present—to an economy in free fall and the attendant repercussions in the cultural intercourse of common and public activities.

THE MUD COLLECTIVE AND TALK
OF BETTER DAYS

In mid-December, after exchanging greetings, a favorite expression of villagers was "*Loi kop*" ("Lots of mud"). Indeed, when lots of rain and wet snow were coupled with little pavement or asphalt on narrow, winding village lanes and paths, mud fast became a scourge of daily movement—a thing at once so slippery and dense, so cold and exhausting, that it served as a topic for recounting how hard it had been to get around during the day. A common, ridiculous sight and personal predicament came in the form of leaving one's loosely tied or secured shoe in the mud (an occurrence made all the more commonplace by people's use of *kalosh*, or loose rubber shoes intended to fit over boots). After having planted a foot in the mud as an ordinary step, a person would delicately cease forward movement so as to place the now-exposed foot back into the stuck shoe by carefully balancing flamingo-like to avoid plunging back into the mud. People soaked their socks and shoes in the muddy morass, fell so that they hurt themselves and ruined their clothes in it, and drained themselves trying to move about the fields picking cotton and the semi-dried-out stalks of cotton plants (*ghoza poe*) in it.

It didn't take long before I developed the following maxim: Wherever mud was, developed socialism was not. After all, socialism had as much to do with development in the form of paved roads, electricity, and telephone lines as it did with the equitable distribution of resources and the end of the exploitation of man by man. At least that is what the good citizens of such small villages as Boburkent had believed. It was not for nothing, after all, that Nikita Khrushchev, a former leader of the U.S.S.R. during the mid-1950s until the mid-1960s, had declared that the Soviet Union would "bury" the United States (1959), that Soviet science put men in outer space, and that well-nourished Soviet men and women returned from places like Mexico City, Munich, and Montreal every four years laden with precious metals (Olympic medals) as evidence of the superiority of Soviet sport, and ergo the entire Soviet system.

Electricity came to Boburkent only in 1960, quite some time after Lenin proclaimed that "Communism equaled *elektifikatsiia vsekh stran* (electrification of all the [Soviet] countries)." Even today the village's electricity supply is a fickle creature, which is why the order of family life may undergo significant time travel throughout the course of a given day: One minute everyone exists in the wonderful Edisonian era of hot plates, immersion heaters, television, and burning light bulbs; the next minute they return in their time machine back to some decidedly non-Communist century of feet warmed by hot coals, the tea kettle placed in the glowing embers of the hearth, ordinary conversation as entertainment, and candles burning for night-time vision.

A colleague and historian of Central Asia once remarked that the Soviet Union was really just a Third World country with missiles. While I may not totally embrace that sentiment, consider the following exchange about telecommunication:

"In America how far can you call with your telephone?", a young man once asked.

"Sorry," I said, "I'm not sure that I understand your question."

"I mean, how many kilometers away can you call with your phone— like 60, 90, or 200 kilometers?"

Phones never worked very well in the capital city of Tashkent either, and today the cell phone has become much more of an accessible necessity than a luxury, as was the case as recently as the late 1990s. In the villages, however, the roughly 10 percent of families with telephones usually cannot directly dial anyone except their neighbors. Occasionally they succeed in getting through to the nearest town of Noghai, where an operator sometimes places orders for calls to larger cities or towns, including international calls. Experiencing these calling hurdles directly helped me better understand why I received such outpourings of gloom from fellow urbanites when I told them of my plans for kolkhoz living.

Initially, the villagers tried to dissuade me from doing research because they felt embarrassed by their conditions:

- "Why did you come to the village now? It's such a bad time!"
- "Our life is so hard here, and we have no comforts (*komfort ioq*)."
- "It was much better here a few years ago. You know, we used to get coal from Russia, but they don't provide it anymore, so that's why it's so cold in our homes."

From such statements three things are clear: (1) Villagers themselves feel that their lives are difficult; (2) they think that the quality of their lives was better in the recent past; and (3) they recognize that a dependency on Russia helped secure a cold-weather necessity in the form of heating fuel. These issues came to dominate the topics of local conversation throughout the cold winter of 1993–1994 wherever it was that we happened to be among the nearly 300 households of Boburkent, or in neighboring villages and towns. No matter how hard people tried to joke about the difficulties or cast them in a kind of positive light ("This is just a temporary phase on the way toward complete independence and development for us"), it appeared that most adults older than age 35 felt a sense of loss with elements of the Soviet system that were dying away. On the one hand, the material losses seemed to matter most. On the other hand, the despotic aspects of the old order were fading none too fast for almost everyone whom I got to know. Complaints about the glacial nature of reforming acts connected to the economy and politics in this independence era often resounded just as those about the loss of heating fuel and living wages.

WHEN WE SAY "PICK," YOU SAY "HOW MUCH"

Common people, with the exception of an occasional kick or punch, have long waited for commands and orders issued from above, as if they had long accustomed themselves to life within a military installation of the mind. Even so, they are also wise to the style of local rule and implementation of decrees from above. Laws may change, and the new legislation may be progressive, but one's actions in accordance with the new order of things must conform to what the local leadership will tolerate. In reality, the reverse of a filtration process sometimes holds sway concerning urban-manufactured reforms and edicts. By the time they are received and implemented at the local level, many impurities find their way into the existing product. Circumventing the barriers put up to hinder citizens from

Courtesy of Russell Zanca

F I G U R E   3.1   Note the cotton field behind the girls and the stalks picked clean. These children are harvesting cotton in November when the value of the crop is much diminished. Children's contribution to the national cotton harvest tends to be minimal.

attaining certain wants or ends, for which the laws have been enacted, requires the kinds of skills, creativity, and resourcefulness that only insiders from the margins of the ruling sociopolitical structure know intimately. In this section, I illustrate how this command structure works in Uzbekistan.

Few farm scenes are bleaker than Amir Temur Kolkhoz's vast acreage of cotton fields in winter. Nearly 1500 acres, or approximately 70 percent of the farm's arable territory, are still sown to cotton. This is actually a decrease of nearly 20 percent from the time of peak cotton growing in the 1980s. Significant reductions in the amount of land devoted to cotton began only after 1989. In the Ferghana Valley, long before today's villages were collectivized (fully by 1937), the great cash crop transformation of agriculture had begun in earnest by the turn of the twentieth century (Jamalov 1947:5). Today's exacting demands often appear to be more an exercise in Soviet methods of control rather than the pursuit of lucrative export trade, because the command to fulfill quantity quotas means that much of the cotton will be of little value. The following example illustrates this point:

> On a morning toward the end of December, about 25 men with apron sacks and tattered, heavy clothing wait along the village's main road for a couple of rumbling trucks approaching southbound from almost 100 meters. Although they appear grim and haggard, many with puffy, sleep-deprived faces and bandaged hands or fingers, they chat with one another, smoking and relating comical events. One alert, refrigerator-shaped man, dressed in good winter clothes, issues rapid commands, makes notations in a ledger, and confers tersely with a couple of other men, who also are standing at a considerable remove—with their fedoras—from those about to board the trucks. As snow gently falls, men blow into their cupped hands or rub their hands together.

This description outlines a preparation for late harvesting. People would tell me later that during some years, in an effort to fulfill state targets, measured in metric tons, they were required to pick snow-laden cotton into the beginning of January. Most interviewees saw cotton picking at such a late time as a sham, and the opinions of local authorities, the distinguished men from above, were about the same. "*Majbur*" came the tight-lipped response to the question of "Why do it?" The word *majbur* means "forced," "no choice," "got to do it," or something similarly grim. It pops up most often in talk concerning why a seemingly senseless thing was, is, or will be undertaken.

Because the best and most valuable cotton is harvested much earlier in September, the quality of such exposed cotton is of little value to the state, to say nothing of the kolkhozniks who must endure the harsh conditions to pick it. In the past, when state planners determined a harvest target for a given crop on a given farm, everything humanly possible was done to meet the target. Kolkhoz wages and payments in kind (wheat, cooking oil, and rice), in addition to improvements and upkeep to infrastructure, depended on the villagers' ability to harvest enough of a crop to be as close to plan as possible. Nowadays little change occurs either in the command-administrative system of harvesting or in the methods used to extract as much of the crop as possible.

TALK OF "TRANSITION" UNDERMINED
BY COMMUNIST ETHOS

For several years after the breakup of the socialist bloc, many journalists, politicians, and scholars spoke generally about the "transition," ordinarily equating the collapse of socialist one-party rule with the beginnings of a switch to pluralistic polities guided by a certain degree of free market practices. Certainly, this has proven to be the case for many ex-Communist states. Uzbekistan, in contrast, has witnessed few political and economic reforms that would really qualify it as a state that has made a "transition." In fact, prevailing wisdom holds that Uzbekistan has become more dictatorial than democratic since the Soviet collapse. The situation on farms really seems to hamper the emergence of any sort of transition.

In the face of the increasing absence of all sorts of consumer goods and state-subsidized services that had, perhaps, made harvesting wet, frosty cotton worthwhile (from the 1950s until roughly 1990), little seems to make this task bearable in the independence era. Again, it seems, the *dehqon* (peasant) is being had; again he finds himself standing out there, shaking his head and saying, "Not again. I can't believe I fell for this nonsense for the umpteenth time."

Courtesy of Russell Zanca

FIGURE 3.2 A local cotton technician surveys cotton plants in September—peak picking time.

And so at the time when a visiting anthropologist dropped into their midst, villagers were more than ready to respond to the simplest, most naive type of agriculture-related questions—to wit, "What do you think about kolkhoz farming now? What percentage did people pick by hand this year?"

Economic transition and economic breakdown are not the same thing. Economic chaos, moreover, seems even further removed from a transitional period. The villagers whom I knew mostly likely did not awake each morning thinking to themselves, "Well, another day with no coal, no natural gas, no gasoline, expensive food prices, no reliable bus service to transport me to the market, no products worth buying in the local grocery store, no new pair of shoes for my child to begin school this year, no affordable medicine to treat my ailments, no salary for the eighth straight month, and no money in general. Well, these hard times will pass soon, because I'm living in the transitional period; things will pick up soon." For optimists, the concept of transition implies a change from one state to another; although it may involve short-term hardships, it is perceived as leading to an experience of the glories of nation building as a concomitant of national independence and the institutionalization of the free market. Naturally, many villagers look forward to the future with the belief that national sovereignty will prove the right course for their country in the long run—and yet even many an optimist questions the wisdom of the way in which the U.S.S.R. disintegrated.

The local leadership seized upon the "transition" as way to cover up its own misrule and intransigence through its embrace of corruption, negligence, and autocracy. Only recently have international players, including the United States, taken positions critical of the Uzbek leadership. Until recently, political criticism was subordinated to the idea of enabling Uzbekistan to make its transition from Communism. Therefore, organizations such as the World Bank and USAID urged on the "transition" by advising that the Uzbeks stop subsidizing prices for essentials, such as milk and bread, and float their currency. Not only has the country's leadership failed to enact such policies, but it has also invited much investment in commerce that may not necessarily help the vast majority. Thus much new business centers on tobacco cultivation and manufacturing as well as soft drinks and sweets concerns. Putting people to work creating cigarettes, cookies, and fizzy beverages for domestic consumption may not bode well for the (literal) health of the country. Out in the fields, the transitional phase has become something of a fiction inspired by bureaucrats, or, seen in a more positive light, the transition may be working for urban folk who at least have lots of petty commercial options. Nevertheless, nobody doesn't like Coca-Cola!

Coercion has always played a major role in the entire process of the cotton harvest. To some extent, the increase in harvesting activity observed in recent years may be a function of the decline in machinery use (which was happening in many Uzbek areas through the mid-1990s), in that the process forces more people into the fields for picking, including children age eight and older. Interestingly, there is almost an inverse ratio between the degree of coercion and the material rewards for complying with state demands. That is, the more coercive and ruthless the state apparatus is, as exercised by police and local officials, in its drive to force people to pick and pack as much cotton as possible, the more the cotton farmers receive in terms of material goods. At least that was the Soviet model. Today, the state-financed and controlled harvest model is used to try to coerce villagers into devoting more time to the harvest, but villager willingness to acquiesce is minimal because of their subsistence and marketing concerns. Such worries foster a greater dependence among family members as they seek to pool resources and maximize their household's economic diversity—a diversity that reckons kolkhoz labor as among the lowliest forms of possible income-generating strategies. The lack of remuneration is the major factor here. In fact, in the first years of the new millennium, peasant exploitation has become so extreme on the "plantations" that people are paid a value that is equal to only a fraction of what their counterparts receive in neighboring Central Asian states, such as Kazakhstan—about 5 percent!

Informants told me that by the late 1980s, the benefits from cotton began to ebb. This slowdown corresponded with an economic crisis throughout the Soviet Union characteristic of the late *perestroika* period. At that time many people from minority ethnic groups, such as Tatars and Ukrainians, began moving to other parts of the former U.S.S.R. or abroad. In the area in which I conducted my fieldwork, surrounding towns never included large minority populations; the district's population was nearly 90 percent Uzbek. Nevertheless, the departures of the minority groups were significant in that those leaving bought up available consumer goods, and, subsequently, an individual's ethnic or national status began taking on a new significance. Republican politics quickly became more nationalistic, and occasionally anti-Russian, and minority groups realized that Soviet cultural dominance was giving way to feelings and policies bent on subverting it. The openness of *glasnost* unleashed by Gorbachev made nationalist feelings and expressions acceptable in the face of economic troubles (Motyl 1990:159), although few therapeutic benefits accompanied the free expression linking cultural rights and economic autonomy to nationalism.

As more political rhetoric focused on the exploitation of Uzbekistan as a great cotton plantation at the hands of Soviet development, and as more politicians and intellectuals began to make speeches and publish articles about the environmental and human costs of cotton growing, certain villagers became expectant, hoping that new measures would be introduced to transform the kolkhozes themselves radically by substantially reducing their reliance on cotton and by giving residents choices about the sort of farm work they might pursue. They had reason to believe so in the late 1980s and early 1990s, when such issues were a matter of routine conjecture and disputation in national newspapers and magazines. In fact, one of my chief informants who regularly read periodicals in those years remarked:

> The newspapers were exciting for a time there [1988–1992]. They published so many articles about history and the wrongs committed against us by the Communist system. Some of the articles even discussed how the country could take a variety of paths to independence, changing the economy, changing agriculture, and so forth.

Courtesy of Russell Zanca

F I G U R E 3.3 In the post-Communist period, more and more picking became nonmechanized, as evidenced by this woman's work.

Indeed, the media daily demonstrated how closely they would stick to older formulas regarding agriculture after the heady days of relatively free expression and divergent viewpoints had been effectively ignored and censored from publications and news reporting by 1993.

None of this was lost on villagers, whether they followed changes in the media closely or not. Although acreage sown to cotton was reduced along with the plan target ratios—relative to the new dimensions of the farmed territory—most of the least appreciated methods for changing the existing system were based on the following measures:

- Brigade assignments for farmers
- Assigned hectares of cotton that continue to be reserved generally for sizable households
- Tying of farm income and budget of the kolkhoz to an imposed plan target (something that could prove well nigh impossible to meet given the lack of industrial inputs and poor weather conditions)
- The farm's inability to pay farmers either in cash or in kind based on state allocations, even though many administrators from within the village seemed none the poorer for the hardships endured by ordinary families
- An information blackout about what their cotton was truly worth and how much the state made from the cotton people picked

I once asked a brigade member why she did not know about prices for cotton on the world market, and why villagers generally seemed to know nothing about whether they were properly compensated for the wealth they generated year in and year out for the state:

> How should I know? I don't think anybody here in the field knows that. We just know what they say they're going to pay us and what percentage of the target plan the farm must fulfill [*bajarish kerak*]. All the rest … it's secret. Who knows about it?

While this woman's statement doesn't tell us how she feels about her own lack of awareness about prices of her cotton income, we might conclude that the state makes sure to keep people outside the loop about the exchange value of their labor. I learned this time and again by asking similar questions about profits and income related to the harvest from other informants who were more knowledgeable than the woman quoted here.

By the mid-1990s, the average cotton kolkhoznik earned only a fraction of the value that he or she earned for the same work in 1973, for example. However, there was also far less to buy with either the moribund ruble or the new *som* (the unit of Uzbek currency introduced following the country's independence) in terms of goods that people needed and wanted. Imported goods, especially from China, began to appear in local marketplaces as a kind of mini-capitalism flourished. The "excitement" over many of these newly imported products wore off quickly once people recognized the inferiority of the goods in contradistinction to their Soviet counterparts. Coupled with this disdain was dismay at the great expense of everyday items, such as cigarettes, laundry detergent, candies, alcohol, combs, calculators, shoes, and kerchiefs. And yet with the burgeoning surplus of agricultural labor, and with the corresponding rise in the underemployed and the unemployed, especially among the youth (50 percent—conservatively), few to no alternatives are left for making money. It seems implausible to equate the staffing of ramshackle kiosks and tables, and even pieces of cloth laid on the ground, with the rise of the free market, but what other conclusion is one to draw from the rural sector?

Farm residents who criticize the country's leadership hint that many of the moves made to decrease the intensity, enormity, and dangers of the cotton harvest occurred only as a result of "hell raising" by intellectuals, journalists, and health professionals during the 1980s. Only then did a widespread outcry against many of the environmental and ecological hazards of pesticides and other farm-related chemicals (spread over nearly 2 million hectares of collective farm land) emerge (Ahmedov 1990:22–23). The state's response at the time consisted of little more than calming some of the growing outrage—some adjustments here and there, some anti-Soviet remarks thrown in for good measure—but then most workings reverted to business as usual.

Optimistic residents, conversely, say that the difficulties, the rise in dictatorial tendencies, and the increasing levels of corruption throughout institutions merely form part of the inevitable "transition" process. They show confidence in the state setting its sights on capitalist welfare as it works to improve overall welfare.

Following are two of these diverging viewpoints that people expressed to me—first a critical voice, and then a supporting voice:

I expected bigger changes by now [1996]. In some ways it's inevitable that the country is poorer; this can't really be helped. We had to anticipate that, but they (leaders) act just like Communists; that's who they are after all. The news (newspapers and television) is full of bootlicking, too.

You hear a lot of people say that we need democracy. Democracy! Now how could that possibly be important at a time like this? This is a period for order and hard work. We should be disciplined rather than concerning ourselves with politics. I think our country will turn around soon. The president needs support more than anything else.

You know, they owe me almost three years worth of wages (kolkhoz work), but I'm not complaining. I'm sure that they'll pay me back. In time you'll see that our country is rich and has much to offer the world.

Of course, these are just two views—and even in a village of 1300 people, feelings toward a new dispensation will inevitably vary. My own observations through 2004 were that the level of dissatisfaction and anger with the state and the leadership coming from rural areas had grown to the extent that people complained more openly than ever before.

WOMEN AS FULL-TIME COTTON PEASANTS

Kolkhozniks constitute that group of collective farm residents whose jobs consist mainly in working the earth and earning their keep from the kilograms of cotton that they pick. Among these people, one would be hard pressed to find even one person who isn't dissatisfied with his or her material well-being. Nevertheless, the prevailing attitude among them is resignation toward the current system, just as it was resignation toward the former system. The kolkhozniks' position stems from an attitude that sees complaining rather than working, or trying to beat the system by striking out on risky commercial ventures, as one of practical futility. This is generally true of those who were raised in the Soviet system. Younger people naturally have their ambitions, several of which concern leaving the collectives altogether.

I draw these conclusions based on evidence gathered through many conversations with men and women of different ages. In some small way, the beleaguered kolkhoz system continues to provide them with sustenance both for themselves and for many other members of their respective households. This happens as most people work increasingly for what amounts to food. I have listened to people tell me, "I'm a peasant [*dehqon*], and I can't worry about politics and all of that talk. In the end, I've got to keep on working." Indeed, as the lowest-paid workers of all agricultural or rural personnel, these people rarely take the time to reflect on labor options. As a friend in Tashkent put it:

Maybe in your country people think about opposing what they dislike, or forming a movement, or protesting. We don't really think that way here. Whatever we think of our system, our most important priority is to figure out how we can fit into it and move with it.

More than 65 percent of *kolkhozchi* (the Uzbek variant of the Russian *kolkhoznik*) are women, and their labor options are more restricted than men's. Outside of the fields, women with jobs work almost exclusively as schoolteachers, in pre-kindergarten programs, and as nurses; they also service schools and medical clinics as cooks and cleaners. Although there are exceptions, women tend to be less vocal than men in making themselves heard by local authorities—that is, they are rarely wont to complain about political decisions affecting their livelihoods. Privately, however, women are more inclined to voice their frustrations.

It seems striking that men often opine negatively about the fact that the Soviet system in "liberating" women in Uzbekistan also "forced" women to work in public, yet rarely rush to take over women's work in the cotton fields. Furthermore, the symbol of the undermined society, owing to the Soviet placement of women in the public sphere, is turned on its head to a degree because a woman's movements are restricted again to this one locale, however out in the open it is (Massell 1974; Bacon 1980; Worobec 1991). The counterargument is that placing women in the fields paved the way for them to work in markets or as service workers in nearby towns. While more women have taken an active role in public

Courtesy of Russell Zanca

FIGURE 3.4 An Uzbek woman weighing her pickings. She will be paid in pennies per kilogram.

life since the 1920s, it must be admitted that they were a part of public life before the Soviet period, although they were a much more "invisible" presence owing to veiling, which is a point nearly absent from the modern scholarship of Central Asia.

Women kolkhozchi know at least that they really don't count for much in terms of their value to the state. To what extent independent Uzbekistan practically pursues the creation of new educational and professional opportunities for girls and women remains to be determined. Full equality between the sexes, however, is guaranteed in the Uzbekistan Constitution. On a practical level, without substantial monetary and material inputs to agriculture, and without efforts to increase payments to kolkhozchi in the near future, it is unlikely that these people will live as well as they did in the 1970s for a long time to come. In fact, the country's gross domestic product (GDP) in 1995 relative to 1989 stood at −5.0—hardly a promising indicator (de Melo & Gelb 1996:266)

HERE WE ARE NOW—ENTERTAIN US

For all of the abuses perpetrated by the state against the populace, the idea of the state simply abnegating its *obligations* to villagers really upsets people. It is arguable whether people have become overly dependent on the state and, therefore, are now unable to think as individuals. Village folk are neither averse to innovation nor incapable of individualistic acts of economic originality. (They do, however, need to be convinced that the innovations make sense and are workable.) In most cases, households—the smallest corporate units within the social structure— have little money or essential resources that would enable people to invest in new job-related ventures. Naturally, those who have served the state for many years cannot but look to this very same state (independence notwithstanding) itself for relief during a period of deepening crisis. Villagers may be entertained by nationalism, independence, new laws about private property and ownership, and the newly vaunted status of their mother tongue and re-created national culture, but, as with most forms of entertainment, they are but a single, finite sphere of cultural life. One cannot inhabit indefinitely or find permanent sustenance in the realm of entertainment. After all, when performances end, material concerns must be faced; the kolkhoz must provide.

And what to make of less symbolic or allegorical types of entertainment other than what is transmitted via the airwaves, via antennae, and in the popular press? That which Westerners might be inclined to call "cultural affairs," "leisure time," or "cultural upbringing"? On the Amir Temur Kolkhoz, this issue is also bound to the cotton growing cycle; it is bound to the collective farm budget itself.

MADE IN INDIA

A village-wide screening of a *Hind* film took place only once during my stay. Such Indian movies are among the most popular in Uzbekistan (along with karate flicks from Hong Kong and American action movies). The Indian movies seem to have the widest generational appeal. Indian movie stars are so admired that in people's homes, offices, and workshops, one will find numerous magazine cutouts adorning walls and windows. Adolescents told me that the films were shown about once a month through 1991 at the kolkhoz's central auditorium (part of the farm's administrative complex).

The one film showing that I experienced occurred in the frigid surroundings of the kolkhoz's auditorium on an icy night. The projector kept failing, the screen was badly torn, and I couldn't help but feel that I was taking in a drive-in showing thanks to all of the broken windows. With all of the additional breaks in the showing, I had plenty of time to talk and joke with the children who made up most of the audience.

On either side of the crumbling auditorium (constructed in 1964 and falling apart in much the same way as the local railway station, and local rusting factories of similar "vintage") hung badly reproduced paintings of Marx and Lenin. My wife and I decided to quiz the children about these titans of world communism. Unlike with children of the previous generation, it became clear that "classic" Soviet instruction had fallen by the wayside. The children, ranging in age from 10 to 14 years, certainly had heard of Marx and Lenin, but thought that the two men had been relatives. Some said that Marx had been Lenin's grandfather; others said that he had been Lenin's uncle. When we asked the children what they thought of these men, a few replied that Marx had been good but that Lenin had been a stick-up man who robbed banks. Whatever else this auditorium was being used for, it seemed perfectly clear that it no longer functioned as a meeting place for making speeches and holding meetings about the glorious founding fathers of proletarian revolution.

Indian movies often made it on to local television stations, because these films were well liked throughout the U.S.S.R. in the past. At a certain point on that January night, however, we simply couldn't stand the cold a moment longer, so we bolted from our seats, leaving behind the teasing images of sultry India and all of the wonderfully rhythmic songs and seductive dance numbers. Once we arrived back at the home where we were living with a single mother and two small boys, the youngest shouted, "Home is good; home is where it's warm." Indeed. Home was the one redoubt from the misery and unpredictability of winter and the discontents thereof in this village. As their mother stuffed more cotton stalks in the small iron-cast stove, we basked in the heat, recognizing the foolishness of ever taking our gas heating for granted back in Chicago.

Later, I took the time to ask why and when Indian films had become so popular among Uzbeks. "From the late 1950s on" answered the "when" question. In regard to the "why" question, in general people said they loved the romance and the singing and dancing. Indian movies are uplifting, usually ending with the righting of unhappiness and injustice. Informants told me that they enjoyed these movies so much because they believed that the characters depicted shared a lot of their own problems, especially poverty, hard work, and parental opprobrium, yet the characters worked through their problems by doing exactly what they wanted to do, while still managing to reconcile with their families in the end.

That those Indians depicted in the films are not Muslims, by and large, has little apparent effect on cultural affinities despite the Uzbeks' Muslim background. Villagers never noted the distinction of religion as a barrier to understanding or empathy among themselves and Indians. Perhaps this situation holds because there are many cultural universals or shared dilemmas between Central and South Asians—so many, in fact, that they supercede religious divisions. Furthermore, even today many villagers in the FV are Muslim in a nominal or almost secular sense.

Once during a ride around Tashkent a young acquaintance popped a cassette into his car stereo. We drove through the wide, bumpy streets in his battered Moskvich car while Indian movie music blared for the whole city to hear. My companion knew that as an American I very possibly neither knew nor liked this music. After a while he asked me if I thought it bearable. I assured him that I enjoyed its exuberance and deep, enthralling percussive sounds. He added his own thoughts:

> Whenever I feel sad, I just go see an Indian movie or listen to the music. It makes me feel better right away. After you've seen a movie or played a tape, you just feel better about life, about everything.

Powerful stuff from seemingly "mindless" entertainment.

Between the realms of cotton farming and popular types of entertainment, I now consider three instances of interrelatedness—celebrations of the new year, Uzbekistan's independence, and weddings. This overlap sheds light on how official politics and new agricultural policies have a direct effect on a given household's, family's, or individual's ability to enjoy the local cultural life. It seems likely that many a villager took this bare and not terribly insightful fact for granted during most if not all of the postwar period.

New Year's Day (Navruz)

The local celebration of the millennia-old Persian New Year, *Navruz*, endured throughout the Soviet period. Although many villagers continue to think that it is a Muslim holiday, in fact its pre-Islamic origins may have had much to do with keeping it from being banned during the Soviet period. Frankly, Navruz was never recognized as an official state holiday until Uzbekistan achieved political independence, but Uzbeks always celebrated it.

Unlike in the past, today's marking of a holiday such as Navruz includes state support, state expenditures, and institutional promotion of the holiday. The last phrase, "institutional promotion," in the village context means that the school stages performances about the holiday that have been created by teachers and students from each of the school's 11 grades. Both groups also bring favorite dishes from home and work together to design costumes and decorations to make the holiday as festive as possible.

Speeches take place near the administrative buildings, and cottage industry items and farm products are presented for attendees to admire. Children read poems about spring aloud, followed by music and dancing on the square adjoining the complex. All attendees don their best attire and participate in what seems to be a huge block party. People enjoy the chance to talk with those

Courtesy of Russell Zanca

F I G U R E 3.5 The Kolkhoz "Klub"—a meeting and entertainment auditorium for speeches, movies, and holiday celebrations.

whom they see in more formal or quotidian neighborly settings throughout the year. The degree to which people enjoy such celebrations, often taking little heed of the *cause célèbre* itself (as was true of May Day or the Great October Socialist Revolution anniversary), is in part determined by the lavishness of the outlays, which local people would define based on the quality and quantity of appropriate foodstuffs and beverages.

Concerning Navruz, several informants said that it was all fine and good that they were learning more about the holiday's history, that they got a day off from work, and that the state re-created the holiday to boost national pride. Nevertheless, it seemed to be just as good, if not better, years ago because one didn't have to be so preoccupied with the costs of food, clothing, and gifts to do things up nicely. According to one informant:

> The state would like you to think that thanks to them we can celebrate Navruz. Sure, it's turned into our real New Year again. Well, let me tell you that we've always celebrated Navruz, and in some ways it was better before because everyone could afford the holiday. We didn't even think about the costs when guests visited; there was always enough.

Independence Day

On September 1, Uzbeks celebrate their independence day. Similar to other former Soviet holidays characterized by patriotism and nationalist vigor, or a giving of thanks to abstract notions such as freedom, these holidays are marked by government-orchestrated activities (Adams 1999, 2007). Along with the masculinity of such holidays are the private and cozy manly *soirees* of the villages where the "patriots" eat and drink up a storm, losing themselves in the bottle, and in turn giving themselves up to abandon, relaxation, and revitalized camaraderie among old friends that may barely outlast the effects of the libations. Younger men and boys will even assemble together with a pilfered bottle or two and homegrown marijuana to rise to their own plateaus of pleasure (*kaif*).

Unlike with Soviet holidays, people no longer worry very much about attending or not attending the main festivities taking place between the new mosque and teahouse (*choikhona*). In the "old days," it was possible that farm or state agents would take note of those absent for May Day celebrations or for celebrations of November 7—the October Revolution holiday. Today, however, agents are rarely on the prowl for anti-independence dissidents or activists. After all, it wouldn't make much sense to be anti-independence, because most people would see it as being anti-Uzbek. Very few people oppose the reality of Uzbek independence; villagers are generally proud of the realization that they live in their own eponymous nation-state.

In the post–World War II period, the Soviet state laid it on thick at holiday time. I speak not of crimson banners, fresh coats of paint, or a "bit of bunting" to placate the "natives" (Cohn 1991:195), although those things were laid on thick, but rather of better stores and varieties of food and booze that were made instantly available during the holidays. Even the cotton farm peasants were compensated.

Today Independence Day events take place in the Uzbek village in ways that do not seem to differ all that much from July 4 celebrations in small-town America, minus the barbecue grills and fireworks. People assemble in the central square to take in the entrancing antics of a local strongman, a team of clowns, wrestling matches, some performances by children, and then tightrope walking. Older men and local *mullos* (religious leaders) gather at the teahouse for prayers, a benediction, and a meal. The overall atmosphere is full of permissiveness and heedlessness.

For the elites in Tashkent, to contrast scenes for a moment, a huge spectacle unfolds on the city's sprawling Independence Square, where a new massive globe statue has replaced the big one of Lenin. Hundreds of political leaders and thousands of celebrities and distinguished guests attend to take in the mammoth, glittering floor show that entertainers from all over the country will have rehearsed for months in advance.

The pageant is broadcast live on television for most hours of the day. As cultish and all embracing as the national celebration appears, one cannot help but be impressed, even if cynical folk think it all a waste of money or a means to express a nation's will about independence properly via sumptuous choreography and musical variety, incorporating "traditionalist" and modernist genres of national art. Uzbekistan has 12 provinces, and they are all represented in the creative acts, thereby promoting the theme of national unity and integrity through diversity of regional or provincial uniqueness. Among those turned off by the nature of the official celebration, muttering can be heard: "This is all for Karimov" (Uzbekistan's president). The implication is that the leader's lackeys put the pageant together to keep him happy. Such sentiments hark back to Stalin's reign and the spectacular performances put on as much for him as for the nation on a whole.

Late one August I interviewed a few women who were part of a neighborhood of young families on the outskirts of the village—an area snidely referred to as the *mikroraion* (micro-region), which refers to the apartment buildings that are crammed together on the borders of many Soviet cities, forming a kind of inner-city atmosphere on the city's peripheries. In asking questions about current conditions and income levels, the women (mostly in their twenties and thirties) let me know that they were fed up with the "lack of everything." One blurted out:

> Look at how we live. We have nothing. Now we're going to be celebrating our independence day. Some holiday! What have we got to show for it?! How can we enjoy the holiday with the way things are?

These women—who were either young mothers who weren't working or kolkhozchi awaiting the start of the cotton harvest—clearly felt that they had yet to benefit much from the reforms, privatization, and the other trappings of independence. While young families always had to struggle in the Soviet Union, especially for adequate housing, the impoverishment of these young kolkhoz families seems to be part of the development of the ambiguity surrounding de-collectivization.

Although modern anthropology would veer away from terming the kolkhozchi a "peasant," owing to established notions about peasants utilizing little to no mechanization (Wolf 1966; Kearney 1996), it's hard to see most Uzbek villagers as much else in terms of their relationship to state power—that is, given their basic inability to exercise their own economic prerogatives. In trying to take part in expressions of popular culture of late, it seems that villagers find themselves in a kind of headlock: The few economic reforms squeeze the collective farmers today just as the massive planting of cotton that began more than a century ago began doing, and just as the drive for all-out collectivization of agriculture did more than 75 years ago. Though it is perhaps not an instance of history repeating itself per se, the villagers perceive these events as an *interrupted* chain of dominating political and economic strategies deployed against the country's most marginal sector. The effects of this latest phase of prolonged downturn appear to impede the most basic kinds of recreational/celebratory activities. When one has to pick cotton in January, the likelihood that the quality of social events that local people most cherish will be affordable and carefree is most unlikely. As a consequence, the cotton lifestyle becomes increasingly distasteful, and the ultimate result is more people abandoning the brigade method of picking altogether.

Weddings

Finally, we round out discussion by considering the ill effects of the harvest on weddings. We will resume discussion of weddings in further detail in Chapter 5, so here I restrict my observations to appraisals of the material context for contemporary weddings.

Uzbeks take part in more weddings than any other socializing events in terms of ethnic culture. People do not hesitate to leave their jobs and children to leave school early (with or without permission) whenever a wedding is announced. Those who must organize and host weddings tend to spend more of their money and resources on weddings to make them successful than on any other family-oriented and community-oriented event.

In addition to the previously mentioned remarks about how I had "come at a bad time" in terms of the economic hardships faced by the villagers, similar types of statements were made about the first weddings I attended in the winter and spring. In short, it was a case of not being able to take part in them when people considered that they lived comfortably or "normally." In those years weddings simply featured more of everything, and hosts could demonstrate to entire communities that nothing was too good for their children, even if this meant bankrupting themselves or putting themselves into debt for the short term (Lubin 1984). Men would explain the decline in terms of fewer kilos of meat and fewer bottles of champagne and vodka, and women would mention the rollback in terms of fewer sweaters and tea sets.

That their children are now able to marry religiously with no fear of political reprisals is all to the good, but needing to borrow money from friends and relatives means that the wedding celebration takes on an unbecoming air. More than ever, Uzbeks have to scramble here and there to find fair prices for the fixed capital they may sell (a sheep or cow) and to buy necessary products (a clothing chest or a case of Coca-Cola), which causes ordinarily taxing preparations for this event to become more burdensome still. To a greater degree than people claim was true a few years ago, wedding hosts have begun to charge close friends with the responsibility of procuring a few extra bottles here, a few extra sacks of rice there. While it may be all good and neighborly insofar as it happens among people who like one another, hosts do not enjoy finding themselves in the position of having to ask friends for help in this way. Relative to U.S. society, the situation in Uzbek villages may be slightly easier to bear because the situation reflects long-established reciprocal patterns and is generally shared.

In these three instances of what we could categorize as the most localized or particularistic forms of village society, readers should gain some inkling about how the farm's fortunes are wedded to the fate of the most basic happenings in village life. The positive side of this trend is that so many people are sharing these dire experiences, and intra-village stratification is only now developing.

POVERTY, COTTON, AND A PATH TO THE PAST?

Adam Smith contended in part that individual selfishness accounted for the prosperity of eighteenth-century England, and that the success of economic life would be best ensured by the mechanism of the "invisible hand," a way of saying that governments shouldn't intervene too heavily in maters of commerce.

Earlier in this chapter, I pointed out the curiosity of Stalinist collectivization and post-Soviet decline functioning to bring about a leveling of village society through vastly different methods. While it is not entirely fair to refer to the post-Soviet period as a "capitalist" phase, the state leadership itself clearly favors the market economy approach. In many a FV village, however, Smith's "hand" has spasmed into a tightly clenched, battering fist.

Nearly a decade after independence, a member of the farm's Neighborhood Committee (*Mahalla Komitet*) told me that at least 20 percent of village families live in chronic poverty (*otqir kambaghallik*), which means that people must depend on a degree of funding from the district administration to secure basic necessities. Of course, it is difficult to define poverty objectively, especially in a monetary sense (owing to village adaptive practices). The results of my own household survey indicated that poverty was practically total in the Uzbek countryside. Most of the people simply lived without regularly paid salaries and pensions. Certain categories of persons, such as mothers with children younger than age 12, received the equivalent of approximately $2.50 per month for each child. Given this kind of stipend, babies would show greater malnourishment were it not for breastfeeding and well-masticated supplements of bread and rice that mothers give to their infants and toddlers.

Cotton is likely to remain the backbone of this rural economy for years to come. However, diversification will grow at the household level and at the farm enterprise level (as socialist collectivism expires) once the Soviet system is gutted. What remains to be seen is the direction taken and the leadership's

Courtesy of Russell Zanca

FIGURE 3.6 Cotton from Amir Temur Kolkhoz that has been cleaned and baled; it is ready for processing and shipping to domestic and foreign markets.

willingness to dismantle the command economy. Will small family farms become the norm, or will prominent bureaucrats gobble up the best lands and create modern plantations that are supported by a kind of kleptocracy (a political system of theft)?

Reasonable social scientists usually steer clear of the prediction business. Our analytical zeal, to the contrary, must focus on changing relationships, roles, and responsibilities among household members. It is doubtful that the Uzbek villagers will orient themselves or direct their own activities around cotton production and the reproduction of the entire harvest cycle with the kind of dependency characteristic of the recent past unless the interventionist role of the state remains oppressive and thwarts independent activity. The trend, however, shows a state unwilling either to redesign its entire economy radically or to deregulate its major crop industry. Uzbekistan appears headed for greater combustibility between state leadership and agrarian society.

Bureaucratic helmsmen, however visionary, still have not proven themselves to be wealth-distributing humanists. Indeed, why should they give up control over a spectacularly profitable industry (replete with export monies that line the pockets of the elite) featuring a commodity bound to be in growing demand for an indefinite period? Whatever carrot the leaders offer to villagers is sure to be followed by a stinging stick. After all, people have been given their "freedom." No one is telling them that it is wrong to be rich or putting them in jail for becoming so legally, but necessary farm inputs, resources, credit, and the ability to convert tiny amounts of capital into hard currency are all hard to come by for the kolkhoz resident. If nothing else, this stranglehold serves a short-term guarantee that the kolkhozchi will continue bending over to plant, weed, pick, and pack the "master's" cotton.

With each passing summer and fall, local anger and frustration frequently give way to hopes, industriousness, and the hedonism associated with weddings. For most people, time brooks no discord, save perhaps for flickering moments. By mid-August, the handwriting is on the wall: The wheat is in and predictability for cotton yields comes with accuracy. People consume themselves with talk of the harvest, and the brigade leaders, agronomists, economists, and the farm chairman meet to hash out where matters stand.

Beginning at this time and following for at least three more months, roadside or neighborly conversation often begin with talk of the harvest. Here is a typical example:

Dalada nima bor? (What's happening in the fields?)

Hosil qandai? (What kind of yield do we have?)

Ob-havo emon ekan. Iana issiq bolish kerak. Fikrimcha ortacha/unchalik emas. (The weather seems lousy; it should be hotter. I think the harvest is average/not too good at all.)

Bugun nech kilo terdingiz? (How many kilos did you pick today?)

The same kind of talk occurs from year to year. Even as controls over the forced nature of picking have been relaxed from the Stalinist and neo-Stalinist eras (this

Courtesy of Russell Zanca

F I G U R E 3.7 Village boys load up on Russian-style bread (*bukhanka*) during a rare snowstorm. Since the early 1990s, bread has become an even more essential staple in the Uzbek diet.

includes the post-Stalin rule of Uzbek Communist Party boss Sharof Rashidov, who ruled the republic from the 1950s through the 1970s), however, the importance of the end result has not lessened. Perhaps it has increased due to the very absence of safety nets, and the knowledge that when it fails one's palate had better be prepared for bread and tea only—for weeks and months on end.

A well-known economic historian of Russia and the U.S.S.R. has stated that a hallmark of nineteenth-century peasant society was these individuals' reliance on bread (Wheatcroft 1991:83). In Uzbekistan, the same reliance exists. Save for occasional short periods in Eurasian history, this tendency toward household meals characterized by breaking bread, followed by more bread, best describes a long-term pattern. Today, fortunately, rice production and consumption are also rising, given the Uzbeks' extraordinary love for cultivating and eating varieties of this grain.

Middle-aged and elderly Uzbek informants often told me that they had not eaten so poorly since the late 1940s through early 1950s. Moreover, there were certainly difficult years during the 1950s and 1960s owing to failed harvests, so this admission carries great weight. People seem headed for a future that looks much like the pre-postwar past. In describing and explaining the commencement of the socialist collapse with its turn toward household-centered and subsistence activities for a farming community, it seems clear that the process affects almost all layers of the village society—not just villagers who engage in cotton farming, but also people from other vocations, including schoolteachers, barbers, and electricians.

Back in the 1950s and 1960s, as difficult as it sometimes may have been, people could rely to some degree on the Soviet "redistributive" system as well as Moscow's material support of the southern-tier republics. As Ellman emphasized, one substantial achievement of Soviet power in the postwar era was the virtual elimination of the famine to which Soviet peoples historically had been subject (1985:220). Of course, we must also keep in mind that the Soviets were at times importers of massive food shipments. Now, however, it seems that villagers have little confidence in the new state to ensure that famine is a thing of the past; people genuinely worry about the possibility of going hungry again.

This chapter has concluded with references to poverty and the importance of bread for the cotton kolkhoz. The next chapter resumes with discussion of practical and symbolic significance of bread, as we explore both the sense of loss with the decline of the socialist system and the optimism associated with a new orientation toward the world through cuisine and ceremonial life.

CONCLUSION

Chapter 3 emphasized the importance of cotton as going beyond agriculture, a person's work, and the overall Uzbek economy. Cotton permeates so many sorts of activities and elements of social life that it literally forms a part of the Uzbek people's diets. As discussed in this chapter, peasant relations toward cotton are complex, including how the workers see their own well-being as tied to its production. A glimpse into what we might call the anatomy of kolkhoz life, especially in adverse conditions, reveals the challenges faced by modern-day Uzbeks as they continue to wrestle with their ongoing dependence on the cotton-based economy. Nevertheless, the Uzbek people continue to find ways to cope during the hardships that accompanied the disintegration of the Soviet Union, and younger families in particular have cast a jaundiced eye at the most recent political and economic changes affecting kolkhoz life.

QUESTIONS

1. Ultimately, what are the biggest pros and cons of cotton production in the minds of the Uzbek villagers?
2. Why will cotton continue to be important for Uzbekistan's future?
3. What are the main sources of entertainment for villagers?

4

Cuisine, Celebrations, and Ceremonies

INTRODUCTION

Recently, anthropologists and historians have researched and written on food-ways (the foods that peoples cultivate and then process and prepare as their cuisines) in a variety of places and contexts. Some have approached the topic historically, whereas others have looked at foodstuffs with an emphasis on how processes and products have not only affected culture change but even have influenced the course of world history (Mintz 1985; Turner 2004; Montanari 2006). While there is a long tradition of writing about food in ethnographies extending back to Franz Boas, it really is only recently that food or culinary studies in anthropology have become a popular subdiscipline within the science.

Discussions of food provide scholars and readers with the kind of knowledge that most of us interested in anthropology would be generally keen to be informed about, simply because foodstuffs and meals tend to be both particular and varied within any society or cultural group. This information makes up a key part of anthropology's knowledge fund. In addition, being informed about what people eat and how people eat can take us deeper into the lives and world-views of people than can mere descriptions and discussions. A focus on cuisine tells us which foods people are willing to eat, which foods they prefer to eat, and how they prepare their foods. We also learn about how people flavor basic food-stuffs, which can serve as a gateway to inform us about how and why people have developed the particular tastes that they have.

Working with informants and consultants on food, in a variety of forms, enabled me to broach topics that might have made people uncomfortable in other types of informal or formal interview settings. This power of food to yield valuable data became a revelation to me, for I had not considered treating food very seriously when I initiated my fieldwork and thought about appropriate top-ics. However, I learned in the course of fieldwork (and when I returned home

90

and began studying what other anthropologists had written about food) that food and its preparation have implications for nearly all realms of culture. When people eat, we do so in particular and habitual ways. We may or may not use utensils; we may or may not eat with members of the opposite sex; we may not eat things considered uncooked, or, conversely, we may enjoy foods that have received the most minimal processing (little to no cooking); we may sit or comport ourselves in a particular manner; and we clearly distinguish the importance of certain meals over others, whether this owes to company, occasion, or time of day.

Because procuring food and then preparing it involves work, people the world over practice divisions of labor; girls and boys do certain things, while women and men do others. Where people sit during meals might tell us much about notions of respect and hierarchy, and the things that people are willing or unwilling to discuss at table can provide anthropologists with all sorts of insights into people and their attitudes in a given locale that might otherwise be difficult for them to understand outside of this intimate context. So, among many other domains of cultural life, food and cuisine inform us about the local economy, division of labor, gender, status and authority, a family or group's sense of interfamilial dynamics, and even local, national, and international politics, among myriad issues that might be discussed daily, and perhaps only at dinner time.

Frankly, interest in what and how people ate in Boburkent enabled me to access intimate knowledge of local affairs and animated opinion about all sorts of politics that I had trouble learning when I approached people formally for interviews or tried to get them to speak on said topics during the course of their working days. If no single factor accounts for why this is so, perhaps it is a matter of common sense to reason that mealtimes—especially dinner time—are one of the least tense periods of any given day, and a time when people seek to create the strongest social bonds as they nourish themselves and share thoughts with a visitor and guest. I cannot think of any other social context in which I gained more insight into what we call culture than during my time spent around various tables or, more accurately, tablecloths (*dasturkhan*—Uzbeks often eat while sitting on cushions or quilts atop the floor from a rectangular tablecloth). I also have to admit that occasional prodigious bouts of alcohol consumption (mainly vodka and fortified sweet wine) during dinners and feasts lubricated many a tightened tongue.

Specifically on the cotton collective, three realms of investigation into cuisine seemed important enough to research, especially as they impinged on daily life, celebrations and ceremonies:

- The notion that perceived changes to their diet—specifically eating lots of bread—reflect a precipitous descent into poverty, even as official policies encourage people to plant more food crops, especially rice.
- The kinds of meals that people prepare and eat, and the related social world of meal taking among family members or a group of friends. This subject matter exists in barest form in both Soviet and Western ethnography.
- The local and external food connections via marketing and trade relations in which many villagers participate as buyers and sellers. In other words, which foods and products do people choose to buy or sell at local bazaars, and

Courtesy of Russell Zanca

FIGURE 4.1 Men praying—saying grace—at the *dasturkhan* during mealtime.

why? What might they prefer to buy rather than raise? What are their imported tastes and desires?

OSH EIMIZ! (LET'S EAT PILAF!)

Daily meal preparation involves heavy-duty female labor viewed through the lens of American standards. Uzbek girls and women form small teams to prepare and cook, usually without the benefit of indoor plumbing or piped-in fuel. Prepping for dinner often takes on the appearance of a small-scale project, especially when an average family amounts to six or seven people.

Rice figures as the basis for most dinners. It arrives most often to the table in the form of pilaf, which today is as much the national dish as it is the national obsession, because Uzbeks never seem to tire of talking about it or eating it. According to my data, Boburkent women served a pilaf (known alternatively as *palov/osh* in Uzbek) more than 60 percent of the time for dinner because as several women told me, "It's so easy to make." Owing to its popularity, children learn from an early age what goes into a tasty *palov*. Lots of children older than age 7 spend time helping their mothers ready the essential ingredients while sitting with them in the kitchen or by the hearth.

Historically, pilaf was a dish reserved for wealthy landowners and rulers. Peasants rarely ate it, having a taste during special occasions, such as weddings, or owing

Courtesy of Russell Zanca

FIGURE 4.2 Buying rice—the central ingredient of pilaf (*palov/osh*) at a local marketplace.

to the generosity of the landlords (Tolstov 1962:308). Pilaf's frequent and wide-spread consumption took place mainly after World War II, and today rural people eat *osh* four to five times per week. During my fieldwork, people often pointed out that they ate it less frequently with meat than during the late Soviet period; meat, naturally, is the most savored component in addition to prized varieties of short-grain rice, carrots, onions, garlic, and copious amounts of cottonseed oil.

It takes about two hours to cook pilaf. Depending on the weather, women cook indoors at a hearth (a kitchen area usually comprising an enclosed mud-brick shed-like area) or outdoors in their own courtyard (*hovli*). The indoor hearth often occupies an add-on room of the home, which in turn connects to a small cellar where particular fruits and vegetables, such as apples, carrots, onions, and dried tomatoes, along with canned goods, are stored for colder months. Cooking smoke is vented up a chimney built directly over the hearth.

Dinners that serve families ranging in size from six to ten people require not only the ingredients but also essential supplies that ordinarily would be associated with non-industrialized countries. For example, at least two full buckets of water have to be fetched. Daughters, mothers, and sometimes sons bring the water from a nearby irrigation channel (*ariq*) that typically courses just outside the home. Water from these narrow feeder canals is further diverted to supply garden plot irrigation for the family's own vegetables, herbs, nut and fruit trees, and, less frequently, grains (maize is the most common grain grown by Uzbek villagers). Because not every household has an ariq running by the home, people may have to walk as far as 100 meters to find another water source. The best-equipped families have a water pipe with a spigot in their own courtyards.

Next, cooking fuel has to be gathered. In FV villages, dried-out cotton plant stalks (*ghoza poe*) are the preferred fuel; one can see huge stacks of these thin pulpy stalks bundled up and leaning against the sides of people's houses. Dried cow or sheep dung serves as the preferred fuel in Uzbekistan's pastoralist and herding areas, mainly in the central and western areas of the country. About three or four arm-loads of the *ghoza poe* must be set aside for cooking a meal or baking bread because this fuel burns up very quickly once ignited. Cooking with this source of fuel necessitates constant attention to the fire, for it rages and dies out quickly.

Nearly all meals are cooked in an enormous cast-iron cauldron, known as a *qozon*. This vessel looks like a thick wok, and the average hearth qozon makes enough food to feed from 12 to 15 people. These containers form the backbone of culinary preparation, and also serve as at least partial testament to the communal nature of rural Uzbek foodways, which may be adduced from their size.

Qozons are also invested with a symbolic quality bearing brief discussion here. The word conveys the idea of a household or family unit, as in the phrase "*bir qozondan,*" which literally means "from one cooking pot," but also connotes people who share their resources and, therefore, eat from one pot. As long as a child re-mains in the parents' home and willingly shares income or other earnings/resources with the rest of the family, then that person remains "bir qozondan." If he or she wishes not to share, then the alternative is to leave and live separately from "an-other pot" ("*boshka qozondan*"). Villagers never described their own households as a household per se with this phrase, but a person would be understood if he inquired whether another person lives in a particular house with the question, "*U ham siz bilan bir qozondanmi?*" ("Is he or she from the same cooking pot (as you)?").

FIGURE 4.3 A man serves palov from huge feast day *qozon* (cauldron).

Courtesy of Russell Zanca

Prodigious amounts of cottonseed oil are used in cooking almost all meals—perhaps a pint's worth per family pilaf. People are fond of saying that the best-tasting pilafs are the oiliest. Still others have their own ideas about the importance of edible oil in the diet. One friend instructed me, "If you don't eat enough oil, your brain won't function properly." Because most rural Uzbeks eat pilaf with the right hand (making a kind of scooper with the four longest fingers), they half-jokingly refer to a great pilaf as one that causes oil to drip down one's wrist toward the elbow while eating.

Beyond all of the healthful qualities imparted by the ingestion of cottonseed oil, women sometimes apply it externally, especially to the face and hands as a moisturizer once the summer sun turns skin to what sometimes appears as coffee-colored leather. On a kind of internal/external note, people also speak of how cottonseed oil regulates and eases bowel movements through its lubricating effects.

After the cooking oil has been left on high heat, the rest of pilaf preparation resumes. Cooks cut up onions, peel and cut carrots into match-stick shapes, and clean home-grown rice by rinsing it three or four times in large enamel basins to remove dirt, small pebbles, and bits of husk from the grains. Next, large chunks of cut-up beef or mutton (the latter meat is more expensive, so it tends to be reserved for more special occasions), along with pieces of animal fat, are added to the boiling carrots. Other potential additions to a tasty pilaf include pomegranate seeds, quinces, black-eyed peas, raisins, chickpeas, and hard-boiled eggs, all of which may be mixed into the final mountain of steaming rice.

Rice growing has long been one of the beloved forms of cultivation among FV Uzbeks. Because the rice grows best in regions closest to abundant water resources, certain regions or villages have traditionally been responsible for supplying nearby towns with rice. Today Boburkent produces plenty of its own rice, and villagers are satisfied that so many varieties can be grown successfully in their "own" backyards." A reflection of the old supply system may be witnessed in village marketplaces where sellers identify the sorts and regions whence their rice originates. Because prospective buyers rarely need to be told the sort, they are likely to ask reticent sellers, "*Qaerdan-u?*" or "*Guruch qaerdan?*" ("Where's it from?" or "Where's the rice from?"), as they pick up a handful from a burlap sack and let it slide slowly through their fingers.

Uzbeks now consume so much rice that each pilaf for a household group requires anywhere from 2½ to 4 pounds of rice. A family of six to seven people will consume approximately 1 metric ton of rice per year (nearly 300 pounds per person per year). Contrast this figure to the annual average rice consumption for Americans, which is approximately 10 pounds, or roughly half the amount of ice cream consumed annually (Williams 1996:83)!

Table 4.1 provides data about the amount of raw rice or paddy that families are able to obtain from the plots recently set aside by the kolkhoz for families' own cultivation of rice. These plots, though only fractions of a hectare (a metric unit smaller than an acre)—often smaller than 0.1 hectare—have become essential for the overall nutritional intake among those households that have them. Per area sown, rice proves to be enormously productive; indeed, 0.01 hectare sown in rice yields upward of 70–80 kilograms of paddy. The Uzbek families plant in late spring, and the rice is ready for harvesting by mid-October.

T A B L E 4.1   Average Rice Paddy Yields for Four Families by Plot Size and Sort of Rice

Family (Number of Members)	Size of Paddy Plot	Rice Sort	Yield
Maghrupov (8)	0.08 hectare	**Qizilarpa**	±600 kg
Kamalov (7)	0.06 hectare	09	±450 kg
Juraev (7)	0.08 hectare	**Avantgard**	±500 kg
Temirov (6)	0.08 hectare	07	±550 kg

Informants told me that they pay even more attention to their own tiny plots than to the kolkhoz's rice crop—a focus that pays off because the families obtain slightly higher yields on their own plots than are achieved on the larger areas that were set aside for the kolkhoz's rice as a whole.

The different names for the rice sorts obviously reflect different kinds of rice that differ according to size, shape, coloring, flavor, and productivity value. Informants told me of at least six sorts raised on the kolkhoz, and I counted at least ten varieties in rural marketplaces. The *qizilarpa* (red barley) variety mentioned in Table 4.1 is among the most beloved for pilaf—people favor its short, fat, flavorful grains. The rice that Uzbeks seem to privilege above all others is *devzira*, and Uzgen district (in Osh province of southern Kyrgyzstan) and Jalalobod province (also located in southern Kyrgyzstan) are most renowned for producing this particular sort.

Once the three to four quarts of water in the cooking pot have boiled down and evaporated, the cauldron containing the pilaf is covered by a bowl that is tightly pressed so that little steam escapes. During the final moments of steaming, bulbs of garlic may be added as a favorite condiment (softened, steamed garlic is eaten by the clove after mashing it into one's helping of pilaf). A woman then typically piles the pilaf on a large platter and brings it to the dining table. Preceding, accompanying, and following the meal will be pots of green tea.

FV Uzbeks ordinarily do not use chairs, but rather sit on quilts (*kurpalar*). People sit cross-legged as they take their meals or sit erect on bended knees. Over the course of longer meals or socials, changes of bodily position occur frequently to improve circulation to legs and feet as well as to maximize comfort.

MEALTIME ETIQUETTE

FV Uzbeks typically practice sex segregation during their meals: Men sit and wait in the main recreation or guest room of the house, while women cook and serve the men. Very young children, regardless of sex, are likely to sit with their fathers at dinner. These patterns varied to a slight degree in the more than 50 village households where I ate and socialized.

Age groups, contrary to common wisdom, do not always reflect liberal out-looks according to the way in which people have been socialized. Education level and commitments to socialist equality, or ideas about "proper" Muslim behavior, however, do influence liberalization (or lack thereof) among individuals in this sense. If one couple (man and wife) were to visit another, it would be likely that the woman guest would sit at the dining table, and that her woman host friend would continue to serve her while socializing with her as if they were taking it easy on their own. In certain conservative homes, representing perhaps 10 percent or less of the total number of households, women guests will head directly to the kitchen area, where they will help host friends prepare and serve. Later, these women will eat together and socialize in the kitchen area. To some extent, such practices reflect more lenient versions of the harem/haram (Warnock Fernea 1965), although there has been no strict observation of rules reflecting the seclusion of women among sedentary Central Asians, save in some urban neigh-borhoods within the historic cities.

After meals, it is again the responsibility of women and girls to clear off the dishes and clean them. Daughters often perform the washing-up task at the near-est ariq, using only dried fig leaves and ash to scour and clean the dishes. Soap and hot water are almost never used to clean utensils, plates, or cooking pots. Ash scours and soaks up oil, and the dried fig leaves appear from time to time as an additional abrasive in the hands of girls and women who squat by the little canals to do the clean-up.

Boys who have reached the age of 16 or so often do not eat with their fathers and their fathers' friends, but rather eat with their mothers and sisters in the kitchen area. Because parents dote upon young children, especially boys younger than age 10 and little girls, these youngsters will often stay for some of the time with a father and his friends.

When men entertain other men, it is extremely unlikely that either the host's wife or any other female relatives (with the possible exception of the host's mother, owing to her seniority/authority) will intrude on the temporarily desig-nated "male space" in any capacity other than as one waiting on and serving the men. There is an inviolability attached to the temporary male domain whenever men gather together, although there is no such enforcement of practices that all recognize and respect. That is, there are few express prohibitions from entering gendered space, but certain kinds of intrusions would nevertheless be considered brazen and improper; such intrusions on temporarily engendered space would flout the norms of practice, such as wives or daughters walking in on a men's evening social to socialize or watch television.

During breakfast (*nonushta*—the breaking of or passing of bread), such sex segregation is not generally practiced, especially if all or most of the family will shortly head off to work or school. Women still take care of preparations and any cooking that they may need to do for breakfast, but everyone eats together quickly. Breakfasts, just as their Uzbek name suggests, tend to be spartan affairs. Bread and tea, plus perhaps a few walnuts and raisins, are the staples. Sometimes bunches of grapes (mostly in the summer and fall), or honey and cups of boiled milk or cold cream, make up richer fare. Of course, much like in families in

Courtesy of Russell Zanca

F I G U R E 4.4 Sex segregation is common at mealtimes. Here women enjoy a late-evening tea.

other agricultural settings, the morning schedules of the various individuals in the home are not the same. School-age children, members with jobs in nearby towns, and collective farm brigade field workers do not all begin to eat or leave the breakfast table at the same time. Even so, there is one breakfast for the entire household.

THE IMPORTANCE OF FEELING FULL

Into the new millennium few villagers express satisfaction about their diets and daily fare when they compare their eating habits and availability of foods to the recent past of the late Soviet era, especially up until the late 1980s. Today people say that their choices are more limited, and they report that their domestic foods are not substantial enough. In this regard, they are talking about the lack of meat in their diets, or, if not meat per se, then meat products—some type of animal fat and animal protein in their meals. Even so, general complaints about food exceed complaints about the lack of meat. Uzbeks, as alluded to earlier, when speaking of greasy pilaf, have what one could call a fundamental belief in the need for rich foods that by American standards would be considered too high in fat, cholesterol, and calories. In fact, villagers speak of foods being most delicious because they are *"kop/mnogo kalorniye"* (a mixed Uzbek/Russian phrase meaning "high in calories" or "rich"). I point to a reversal in concepts of what

T A B L E 4.2   Average Yearly Consumption of Meat and Dairy Products for Agricultural Workers During the Course of Three Years

1991		1992		1993	
Meat	13.4 kg	Meat	10. 8 kg	Meat	10.5 kg
Dairy	148.2 liters	Dairy	84.3 liters	Dairy	70.8 liters

is healthful and nutritious half-seriously: There obviously is no mystery as to why it should be the case.

Basic nutritional intake declined throughout most of the old U.S.S.R. beginning in the 1990s, and the Uzbek villages have not been immune to this trend. The downward trend began about 1990 and intensified with failures in the agricultural sector and the Soviet breakup in 1991 (Fridman 1994:31–68). Although some villagers were able to rely on their savings to some extent during and after the decline of agricultural production and subsequent inflation, this option ceased to be available after Uzbekistan was forced to leave the old Soviet currency zone (based on the Russian ruble after 1991) in 1993. To enjoy a substantial meat intake only once a month when one remembers enjoying it twice weekly has become a letdown. When this loss is combined with significant declines in the availability of cooking oils and dairy products, villagers think that their overall alimentary situation has worsened.

Consider Table 4.2, which summarizes the declines in meat and dairy consumption for the whole of Namangan province—the province of most of my research work—for three years from 1991. While I was not able to access these same kinds of statistical data in the late 1990s and into this past decade, friends have assured me that their situation has not only failed to improve, but possibly become worse. The design of Table 4.1 is modified from the one shared with me by the Namangan Province Statistical Bureau.

By 1994, all statistical data for the major food industries of the province showed even more dramatic declines in metric tonnage. For example, the overall meat output declined to 58.7 percent of what it had been in 1991 (2700 metric tons versus 4600 metric tons), and dairy production fell by 36.8 percent from the 1991 figure (18,300 metric tons versus 24,000 metric tons).

The vast majority of villagers from ages 10 to 65, if able-bodied, spend a great deal of their waking hours moving about and working hard. On average, villagers walk or bicycle from 3 to 8 kilometers per day (less in the winter months). They engage in arduous physical labor, ranging from cooking preparation to carrying heavy sacks of provisions to paying constant attention to the land itself—hoeing, cropping, digging, draining, and so on. In short, the high-calorie diet most people recall and wish for is commensurate with the demands of their lifestyles.

As mentioned, in visiting the FV during the summer and autumn months, one would think (and rightly so) that people eat well. The winter and spring seasons, however, mark different periods in nutritional intake. During the mid- to late 1990s, some families experienced the kinds of food shortages that the village had last experienced only a few times after bad harvests in the post–World War II era. Approximately 25 percent of the village's families experienced a situation akin to hunger (people mentioned that they sometimes simply didn't have enough food at home) during the spring and winter periods of 1995–1996. While this condition hardly is uncommon to agricultural societies throughout the world, it still seems peculiar in an industrialized country that had been part of a superpower nation until very recently. Furthermore, this condition arose in a country where there have been no natural disasters, such as prolonged droughts over the past few decades.

One September afternoon, I recall joking around with a friend who had prepared a sautéed mixture of corn, potatoes, carrots, peppers, and eggplants from his own garden. My friend announced that he was going to try an "experiment" before he set to cooking. The "experiment" turned out to be a meatless meal—to Uzbeks, no meal really is considered manly or hearty enough if it contains no meat. As one can see from comparative research into Mediterranean and North African societies, hosts may feel mortified when there is no meat to be had for their guests (Herzfeld 1985:136; Bourdieu 1990:252). While we were eating, I praised the meal and told my friend how I appreciated his culinary innovation and that I knew American vegetarians who would really go for his meal. He proceeded to ask me if most Americans were vegetarian. I said no, explaining that it is difficult for American vegetarians sometimes, because meat always intrudes on their dietary plans whenever they are not in full control over the preparation of their own meals. My friend nodded as he listened, and then said, "Well, you go ahead and let them know what an easy time of it they'll have in Uzbekistan; we're all vegetarians now." We laughed for a while but both wished for a piece of meat at that moment. We also recalled the old Jack London short story about the withered and impoverished prizefighter longing for a piece of steak to give him the strength to defeat a youthful challenger.

LIVING BY BREAD ALONE

After the early 1990s, bread assumed unprecedented significance in Uzbek diets. Grain-based foodstuffs of the carbohydrate-laden diet consumed in Uzbekistan consist mainly of wheat and rice, with smaller supplements of maize and sorghum.

Uzbeks eat enormous amounts of bread. Because women make bread and other dough-reliant foods, I inquired about the total amount based on local calculations, given that people do not usually sit around thinking about how much they eat in the manner of a statistician. At any rate, results show that a family of seven to eight people will consume nearly 90 kilograms of wheat flour in a two-week period, which means that they will consume more than a metric ton of wheat in the course of a year! A day's total, based on informant information and direct observation (to say nothing of personal consumption), is approximately a little more than one kilogram of wheat flour per person. In terms of bread alone, a neighbor woman told me that she bakes at least 20 loaves of bread every two to three days for her family of six.

The loaves baked in the *tandir* oven (a large circular oven made from mud and wool) are heavy and dense. These loaves often get shared among neighbors, so not every loaf is eaten by a particular household's members. Village women have a system of "bread giving" and "bread taking" that operates on internal concepts of neighborliness and friendship. Not to bake bread and savory pastries (*somsalar*) with others in mind would not be well regarded.

Lest it be thought that the dire necessity, passion, and all-around obsession for and with bread is a distinctly rural phenomenon, I can attest that experiences in urban settings show the contrary. In cities such as Namangan and Osh, few urbanites have or frequently use tandirs, especially those living in high-rise apartment blocs. Bread baking in the cities is left to professional bakers, or at least to people who bake all the time so as to meet street or neighborhood (*mahalla*) demands. Most city bread is lighter and fluffier than whole-wheat bread baked in the villages. Refined flour and other ingredients, including egg and milk, make for a very tasty, but less substantial bread. City people even will say, "We don't eat as well as villagers [meaning fewer vitamins and nutrients from bread]. Our bread has no substance, and theirs is so solid and dark the way it should be. Life is harder there, especially for the women, but all the same they're healthier than we are."

Nevertheless, rural people—and children most of all—enjoy the opportunity to have bakery bread (*nonvoi non*). The kolkhozniks buy this kind of bread in bulk (perhaps 175 to 225 loaves in a variety of tastes, shapes, and styles) for weddings and special occasions whenever tens of people gather at one house. Several small children once confided in me that their gastronomic fantasy was nonvoi non with *shashlyk* (skewered pieces of marinated mutton or beef and fat that have been grilled). Their response came as an answer to the question, "What's your favorite holiday dish?"

Another anthropologist who has noted the centrality of bread in the lives of a mainly agricultural society is Counihan, who conducted her fieldwork off the coast of Italy in Sardinia. Her work shows that bread affects many spheres of social life besides ordinary consumption (1997:283–295). Bread's role is also multilateral in the village: It physically sustains Boburkenters, is a thing of pride to those women who bake well, and serves as a means for labor organization and social intercourse for those involved in preparing it.

Moreover, bread has essential symbolic roles to play. Anyone leaving home for even a short overnight journey must bring at least one loaf from home, and it is crucially important that bread accompanies a person if he should be heading off for a long or distant trip, or for a long time. Uzbeks believe that bread delivers comfort and happiness. Moreover, if one suffers from nightmares, a recommended method to alleviate fright is to place bread under one's pillow because it will guard against demons. Villagers believe that birds may come and take this bread from underneath the pillow, flying away with the demonic spirits it absorbed through the nightmare. Such symbolic associations of bread's protector-like status have also been noted by the anthropologist Arnott working in Greece, in the Peloponessus (1975:303).

Uzbek villagers eat bread all day long and would never dare throw away stale bread, an act considered obscene and sinful given the relatively recent experiences with hunger. Of course, such attitudes are not only a product of history and famines, but also are shared by Muslim peoples throughout the Near and Middle East. Stale bread is broken up into soups, dunked in tea, or simply placed in bowls of water for softening (this last method is known as *ordak shurva,* or "duck soup," because the pieces float as they absorb water like ducks on a pond). These methods of eating bread are essential to older people, who often have few, if any, teeth.

Bread's all-important role as nourishment mirrors patterns found throughout the Mediterranean (Balfet 1975:310). In peasant households, few meals commence without someone (generally the oldest male relative present) announcing, *"Non sindiring!"* ("Let's break bread!"). Pieces are torn from each loaf with the hands (using a knife to cut bread is considered bad form, as if one is doing violence to the bread). Then the host carefully places equal amounts of bread in front of each diner. Later, uneaten pieces are collected from the sitting, carefully stacked together, and put away. This cycle repeats itself at the next meal.

By the mid-1990s, research by the United Nations indicated that the average rural Uzbek was consuming about the same amount of calories prior to political independence in 1991, but the key difference was in carbohydrates intake, which increased rapidly at the expense of proteins and fats (UN Human Development Report 1996:76). As the trend continues, more and more children and young mothers are placed at risk for malnutrition. Important foodstuffs are now being rationed throughout cities and villages. It may take some time before we are able to explain exactly why this happens in a country that produces adequate food for the entire population of nearly 27 million people—perhaps until the current state regime no longer rules the country.

One historian of Soviet agriculture, Geoffrey Wheatcroft (1991), delved into nineteenth-century Russian history for comparative purposes. He analyzed peasant diets, and found evidence that in the late nineteenth century a distinguishing peasant characteristic was reliance on bread and associated grains. Today it appears that we are witnessing a kind of return to at least a peasant-like diet connected to a history that now helps to define negative attributes of rural Uzbek living after the collapse of the U.S.S.R. and, specifically, the collapse of the collective farm economy. Dependency on bread, along with the anxieties and fears connected with each harvest period, betray the underdevelopment of Uzbekistan's agricultural system. The post-Soviet experience of these past 15-plus years has thrust the state farms' workers—or, more accurately, "sharecroppers," as discussed by Marx (1974:802–813), Lenin (1964:198–210), and Gramsci (1989:76)—back to circumstances akin to the pre–World War II period when the benefits of the system that helped rural people to become something other than peasants were inchoate. Today they appear to be largely in abeyance. Formulating this trend more simply, the more people are eating bread to the exclusion of other substantial foodstuffs, the worse they are doing economically at almost every turn, and this necessarily limits opportunities for rural people.

Courtesy of Russell Zanca

FIGURE 4.5 Market woman selling Uzbek flatbread (*non*).

ELECTRIFICATION (SORT OF) AND THE PEOPLE WHO DIDN'T STARVE

Few topics serve as better indictments of the present system and government of Uzbekistan, to say nothing of the nation's creeping impoverishment, than that of food. Both the talk surrounding food and the act of having one's meal sometimes combine to bring out opposition to the new political order. Food itself (meat in particular) has become a trope in support of Soviet power, notwithstanding the fact that people hated many other aspects of Communist rule. Contrasting how one eats today to how one ate 20 or 25 years ago invites comments about the relative "good life" of times past. As one of Boburkent's senior school teachers related:

> I used to be able to afford meat once or twice a week then. Now I can afford to buy it maybe once a month.
> When Brezhnev [Soviet leader from 1966 to 1982] was the *podshoh* [leader/sovereign], our celebrations were "up to here" [drags tip of thumb across throat to symbolize plenitude]. We could afford everything and didn't worry very much about prices. Those were good years.

Considerations of foodstuffs and food preparation constitute one of the most lively and enjoyable aspects of social interaction, but even this topic cannot but become political during anthropological investigations involving an American and post-Soviet citizens. Food as a consumer good became an important tool in the Soviet quest to deliver the U.S.S.R.'s people from the hunger that had prevailed from the 1920s through the 1950s. The state knew that for socialism to succeed, it had to put food on the table, especially foods that people coveted, such as meat, butter, fish, and eggs—the items richest and highest in calories. In fact, from 1960 to 1990, the gross agricultural output of the U.S.S.R. grew at twice the rate of the country's population (Severin 1993). All the while, this very system—specifically its financial, productive, and distributive parts—were heading for disaster (Van Atta 1993).

From an ethnographic perspective, one has to consider both the pertinent facts from the macro-economic side, meaning the bungled planned economy of food production, as well as the micro-economic perspectives and local perceptions of the accomplishments achieved in filling stomachs by the old regime. With the exception of during World War II, other countries of the formerly Communist world (the so-called Second World)—notably, the Czech and Slovak republics as well as Hungary and the German Democratic Republic—probably have not experienced the kind of long-term poverty and hunger that have plagued the peoples of the countryside in Russia and Central Asia since World War I.

Lenin once remarked that grain was the "currency of currencies." In the 1950s, the Soviet leadership began to promise untold peace-time riches, which would have a lot to do with the greater exploitation of the country's vast resources, and the ocean of wheat in which citizens would soon be awash with the kickoff of Khrushchev's (leader from 1954 to 1966) Virgin Lands campaign in 1954 in northern Kazakhstan. (The idea behind the Virgin Lands initiative was to grow vast quantities of wheat on dry grass lands, mainly used by nomadic herders at the time.) For the first time in decades, the mid-1950s marked a period in Soviet life when various leaders spoke openly about past mistakes and crimes, not the least of which were those dealing with the falsifying of agriculture and livestock production figures and developments. For example, from 1928 to 1953, the Soviet Union lost nearly 9 million head of cattle (Crankshaw 1959). Furthermore, the leadership began declaring the importance of consumer needs, especially quality foodstuffs. More than likely this new notion may have had a mesmerizing effect, as people could start to salivate over illusions of steaming bread and skewers of roast mutton as opposed to visions of power plants and pesticide factories.

In an effort to understand what genuine wealth differences existed between themselves and Americans, informants and strangers never hesitated to ask about my annual income. However, the amount of money alone did not satisfy people's understanding; they wanted more concrete understandings of what American dollars buy. The importance of affordable food, demonstrating a good quality of life, was brought home to me when people would probe further with standard questions, such as the following:

- Okay, but how many kilos of meat does $2000 buy you each month?
- Alright, but how much is a loaf of bread?

Once I answered these questions for informants or strangers, they would start calculating immediately how much of a given food product it would buy. Questions about rent, cars, stereos, entertainment, and other purchases followed those about food values.

Back in the United States, when I later hosted a visiting Uzbek scholar in Chicago whom I had brought as a guest to a wedding, he announced toward evening's end, "I think there is more meat at Uzbek weddings." My wife and I exchanged bemused glances. Talk of food as a measure of the relative wealth of economy—political economy, really—appears to be anchored in the rural social structure, and this may reflect more a Soviet–Uzbek identity than one wholly rooted in historical patterns. Quantification seems essential to any wealth calculus.

In the post-Stalin era of the early 1960s, according to informants' comments, people in Boburkent began to eat better, more varied foods. So extensive and well developed was the state's monopolistic control over food production and distribution at this time that many collective farm families did not have their own cows. It was not that such ownership was forbidden in the postwar period; rather, it was a more a matter of the kolkhozniks having good access to farm products from nearby marketplaces and state stores, including dairy. In other words, the cattle and sheep that are typical of current village households were actually rarer 20 years ago. I learned this only as I interviewed a schoolteacher (ST) from Boburkent who worked in a nearby town. I had asked her why she frequently complained to me about kolkhoz life, and which chores around her mother's home she most disliked:

ST: Milking the cow is always unpleasant.

RZ: Why, is the cow ornery?

ST: It's not that; it's just that it's another thing I have to do for my girls [two young daughters] in the morning.

RZ: But why is that any different from what you've always done?

ST: I didn't always milk cows! We didn't have a cow until a few years ago.

RZ: Really? That must have been hard. How did you get milk or yoghurt? From neighbors?

ST: Oh, no, not at all. I used to be able to buy those things from the store or at the market. Now the only thing I see from time to time is powdered milk (in shops). Without the cow it would be worse.

This schoolteacher continued on, telling me that dairy stores had been consistently well stocked when the livestock sector was well provisioned and cared for. Before the decentralization of the kolkhoz economy and infrastructure began after the Soviet disintegration, much of the milk was trucked to the regional center and to the provincial capital, Namangan, but a portion usually remained for distribution and sales to villagers. Similar to many other confounding matters connected to the overall decline, I had serious difficulty pinpointing why milk products should have vanished over a short period of time (no more than five years, although the decline was not sudden). The pat answer, of course, is that as the state lessened its procurement demands from the kolkhozes, the kolkhozes ceased to work diligently to fulfill orders that nobody cared about. Consequently, the role in fulfilling consumer demands created by the Soviet state through the establishment of the *khozmag* or *oziq-ovqat* (agricultural products or grocery) shops ebbed: Who needed the shops if there was no longer a support network to run them (referring to the breakdown of the centralized system of production and distribution)?

Many people would shrug their shoulders and say, "I don't know," if asked why fresh dairy products are so hard to find on a farm that still has a pen with nearly 500 head of cattle. I cannot say that no one knows why, only that I am not sure why, and that ingenuous questioning yields few concrete responses. The vagueness may have something to do with the fact that people feel ashamed when confronted with difficulties that they agree should not exist, difficulties that appear illogical and a product of the practice of state administration. As a foreigner, my inquiries into the problem about the shortages took me out of the insiders' loop: Circuitous or nondefinite answers were one thing, but immediate, direct responses rarely were forthcoming. Some topics, no matter how controversial, are fit for discussion, whereas those that seem approachable are avoided as much as possible. I met many foreign and local scholars who either had similar frustrations when trying to obtain statistics or explanations for negative trends or phenomena, or who knew how to handle me with the questions I put to rural people. In the case of local scholars, they—like so many other Soviet people—had decades of artful experience as dissimulators in efforts to protect themselves.

This is not to suggest that answers—perhaps truthful answers—are impossible to secure. Hardly. More than likely, if one badgers informants relentlessly, they will reveal guarded kernels of causation, for some problem or other. However, anthropology parts ways with journalism in this sense; it is not always worth it for anthropologists to get the story at any cost. Anthropologists want to gain a significant degree of trust so that the people to whom questions are put feel at ease telling anthropologists things that do not cause them undue discomfort just because their statements might show Uzbekistan's political and economic system to be blameworthy for contemporary problems. When villagers resisted my questions, I read their discomfort as a warning to change the topic. The suspicions and fears such people were long taught to harbor in regard to Americans (or any type of authoritative, information-seeking folk, for that matter) did not simply die with the collapse of the Soviet Union. Likewise, because independent Uzbekistan remained little changed from the Soviet brand of governance (complete with the continued activity of state security forces in the village), my reasons for treading lightly were brought home to me in even stronger terms.

CURTAILING EXCESSIVE WEDDINGS

If procuring dairy products in daily life engenders a new set of economic hurdles in the post-Soviet world, getting married and planning wedding parties are on an altogether different scale in terms of how Uzbeks look at the gist of who they are as a people. The rural wedding has long been a point of pride. Typically, it features hundreds of guests who feast, dance, and display all sorts of important gifts for the new couple (mainly new garments and new household items) as the newlyweds start out on the road to family life.

Excess or abandon at weddings, even among families who can ill afford to spend so lavishly, has been noted in the historical literature. It certainly became an issue that even the Bolsheviks wanted to tackle much earlier in the twentieth century (Kamp 2007).

Few cultural practices are marked by the kind of cultural extravagance that the *kelin toi* (daughter's wedding preparation ceremonies and party—the main wedding celebration) is. Uzbeks themselves consciously engage whatever doubts or self-questioning they may have about spending so much money and expending so much effort on these weddings by ensuring that the affair goes off in a way that garners respect. Just as it gives the daughter pride in her own family, so it also helps her parents ensure that the crucial relations to new in-laws get off to a proper start. Of course, this is the ideal; the reality may be somewhat different.

Uzbeks sometimes talk about being trapped by weddings, saying there is no escape from the burdens (especially the dual-sided contributions of bridewealth and dowry) they entail. Smart are those parents who plan for the festivities years in advance by collecting the items required to help furnish the new union. Thinking about and planning for these weddings is so developed a field of cultural reproduction that every adult can provide outsiders with a quantified list of necessary items. Gift endowments are based on strict plans, too. Table 4.3 provides a partial inventory of some of the most important items.

Today a major difference in items selected (a trend begun from the mid-1990s) is that they are neither Soviet nor Uzbek products, but rather foreign imports. Naturally, it is not the brides-to-be who are disappointed by many of these items. Instead, the women of the previous generations often do not think that they are getting the same value for their money as was true some 20-odd years ago.

The small model list in Table 4.3 reflects an overall quality decline of about 50 percent since the mid-1970s in dowry goods, according to local women—the main dowry planners. Sweaters, dresses, quilts, scarves, coats, a storage chest, and sundry items both for the new household (virilocal) and for personal use make up a part of the overall dowry. As degrees of respectability do apply, wedding quantities are assigned.

T A B L E 4.3   Some Essential Material Items Provided for Brides at Weddings

Personal Effects for Daughters (Number)	General Household Items (Numbers)
1. Sweaters (4)	1. Quilts and pillows (20)
2. Coats (2)	2. Storage chests (1–2)
3. Dresses (6)	3. Tea sets (6)
4. Shoes/footwear (4)	4. Area carpeting (1)
5. Scarves (8)	5. Cookware (8 pieces)

Courtesy of Russell Zanca

F I G U R E 4.6 Relatives and friends viewing items for a bride—part of the dowry, items mainly supplied by bride's family. Notice the man filming; Uzbeks commonly videotape all aspects of a wedding.

A woman neighbor (WN) from a family whose daughter was about to be married provided me with a description of the kinds of things and numbers necessary. She walked around a room where the items for a wedding had been set up, most of which had been pinned to a large tapestry. These items included everything from bright red nylon dresses spun with gold threads to quilts covered with dazzlingly tie-dyed *atlas* silk fabric (*atlas* or *hon-atlas* is a primary style of silk dyeing mainly for Uzbek women's garments and furnishings covers). After the neighbor finished showing me most of the main items essential for all brides to bring to their matrimonial homes, I asked her how today's weddings differed from those of her emerging adulthood, some 20-plus years earlier (mid-1970s relative to the time of that period of fieldwork):

WN: Well, I would say the amount of gifts was about double.

RZ: Double? What do you mean?

WN: I mean that then we provided 10 sweaters as opposed to 5, or 12 quilts as opposed to 6, 4 pairs of shoes as opposed to 2—you see?

RZ: Yes, but is that just because of the current economy?

WN: I think so. You know, no one has any money now, and whatever there is doesn't buy much. A toi has a lot of expenses.

Nothing about the nature and structure of the celebration has really changed; it is just that people have had to scale back the level of lavishness. Proportionality has been introduced, and most villagers seem to be aware of new standards that have become self-imposed in a fast but also collective way. Both men and women move within their own jurisdictions when wedding planning and supplying come about. Men ordinarily concern themselves with supplying all nonbaked foodstuffs and beverages to feed anywhere from 85 to 300 people. Part of this inventory includes a cow and perhaps one or two sheep, 50 kilograms of carrots, 30 kilograms of onions, 20 melons, 50 kilograms of rice, 25 kilograms of potatoes, and so on.

There is really no way to tell how many guests will show up at a wedding. Variables that ensure large crowds usually include marriages between a villager and a townsman, the sheer number of one's relatives, the popularity of the host in the community, the influence of one family over the others, the popularity of the betrothed, the hosts' generosity, and the popularity of a singer or the musicians involved. One or two days prior to the wedding, small boys walk from house to house announcing the event. Sometimes their announcements are not too explicit: "My father is calling for you. There's going to be a wedding tomorrow." Ordinarily, there will have been talk in the air for weeks about whose daughter or son is getting married. But even in a relatively small village of 1200 to 1300 people, such as Boburkent, it is hardly possible to keep track of every wedding during the "peak season," from August through November. Sometimes a household head will no sooner hear this announcement than he will say, "Whose kid was that anyway?"

Paradoxically, the consumption of alcoholic beverages is always (subtly) discouraged, but should a family in this particular village not supply the alcohol those in attendance (the men, really) would view the hosts as ungracious tightwads. This matter—no laughing one—becomes so serious that men obsess about their liquor purchases days before the celebration draws close. They worry about who will find the necessary quantity of liquor, which varieties will be available (champagne, vodka, brandy, and port wine), and, most importantly, how much it will cost.

Men claim they have had to cut down on their wedding-related outlays for alcohol by approximately half the level from the pre-*perestroika* years (1985–1991). Today, they purchase 20 to 25 half-liters of vodka (the size of bottles in which it is sold) as opposed to the 40 to 50 half-liters that characterized weddings held during the last 25 or so years of the Soviet era.

My own findings indicate that because men drink, perhaps more heavily now than in the aforementioned period, they tend to supply or provide wedding celebrations with vodka that they have brought themselves and bring to the celebrations as guests, which is a newer pattern. Weddings, furthermore, are one of the few social occasions where people expect to drink and willingly make excuses for those who have drunk a lot of vodka or port wine—the other main wedding beverage: "We just drink for his daughter's happiness." The weddings provide a release from daily oppressions and an outlet for mischievousness within the darkness of the night air, accompanied by blaring music, throngs of people, and the opportunity to rejoice in the happiness (also a kind of relief) for both of the uniting families.

It is unlikely that curtailment of festivities and consumption itself will come to pass anytime soon, because such a transformation would have ramifications for several domains of the social structure. One should not see the spendthrift patterns as merely an example of blindly following custom. Of course, people think seriously about the costs, including how they will budget the available cash on hand, whether they will need to borrow funds, and what their actual spending ceiling is. Having said this, the wedding gifts, dowry, and party form the integral parts of one of Uzbek culture's most important life-cycle celebrations. Not only must an atmosphere of conviviality and generosity be shown to neighbors and new in-laws, but the celebration enables a daughter's parents, and especially her father, to show their child how much they value, honor, and love her, even as they send her off to live with a new family—in exogamous surroundings (i.e., often outside her own neighborhood and village). Understanding why cultural habits and practices are problematic and damaging over the long term probably will not lead to either a change in practice or work in the form of adjustments to the perceived social ill.

At one wedding, near-chaos set in once people learned that the host had run out of food. People were not particularly angry; some found it funny, in fact. Just the same, they wondered aloud why they had come if not to eat a meal with meat. (It is essential to sacrifice and cook a sheep for the wedding feast, which will then be cooked into soup and rice pilaf.) Still others, in an effort to avoid an even greater embarrassment, mobilized to get the cauldrons filled and bubbling away again. One woman (W) who noticed me snapping photos and taking notes during the party got my attention and asked what I thought about the wedding itself:

W: Our weddings aren't like yours, are they?

RZ: Well, in some ways yes, in some ways, no ...

W: Come on! Of course they're not! We're wild, running all about. There's no order to our weddings. Everybody is welcome, but not much forethought goes into the planning. You must think we're backward, right?

RZ: Not really. I just ...

W: Well, it's true. We should plan them. They're so expensive now, but we just don't think. That's why we stay so poor.

As the woman spoke to me, she smiled knowingly, as if there could be no mystery or doubt surrounding the situation. Villagers willingly appear to reproduce the atmosphere and attributes of late-Soviet weddings, even though political independence has outstripped their ability to maintain those wedding budgets. This is not a matter of people wishing to live an illusion, wherein they pretend to convince others that they enjoy a comfortable "normal" lifestyle. Rather, despite the downturn that accompanied independence, villagers are determined to pull out all the stops for this most important event. Imperiling one's own financial well-being involves more than simply keeping up appearances or questing after prestige and respect: the high costs of weddings give a large number of people a chance to celebrate and relax, to bring about and participate in the happiness of others affecting kin and community.

The one thing a family need not preoccupy itself with before wedding celebration days is assistance and resources. One reason why Uzbek wedding festivities are so grand is the great amount of help given by extended family and neighbors. Weddings are never a matter of a single household making all of the preparations; instead, countless numbers of people from various age groups bring it together. Every facet of the preparations, from quilt making to firewood chopping to noodle cutting to securing and hauling tables and benches, involves tens of people who carefully plan out the division of tasks.

But what goes into the actual financing of a wedding with so little money on hand? The family—generally the father himself—must sell livestock or other sources of capital that are not subject to the vagaries of a nonconvertible currency in the marketplace. Thus a sheep, a cow, a bicycle, or even an old auto and electrical appliances may figure into the "war chest" and be used to raise the cash necessary to pay for the provisions and supplies.

One may witness the epitome of village cooperation and solidarity through the pre-wedding party organized and attended exclusively by males, colloquially known as "*sabzi qirish*" ("carrot peeling"). The event takes its name from the enormous quantity of carrots that men prepare for essential wedding meals, such as *laghmon* (a noodle soup) and pilaf (50 or more kilograms). On the night before a household's main wedding party, boys and men of all ages gather at the home of the bride and the groom, respectively, to help out with the food preparation and cooking. The event showcases industriousness and relaxation, in a kind of whistle-while-you-work way. The camaraderie allows for gossip, news, joke telling, and, of great delight to many, the chance to eat and drink in a feel-good atmosphere as the event marks the more joyous and less solemn side of the wedding.

A local butcher and cook will already have been dealing with meat and cooking for the better part of a full day in advance. They may work for the particular household for two to three days and may be paid in a number of ways, including the return of the revered favor they perform—a sort of balanced reciprocity. Naturally, the exercise of friendship and the affirmations of collective identity are not the only rewards for those who show up. The material—or, rather, gastronomic—incentives of a meat dish and booze ensure that there is something for all under the society-wide banner of "share and share alike."

Sabzi qirish usually begins about dusk and lasts until midnight or thereabouts, once the elders have come, supped, pronounced a benediction over the wedding, and led the attendees in prayer. During these preparation parties, boys and men congregate in age groups—that is, they congregate as classmates and former classmates, for it is through their schooling that people make their lifetime friends and form tightly knit groups.

Once the vegetables have been cleaned and chopped, the rice rinsed properly, sufficient firewood gathered, metal tables and benches furnished with quilts for cushioning, and all of the raw foods begun cooking away in two or three 50-gallon cauldrons, the groups relax either inside or outside on raised rectangular platforms, sitting on quilts. Most of the younger men are careful not to drink too brazenly in front of the older men, who themselves may imbibe little, if at all. Once the seniors have exited, however, caution is thrown to the wind. Many men proceed to bolt down teacup after teacup of either *portvine* or *oq choi* (literally "white tea," meaning vodka). Having attained quick highs all around, the remainder of the evening may be dedicated to joking and laughter. Serious discussions and grievances surrounding personal circumstances or the national economy are left behind, although they were fit topics at the beginning of the carrot peeling party.

During one such get-together, a local electronics repairman related his concern and frustration over the fact that his mother had been issued a "check" (a state I.O.U. voucher) rather than the cash she expected for her monthly pension. People routinely travel to the district centers from villages to collect various welfare payments. The repairman comported himself on the *suri* (the raised, square-framed sitting platform), joining others for tea. Commiseration ensued and talk soon turned to why the country had such problems in supplying actual money to payees. The repairman opined that sufficient money existed for most necessary transactions, but that nearly all of it was tied up in "trade," by which he meant that minor merchants of kiosks and shops had bundles of legal tender that they hoarded. The merchants did so, he suggested, because people had few opportunities to make sound or sensible investments. Still other men speculated that the state itself lacked cash, or that it withheld paying money into the provincial district banks because the collective farms performed poorly, becoming ever more insolvent. The implication was that the new state continued to punish the peasant-farmers for poor production just as the U.S.S.R. had, although much of the disappointing crop yields seemed mainly a result of poor government planning and support, or so the villagers say.

This exchange of views underscores the villagers' relative ignorance about the truth of the matter owing to a virtual mass information blackout about problems affecting Uzbekistan. Villagers have had plenty of practice in accustoming themselves to speculation-mongering in the face of such crises from their Soviet past. Media tenseness on such an important issue also indicates how significantly Uzbekistan mirrors aspects of the U.S.S.R. in its lack of transparency. As one of my principal informants was fond of saying, "What distinguishes us from the Soviet Union is our flag."

Even though men and women must work together as they organize and conduct successful weddings, male networks seem to take precedence in the Uzbek village. Concerning the world beyond their *hovli* (house compound), men become more involved in controlling various processes as they assume greater burdens. This is peculiar to everyday life to some degree, most especially in and around the household where women, in all but exceptional cases, perform more chores—and often harder chores—than the men. Furthermore, mothers and grandmothers can and do exercise authority over grown sons and male grandchildren; they have the ability to compel them to do tasks that the males would otherwise prefer to shirk, or do whenever they saw fit.

When Michael Peletz (1988) considered the feasting celebrations of a Malaysian community, he noted the rare presence of women in wage labor settings in his area of study. He concluded that overall women were not active in the public sphere (according to the community's men) because it is considered the men's world. Women in Malaysia are both protected and prohibited from moving within that sphere. Those familiar with the political science literature and the history of the Central Asian countryside know that the new Soviet government (early 1920s) labored furtively to "liberate" Central Asian women from the confines of their households where they were "imprisoned" (Bikzhanova 1959; Massell 1974; Alimova 1990; Northrup 2004; Kamp 2007). To some extent, the Soviets achieved their modernist goals whether or not the "inmates" ever were clamoring for a breakout.

Today Uzbeks, whether approving of the practices or not, are used to women working outside the family compounds and actively participating in the public sphere, whether in schools, in government offices, in cotton fields, or in marketplaces as buyers and sellers. By and large, adult men across age groups dislike this social fact.

Given that weddings are so self-consciously viewed as core events of Uzbek culture—that is, a way to "act" and "be" Uzbek—I would argue that men have preserved their dominance over women's participation and movements during the days of the ceremonies and celebrations. Readying themselves for weddings requires networking and activities outside the home, so men take on these organizational tasks, including purchasing the bulk of the provisions, making arrangements with a *mullo* (local Muslim spiritual guide), and securing the presence of musicians and their equipment. Women may go to market without their husbands or sons, but they do not race around the villages as do their husbands and other male kin who take care of the details concerned with accommodating the vast number of guests. This networking structure demonstrates the "maleness" of any village, owing to its patrilineal roots. Bear in mind that men ordinarily do not leave natal villages; women do.

Most of the cooking and food preparation itself takes place within the male arena. Comparing themselves to their wives, men half-jokingly refer to the manliness (*erkaklik*) necessary to stir the capacious cauldrons that may serve 200 people at the actual wedding.

Because the family name is on the line, it should come as no shock that men in this patrilocal/virilocal society work very hard at executing all tasks that go into ensuring the success of the wedding entertainment and guests' comfort with maximal efforts. To outsiders, Uzbek men may seem lethargic and irresponsible from time to time vis-à-vis Uzbek women, but weddings witness men in action, men with little time for dalliance's ordinary respites on the roadside, over by the canal, or at the auto mechanic's shop. Peer scrutiny forces the man of the house to tap into hidden reserves of energy and creativity; he will be at his best during the wedding preparations and celebration—indulgent and gracious, making sure that all who matter get their due.

When questioned, a young, university-bound man (YM) discussed how it is that older men endure these weddings, what with all of the expenses, impositions on time, the endless stream of guests, and other demands. Then he turned the tables, asking what it is like for American fathers. Although he had some familiarity with American weddings from movies, we established that most American fathers rarely do much cooking for the weddings and do not worry too much about uninvited guests showing up. Continuing with the local issues, the young man was asked about what happens if a man just gets fed up and wants to scale back the excess. He shook his head and explained:

YM: There's no way; that's just not acceptable to us.

RZ: But why? What if you don't have enough, or you're ill prepared for large crowds of people?

YM: Then you're an idiot! Look, these celebrations don't just sneak up on people. They're a part of one's upbringing, and men know about them and prepare for them years in advance. Besides, even if it pains a man, he will not let it trouble him until it is well past.

RZ: Why?

YM: Because we are supposed to look upon the *kelin toi* [literally, "bride's party"] as a happy event. On mustn't worry about not having enough.

This young man's remarks demonstrate that, financial burdens aside, the *toi* must go on. Impressing others, earning respect, and gaining pride may be guaranteed through a successful or scandal-free wedding (scandal could be caused by disputes among the new in-laws, insufficient foodstuffs, disciplinary breakdown, poor culinary execution, or any other untoward events). Keep in mind, however, that the reputation of a family holding a wedding is not predicated on one-upping or outdoing neighbors and friends (at least not for most of the families) in some potlatching style—although everyone wants others, especially the in-laws, to know that there was no skimping on the festivities. Additionally, the high degree of mutual help among friends, neighbors, and relatives during weddings works against individualistic or selfish tendencies that might demarcate groups of villagers by stratification. By and large, Uzbek society remains sufficiently communalist so as not to cause any noticeable non-egalitarian antagonism. Today the situation for a majority of villagers may be said to correspond to a remark made by Clifford Geertz about the Javanese people with whom he worked in the 1960s; he spoke of their "shared poverty." According to Geertz, the Javanese peasants he knew referred to themselves economically as the "just enoughs" and "not quite enoughs" (1963:97).

Referring back to the idea that the wedding ceremony carries with it a popular air of being traditional and quintessential as an Uzbek cultural institution, it is also worth remarking that the costliness of the affairs has a vestigial basis. Peasant prodigality probably dates back no further than the late 1950s. What is more, the historical literature contains few accounts that suggest peasants of an earlier age went into debt over the expenses for family weddings. Perhaps the outlook about these outlays reflects a core value or "traditional" culture, but one must place the supposed tradition in its rightful historical context.

THE *VALUE* OF A DAUGHTER

Outsiders to Uzbek village culture, whether foreigners or urban citizens, sometimes opined that rural fathers cared little about their daughters beyond the girl's childhood and adolescence. Observers within and outside Uzbekistan made hackneyed claims to support their reasoning, suggesting that the daughter had to leave home forever after the marriage; Muslim men are much more worried about their sons; and it is obvious that the *oblast'* ("provincial" or, more collo-quially, "redneck") Uzbeks devalue women. According to these sources, the sooner a daughter could be married off, the better for her father, who would then have less to worry about.

Among my informants, this supposed lack of love for daughters was by and large untrue. While informants confirmed that it is not prudent for fathers to show physical displays of affection for daughters (after the early grammar school level), this restraint has next to nothing to do with how much they love them. "How could I not love my own daughter?" rhetorically asked a father of seven, as if the question was among the most foolish he had heard.

Another man told me that it would not make sense to arrange a marriage if one's daughter is opposed to the choice of groom. Ideally, the most desirable matches satisfy the betrothed, the parents, and the grandparents from both sides of the families who propose the marriage. The same man said:

> If I were to give my daughter to somebody whom she didn't like, to someone who made her unhappy, then I've done wrong by her, and it would make me upset to see her that way.

At the same time, parents—and especially fathers—often try to order their daughters to marry a given man if they think the results of the new arrangements will prove beneficial. When girls absolutely cannot be convinced, parents usually relent, though her refusal may sour interfamilial and intrafamilial relations for a long time. In the very household where I took up most of my residence, to cite one bit of anecdotal evidence, one of the daughters wanted to marry one of the next-door neighbor's sons, although our host's father disliked the neighbors. In the end he did not impose his own desires on his daughter. As a friend of his explained, "They were in love. What could he do?"

ENACTING WEDDINGS AND TRADITIONAL CONTINUITIES

Ferghana Valley Uzbeks, including those who refer to themselves as Qipchoq—historically, a tribal nomadic Turkic people—have led a sedentary existence throughout the lower, wetter areas of the valley for the better part of 500 years (Gubaeva 1983:72). Nevertheless, attributes of their formerly semi-nomadic heritage may be observed in the weddings themselves. Most of the residents of Boburkent claim they are descendants of the Qipchoq group.

Early on in my fieldwork, it perplexed me whenever certain seemingly rit-ualistic behaviors took on an edginess and uneasiness that would suffuse key as-pects of the weddings, especially at the brides' homes. It was hard to be sure that the aggressiveness of young men who were part of the entourage that brought part of the groom-side's gift collection was not all a part of a display or a show.

Was it mere youthful bravado prepared and ready to handle all challengers, or was it possibly a typical and metaphorical association of betrothal ceremonies with warfare? Jack Goody, for example, discusses important aspects of dowry practices and significance, especially in terms of the daughter's relations to her natal family, and the bonds between a father and daughter at the time of her marriage. Goody's analyses concerning these aggressive aspects of wedding ceremonies refer mainly to various Arab groups, but much of what he describes relates to the Muslim cultures of Central Asia, which came under Arab political rule and cultural influence more than 1200 years ago (1990:361–382). At any rate, after my second summer and fall of observing such crucial moments of the ceremonies, I realized that, in fact, the palpable aggression exceeds the bounds of mere jocular display. Here it is important to explain what happens at the time the boys or young men (age-mates accompanying the groom range in age from 17 to 23 years) who travel with the groom arrive at the bride's home.

Generally, on the third day of festivities—the last day—between 15 and 20 of the groom's friends, brothers, or other close male relatives arrive at the bride's home toward dusk with the groom to take her away from her parents' home for the rest of her life. This rite, historically known as *kuiovnavkar* ("groom's coming out"), used to involve the payment of *qalym* ("bridewealth") (Abdullaev 1955:80). Today bridewealth is unnecessary, although it has started to make a comeback. The general atmosphere just before the men's arrival at the bride's home is fraught with anxiety and excitement. A bride's family members, along with neighborhood children, continually leave the compound or courtyard to search for signs of the groom's party.

The groom usually arrives by car (perhaps in a Zhiguli, Lada, or Volga model), dressed in a suit and armed with a bouquet of flowers. Throughout the event, he plays almost a minimal role. A driver—often his best man, or sometimes a person esteemed enough to share his car—accompanies him.

Following just behind the groom or sometimes preceding him is either a truckload or small busload of boisterous youth. As this vehicle drives through the area, the young men shout out at the top of their lungs:

- "We have come from Q.__ to claim S.__ for G.__."
- "Everybody listen: G.__ is the groom today and he has come to B.__ village to take N.__, who is the daughter of R__ov."

These examples illustrate a couple of the wedding chants. And then the men begin to yell and shriek even louder, whooping it up as they approach the gates of the bride's home.

Upon witnessing their arrival, children squeal with delight: "The groom is here! The groom is here!" At this point, all of the older men hurry out to "greet" the party of young men. The welcoming is more professional than cordial, something on the order of sportsman-like conduct, because tacit rivalries are forming as younger men from the bride's side—relatives and neighbors—size up the "challengers" from the groom's side.

After a quick exchange of greetings and congratulations, the young men burst into the bride's home. In a manner that is half-wild, they all try to storm through the gates of the house at once, as if they are locked in mortal competition with one another to get inside. They then proceed to thrust their way through the portal of the home of the bride's parents, continuing with their shouting and celebratory cries.

Still jostling one another to enter the sitting room (which is adorned with the bride's personal gifts) for refreshments, they smile and laugh uproariously, sated with their mock conquest. Once inside, it is no holds barred, as the boys begin to devour the wedding foods, including hard-boiled eggs, with ferocious hunger. Having reached their destination, it is as if they are bent on devouring the host himself.

Actually, their stay is a short one. After they have finished eating, a neighborhood mullo, the bride's father, and a few other community elders enter the main sitting room. Their presence lends an air of solemnity and restraint to the coming of the groom's crowd. After prayers are chanted and a benediction bestowed on the absent newlyweds, the youngest visiting boys begin collecting and taking the gifts and part of the dowry from the bride's side. The whooping and merrymaking gradually return, too, as the young men stomp out and parade about with the married couple's new belongings.

It should be noted that the groom's friends do not remove their shoes before entering the bride's soon-to-be-former home. This is tantamount to barbaric and unclean behavior in Central Asia: Footwear is always removed before entering a private home so as to keep out the accumulated filth from all public places. Thus, in a mock sense, the youngsters show total disregard and a lack of respect for the bride's home. They have come to trample upon it, sack it, and loot it. These actions or the contravening of social convention serve to boost the notion of wedding as warfare.

Were the young men or the groom to remove the bride in the same way, the historical or traditional reenactment of pastoralist nomadic or pastoralist seminomadic wedding parties would be even more complete. Even to this day, kidnapping practices persist to some degree among rural Kazakhs and Kyrgyz, who still engage in transhumance and fixed pastoralism with their flocks of sheep and goats (Werner 2003; Kleinbach, Ablezova, and Aitieva 2005). If nothing else, these rural Uzbeks manifest a linkage of their current culture to nomadism and semi-nomadism on bases other than conjecture, as I allege here; this allegation itself may lend further credence to villagers' claims about their Qipchoq origins.

The bride's actual leave-taking engenders a great deal of weeping, as it brings about momentary sadness. Even a normally stoic father may be seen swallowing hard, allowing tears to escape softly as his daughter blubbers and bellows, "*Dadam, Dadam!*" ("My dad, my dad!"). The bride totters and wobbles from inconsolable sorrow at the recognition that she is leaving the only home that she has ever known. Older female relatives, especially the bride's mother and grandmother, comfortingly intervene to guide the young woman, who is covered with a red velvet veil, into a waiting car. They ceremoniously place a piece of white cotton string in her hair to ensure that her journey to a new home will mark the propitious beginning to a new life.

Some informants (men, not surprisingly) chuckled at the suggestion that the wedding ceremony was a traumatic time for the girls. (Young women are generally married at the ages of 16–22, with the median age being about 18.) One man commented that trauma was not really what the bride feels. For him, it was a matter of feminine histrionics; girls just have to "pretend" that they are sad:

> No, my friend, ha! That's not right. Of course, they cry, but it's all kind of an act. They're supposed to do that. They have to show their parents that they are sad. Really, she's very happy to go with the prospect of becoming a woman, starting her own family.

A while later, when I spoke to a grandmother, one of whose granddaughters recently had wed, she also cackled at the question about the bride's mood and mental state. Nevertheless, her overall response was not quite as dismissive about the way in which roles take on a particular identity, in this case that of the betrothed:

> Well, if you're asking me do girls get upset … yeah, sure, they're upset. They cry because they have to leave everybody and everything behind. I recall that I was scared when I left: "Who are these new people [in-laws]? What will my husband be like?" And I worried about my mother-in-law: "Will she be awful to me?" So, you see, there are lots of reasons why girls aren't so happy when they first get married.

The brides are embarking on a brand-new life with someone whom they barely know (in most cases in villages) and entering a new home to serve and to be judged rather than welcomed. To say this experience often proves unnerving for young women is an understatement. Furthermore, the moments before she leaves her parents for good mark the last possible time a newly married daughter can give free rein to her emotions about that very leave-taking. To cry, look sad, or sulk and mope about in her new home would be so unacceptable as to bring temporary disgrace to her and her family.

Because marriages unite families as much as individuals, all parties must play their roles with diplomatic aplomb, not merely for harmony's sake but also to cement the new bonds that effectively guarantee an expansion in a given family's support network. And when the new union involves a rural–town family connection, the mutual advantages that come via a workable union are obvious. For the villagers, such unions serve as an element that provides them with increased access to all sorts of goods, communications, and improved public institutions beyond their natal communities. Such a union also lays bare the misguided notion that peasants exist in isolated settlements with little knowledge of what happens beyond the homemade walls of their compounds, or beyond those scorching cotton fields of their plantation-kolkhoz. In this particular post-Soviet context, we have now begun to learn that notions about pre-Soviet peasant socioeconomic and sociopolitical autarky are mostly a fiction: Even during the mid-nineteenth century, peasants had to trade for agricultural tools and implements themselves—that is, the products that made being a peasant possible! This includes items such as axes, shovels, plows, matches, and kerosene (Millar and Nove 1976:53).

ХУД КЕЛИБСИЗ

Courtesy of Russell Zanca

FIGURE 4.7 Wedding celebrants dancing. The sign hanging above the place where the bride and groom sit reads "Welcome."

THE "PRICE" OF HOSPITALITY

Hosting guests provides villagers with the unique chance to ask for favors from friends in a confidential atmosphere where a person can carefully detail and explain why he needs a given thing or a particular kind of help. The resources a complete stranger brings also may be solicited for a favor for another. Making such a request on the street—say, in the workplace, or elsewhere in public spaces—would make an indecorous person of the one desirous of aid. To be sure, some people will inevitably damn decorum and make requests whenever they think they may not want to pass up an opportunity.

Inviting a person into one's home as a guest enables the host to show himself and his family at their best. And should the host make sufficient effort, or should he take proper pains to make his guest comfortable, sate him with tasty food, and so on, he then would place the guest in a rather vulnerable position, because he will have set the guest up for the proverbial offer he cannot refuse. How can the guest not reciprocate? At the very least, he will feel a tinge of obligation to do similarly by the host as the host did unto him.

In this particular *mekhmon–mezbon* (host–guest) relationship, it is usually the former who wields most of the power, although the latter controls a kind of power that the host in his turn must grasp and use to his own advantage (i.e., money, influence, accessibility, connections). Here I am pointing to the necessary awareness that the actors involved have to exercise lest they permit themselves to be manipulated when placing themselves in the vulnerable guest's seat (Gledhill 2000:235).

Speaking of this power relationship only in the sense of the guest having to eat when he wishes not to eat, the ethnomusicologist Theodore Levin points out the following about the concept of *dasturkhan* (literally, "tablecloth," but more accurately translated as "the spread or the meal that accompanies the hosting of a welcomed guest").

According to convention, once a guest has stepped across the threshold
of a house, he has committed himself to accepting *dasturkhan*. At the
same time, he has surrendered control over the complexity of the *das-*
turkhan and the length of the séance, for these are entirely at the discretion of the host. Pleading for a small *dasturkhan* on the grounds of
having just eaten has no effect whatsoever. (1996:34)

In fact, in Levin's sense, the dasturkhan figures metonymically as the entire host–
guest relationship. Dasturkhan becomes a practical area of contest between the
host, actively bending the guest to his will, and the guest, often haplessly trying
to invoke his own will.

However much pressure he faces, the mekhmon almost always has a way
out of the encounter once requests have been asked. Regardless of the situation
and pressure, he would be most disinclined to refuse a request outright, whether
or not he is much opposed to the proposal initially. Utilizing a variety of deflec-
tive or defensive strategies to refuse the host, the guest would be more likely to
deliver constructive criticism; he might serve up all of the cons to the idea, and
then earnestly explain to the host that he will have to mull over the proposal
before ultimately deciding.

Actually, both parties want to avoid confrontation at all costs. Argumenta-
tiveness and anger would only succeed in poisoning the atmosphere of the host's
party, and it shames all involved. Unpleasantness will ruin the meal, damaging
everything that went into all of the preparations for the day. Intricacies of civility
in the home environment militate against confrontation, because otherwise the
ulterior motive of the moment must be acknowledged, and it is considered an
affront to the host. Furthermore, both parties then must signal their awareness of
the entire entrapment scenario, which makes them appear ugly.

Pertaining to an outsider—an outsider to the local ways—the chance of the
veiled request being revealed directly and soon after the guest's arrival is much
greater, because the outsider, after all, is unversed in local subtleties of appropriate
conduct in this context. Naturally, I was an outsider in several instances during
my fieldwork before I began to understand my role as a guest, along with the
rules that were to be followed. At the same time, outsiders may also be put
upon in the public sphere because older persons may think the outsider will not
recognize crudity. As is generally true of outsiders, they tend not to stay long, so
the very presence of one at the wedding imparts the need for haste to act on the
part of those wanting something. The host realizes that he has much less to lose if
he is rejected or rebuffed by the outsider; he can afford to take risks with him.

A gift-bearing guest assures himself retention of face, in the event that he
must reject the host's overtures, by honoring the host. The gift preempts harshness in the event of the inability to come through and meet the host's request.
The gift is a simple token of appreciation for the host's kindness, although actually getting the host to accept a gift may prove to be quite an ordeal. The host is
culture-bound to refuse the offering. In local terms, the host is demonstrating
gratitude to the guest for the thought and effort, but must simultaneously show
a sort of indifference to "luxurious" things—and few gifts will be practical items.

To accept a gift without first launching into a series of protestations would be to signify that one is avaricious. Therefore, it is only becoming to initially reject the proffered item. The guest then must express his own will more forcefully and with increased stamina relative to the host's demurrals; the host deep down really wants the gift, or at least is pleased to receive one.

Friends in Tashkent enjoyed recounting a host–guest encounter that speaks to this tussle over the gift-giving process. They once invited two young Japanese graduate students for dinner. The women kindly brought gifts of fruit and cake. Not being well versed in the rejection act, however, they returned home with the gifts they had brought. Nothing seemed more farcical to our friends than the image of the guests leaving and trundling off with the heavy melon and cake that they had brought.

A guest needs to strategize from the moment he sets foot in the host's home. First, one has to consider how long to stay, whether it makes sense to drink alcohol and in what quantity, how much to eat, and other key issues. The host always feigns disappointment that the guest wishes to go and resolves that he will not permit him to do so. In time, the guest learns that the host's game is control as well as decorum, and he has to show respect for the host via the host's authority in his own domain. More accurately, the guest must negotiate his way out of *guestdom*.

OTADAN MEKHMON IUQORI (A GUEST IS HIGHER THAN THE FATHER)

Uzbeks delight in informing foreign guests of the preceding proverb header, as it shows that the guest enjoys the greatest attentions of his host for the duration of a sojourn. The outsider, however, is forever left wondering what happens with unexpected guests whom the host dislikes. To an outsider, it always seems that Uzbeks will welcome anyone into their homes regardless of conditions and regardless of the time. When a guest comes, all work and/or all fun and games must come to an immediate halt. Few things could be as self-disrespectful as ignoring a guest.

After my wife and I had lived for several months with a family with whom relations became strained, the mother of the family announced to me:

I love to have guests. Uzbeks need to have guests.

From my perspective, the subtext of her statement was "I just don't really like you as my guest." There had to be a mixture of humor and incredulity to her remark, as I well remember the less-than-happy state of our relations (my wife and I soon relocated). But why did this woman compel herself to tell her unwanted guest what seems the opposite of the truth in this particular situation? In a sense, she clearly understood why she had a foreign guest living with her, and what his reason for being with her family was. Thus she probably was aware of indicating her sense of self, her sense of her culture, especially vis-à-vis her foreign guest. Quite possibly, her statement was as much about belonging as it was reproducing notions of what characterizes the good social life.

To be sure, one need not be an uptight and individualistic American to understand that having unannounced guests arrive could, under any circumstances, truly dampen one's mood. The thing is that an uptight American person and an Uzbek villager have very different ways of dealing with their personal distastes for lodging and putting up with an unexpected guest. The American might show his distaste by means of overt expressions—possibly through language and comportment—that would include tone of voice, facial expressions, and gesticulations. He might even say bluntly, "Look, I'm sorry, but I have no room for you." For an Uzbek to follow suit, however, the repercussions in terms of reputation would outweigh the responsibilities and extra work that having guests entail.

Generally, Uzbeks do enjoy visits and enjoy visiting themselves, and they rarely make dinner or socializing plans far in advance depending on the particular type of social event; here I speak of those that are least formal. One may say accurately that planned guests are uncommon in the village. A person simply drops by, and the thought of so-and-so not wanting to see him simply does not seem to be a very practical consideration (unless, of course, the two people really dislike each other). Naturally, people work themselves into bad moods for all sorts of reasons, but the host has to snap out of it or fake his way out of any such bad mood from the instant the guest sets foot in his home. It goes without saying that there are different levels of guestdom that have as much to do with the rank and status of guests as with individual likes and dislikes.

The ways in which a host may show his guest he wishes the guest leave are numerous and delicate. For example, the host may contribute little to a conversation, rendering the guest's sociability halting and disjointed. The host, who should always offer a variety of snack foods—at least four different types on four separate plates set properly on a tablecloth (including, but not limited to, nuts, raisins, cookies, and candies)—may make sure that the foods are stale as he presents them with little aesthetic attention. Similarly, he may delay the request of his wife to begin cooking something, which is also culturally binding. While never looking to drive the person from his home in an overt or unpleasant manner, the host may express displeasure with an unwelcome intrusion simply by treating hosting conventions laxly. An attuned guest will easily pick up on a host's preoccupations, anxiety, or distemper. And unless the guest is completely oblivious, he will soon look for a way out. Chances are the host will then protest lightly with the guest's rising and pronouncement that he must go; any protest would likely sound artificial anyway.

Such treatment of a guest usually signifies that the guest is neither a friend nor a person of any advantage to the host. Otherwise, there would be no excuse for such off-putting treatment. As noted previously, bad moods, excused later, will not make up for the original slight. One may apologize for not keeping an appointment, refusing a request, becoming angry, arguing, and other perceived minor sins, but not for making a guest know and feel that he is unwelcome. As one villager once remarked about another, "I have no use for him because I once went over to his place and he practically ignored me. He didn't want me in his house."

Doing right by one's guest in the formal sense also is predicated on numerous styles of welcoming, such as immediately aiding the guest in washing his hands and making sure that the guest has enough pillows, that his cup always has hot tea, that the host not only provides large quantities of cooked foods but also urges the guest to eat more and more, and that the guest is made to feel pride of place—spatially and psychologically—for the time he is a guest. Few realms serve to help Uzbeks pinpoint their identity as a collectivity more than their satisfaction with their host–guest relations.

THE TALE OF THE MAN ON THE ROAD: AN ODD WAY OF RELATING TO A GUEST

I once spent a frustrating day traveling from the FV city of Osh in southern Kyrgyzstan back to my field site (a distance of roughly 85 kilometers). Things got off to a bad start when I attempted to buy a bus ticket in Osh. A police officer accosted me, asking for my passport; after I showed him my document, the official tried to get me to follow him into his office. This diversion seemed to be totally unnecessary, as I had every legal right to be where I was at that moment. Fortunately, a friend had come with me to the bus station to see me off, and it just so happened that he was a relative of the officer. The potential problem was speedily resolved, and I did not have to dip into my wallet and bribe my way out of the country. After greetings had been exchanged through my intermediary, and the customs officer returned with my passport, he said, "C'mon, let's have lunch together." Of course, he knew I had a bus to catch, but this was a cultural response toward diffusing whatever lingering hostility may have existed over the beginning of an incident that might have proved costly and corrupt were it not for my friend's intervention.

Hot and bothered after a slow ride on an old bone-shaker, I became only more frustrated and irritable once I finished the first leg of the journey. I had failed miserably to negotiate what I thought would be a reasonable price for taxi service from Andijan to the field site (about 35 kilometers) to the north by northwest. Finally catching a ride that brought me a few kilometers, I got out when the driver told me that the drop-off site would be my best bet to catch another ride to Boburkent.

Standing on a strip of highway on the outskirts of a town under a broiling sun, my confidence and resolve shriveled. Just then, a small stocky man (SM)—perspiring heartily and burdened with cloth sacks bursting with market goods—asked me where I was headed. Upon learning my destination, he told me that he was headed in the same direction, implying that we should team up and share the costs of a ride (a common practice among rural folk, especially as such people usually do not have any transportation of their own and cannot rely on buses owing to their inconsistent scheduling). The prospect seemed fine to me, for it meant I would not have to speak much (revealing my heavily accented and, at times, grammatically inept Uzbek), and would not necessarily be seen as a foreigner necessarily (ergo I would not have to pay an exorbitant sum of money by local standards).

The sweaty man triumphed quickly in irritating me further. He began to understand that I was no countryman of his. After learning of my nationality and why I had come to Uzbekistan, he asked me what I thought: Which people lived better from our respective countries—that is, did the Uzbeks or the Americans live better? And who had better goods? Given what the previous section described in terms of the host–guest relationship, I found myself in a situation, or a bad mood, where trying to be as tactful as possible taxed my wish to do the right thing. Thinking that for once I just couldn't lie or dissimulate, as I had since the mid-1980s when I began traveling to the U.S.S.R. as a student and fielding this exact question ad infinitum, I told the man that I thought that most Americans enjoyed a higher standard of living than most Uzbeks.

He appeared miffed by this response, as it may not have accorded with the explanation he sought. Then he declared:

SM: Yeah, but who has better hospitality?

RZ: Well, sir, we're pretty good to our guests, and we like to entertain friends and family members at home and in restaurants.

SM: If I were in America and you didn't know me, tell me would you just invite me into your home?

RZ: Well, probably not. Unlike here, Americans won't usually welcome a perfect stranger into the house.

With this, he turned to our driver of the moment and said smugly, "You see, it's better here than in America. We wouldn't just leave someone out on the street like that."

For my fellow passenger, it seemed that the essence and decency of a country had to be distilled from properties constituting hospitality. Wherever there was "less" hospitality in comparison to Uzbekistan, or wherever there was a non-Uzbek type of hospitality, it was clear to him that Uzbekistan just had to be a better place. As glum as I became at yet another invidious comparison that seemed to be a post–Cold War holdover, that hard-traveling man looked out for me, treating me as a companion and my country as an abstract as we continued on our short and plodding journey home. I stopped minding the fact that he saw me as a complete ignoramus—as a bumbler in desperate need of his help every step of the way—but I really had to restrain myself when he informed me that I had overpaid for a roadside melon that I bought out of boredom and semi-scholarly interest after we had been disgorged from yet another rickety vehicle that appeared to drive us only as far as the next scorching piece of asphalt.

Cynics could not see the host–guest relationship as anything other than venal on the part of both parties. Of course, not all such encounters are built upon conniving motives. Naturally, genuine friendships and family affairs are not marked by such exploitation and trickery.

KEEPING UP APPEARANCES

Uzbek society is one wherein appearances mean a great deal, and having guests over to one's home provides the atmosphere most conducive to taking care of business and attempting to complete goals where prying eyes and malicious talk are kept to a minimum. The home is the place of refuge and confidentiality relative to the public sphere. Here one probably need not fear reproach or ridicule owing to unwelcome requests or propositions. Conversations in the home among friends or acquaintances usually do not travel beyond the four walls of a particular sitting room or beyond the outdoor *aivan* (the low, porch-like area that usually faces the courtyard) in warmer weather.

Whereas other men in Muslim societies of the Near and Middle East find or seek little repose in the home (Bourdieu 1977:90) because it has been designated a feminine domain, Uzbeks have masculinized their own spatial and temporal areas within the home. They make sure that women wait on them and clean their sitting area. Children generally are not allowed to bother the men once they have begun to entertain their guests, or once men have decided that the time has come for men-only discussions or recreation. Wives typically play little to no role in these very private affairs of their husbands save post facto, if matters are serious enough to merit the authority of both household managers.

The service and attention that a wife brings to these guest evenings can make or break her husband's relationship to the guests. The importance of women's conduct and efforts factor into the freshness of the foodstuffs prepared. Because no one should leave dis-gusted, the food—from the fundamental breaking of bread and tea drinking, to the long, drawn-out pilaf eating— should at least be tasty. Here a woman may either be a partner to her husband or act in opposition to him. Her housekeeping and food preparation may serve as either a part of his family pride or his scourge. The role of the woman or women in these sessions constitutes a form of power over the men that outsiders can overlook easily at first glance. After all, the women appear and comport themselves as ones who are effaced and subservient, making of themselves a shadow presence as they busily follow imperious directives at the behest of men.

Indeed, hospitality is a family affair. The male head of a family household cannot make the guests feel welcome and comfortable—hospitality's crucible— if his spouse and other relatives do not put their best collective foot forward. Even a guest who is not an insider can feel the tension and sense the anger of a family not living in harmony. This is why benevolence and decency must be expressed characteristics of the *hojaiin* ("master of the house"). He dooms himself if he is neither respected nor liked in his own home.

CONCLUSION

Domesticity, broadly, has been the subject of this chapter. Domestic concerns in Uzbek households include food, nutrition, and ideas about good eating and good meal preparation. These notions segue naturally into weddings, which represent major domestic affairs. These affairs tie together households as production units as their members join children to other families, all the while keeping in mind the importance of emotional and psychological satisfaction that the hard-boiled aspects of weddings as major life-cycle events within the domestic sphere must try to achieve. Conceptions and instances of hospitality—a vaunted aspect of social life for Uzbeks in addition to being a value that they feel strongly distinguishes them from neighboring peoples—mark an important aspect of their identity.

QUESTIONS

1. What are the most popular foods or dishes among Uzbek villagers, and why?
2. What has happened to the rural Uzbek diet since the late Soviet period?
3. Wedding celebrations appear to be a double-edged sword for all parties involved. Why?

5

Running on Empty
Surviving on the Kolkhoz

THE BAZAAR AS MICROCOSM OF
POST-SOVIET LIFE

Chapter 3 discussed the peasant marketplace (*dehqon bozor*) or bazaar, noting how it had taken on the role of heightened prominence over the past decade in terms of villagers' livelihoods and shopping practices. This transformation coincides with the disappearance of useful stock from the handful of state stores standard for almost any kolkhoz village. So how have the marketplaces changed with regard to the physical space they occupy as well as how people organize their activities within this space?

Rural Uzbek marketplaces might be open twice weekly. Small towns within a province or district have varying market days so that, for example, Baliqchi's market occurs on Wednesday and Chorqala's market falls every Saturday. On those marketing days, sellers and potential buyers mobilize because it is the only nearby opportunity that they may have to acquire necessities and luxuries for a full week's time.

In the large cities, the marketplaces operate six or seven days a week, but villagers do not take a lot of time to search for desirable goods in the provincial capitals of Andijan and Namangan (55 kilometers northwest), let alone travel to Tashkent (more than 350 kilometers west) because, as villagers quipped, it was "too far away," or because "transportation was difficult." Villagers occasionally make the trips to obtain electronic goods, motor vehicles, and a large variety and quantities of imported items at lower prices than are available in regional bazaars and stores. Typically, a villager would visit such centers only a handful of times throughout the year.

Within the few square hectares of the officially established marketplaces, there are divisions or sections for all sorts of goods. In keeping with both the

Courtesy of Russell Zanca

FIGURE 5.1 Main entrance to the Adolatabad district peasant bazaar.

legacy of Central Asian history and Soviet-imposed arrangements, the peasant marketplace has sections for livestock, fruits and vegetables, dairy products, footwear, household goods, sweets, clothing, meats, grains, animal feed, spare parts for machinery, farm tools, and other goods. Upon initiation into this little world, an outsider may experience an overwhelming sense of dislocation, claustrophobia, and randomness. But, just as in American supermarkets, it is not the shelved products that cause the chaos and the pushing and shoving; rather, the confused and overwhelmed shoppers do. One thinks he has bought everything he set out to buy, but then realizes he forgot the sugar or the beef or the tea, and once again plunges back into the fray.

The analogy between the Uzbek bazaar to the American supermarket cannot be extended too far; rural marketplaces on the whole are much more crowded and much more haphazard than U.S. stores. Much of this character stems from the confined selling and buying space and, more importantly, the post-Soviet economy of scarcity combined with the low purchasing power of the average Uzbek consumer. Furthermore, bargaining and haggling conditions are intensive and fierce, as perhaps 20 different vendors sell the exact same goods simultaneously. In few other commercial arenas is the phrase *"Caveat emptor"* ("May the buyer beware") better exemplified or better put to practical use than in these bazaars. For that matter, the phrase *"Caveat venditor"* ("May the seller beware") has become fitting, too. In these environments, there are now no set prices for most exchanges, and prices must satisfy the demands of both parties. The seller who doesn't know how to meet consumer demands is doomed. In the old Soviet system, little value was placed on consumer interest. Although

Courtesy of Russell Zanca

FIGURE 5.2 A kolkhoznik selling spare auto and electronics parts.

the kolkhozniks sold goods, workers in state stores and shops expressed little interest in whether people bought their products; they were paid just the same.

The bazaar no longer functions as it did under socialism—that is, as a place where farmers could add profit to their government incomes. Today it is their lifeline: The bazaar often figures as the sole means of employment. In this economy, each shopper's attitude comes close to reflecting frustration at the fact that one has actually to pay something for the goods themselves: "Why not just give me these eggs?" Thus the relations between many a buyer and a seller are characterized not so much by a grudging quid pro quo as by mortal combat—extreme bargaining.

On a Saturday or Sunday morning (major bazaar days in the countryside), the district market town of Adolatobod pulsates with throngs jostling and struggling to move themselves from one part of the market to the other. The crowds breathe in the indelicate scents of burning cottonseed oil, grilled meats, cattle and sheep dung, and dried bits of the smoking vermifuge harmel/harmela (*isiriq*—Uzbek); the last item is used to ward off illness and to help cleanse the spirit. Meanwhile, men with bicycles and carts try to get past consumers burdened with bundles and sacks of new purchases. The men with wheels shout, "*Hosh!*" ("Gangway!"), as they steadily ram their way through the sea of bodies that squirm and bunch together as tightly as possible to let those vehicles pass. Rice sales take place in one corner as men bargain vociferously for a set price at a set weight. All over the marketplace, people concentrate as they scour each table with their eyes. Although everyone is laden with similar kinds of merchandise, they continue to search furtively for the best of the same. "Best" often means cheapest in this context, and "cheapest" requires visiting all of the vendors who have the same scarves or the same galoshes or the same grapes or the same boxes of Indian laundry detergent or Turkish bath soap.

Adolatobod's market has expanded. A sort of feral commerce rings the marketplace outside, along the perimeter, and on the sidewalks, forming the embodiment of a desperate, petty commerce. All kinds of people sit behind small tables, selling all manner of small imported items—from acrylic winter caps to candies, soft drinks, and cigarettes. The sidewalks of the town itself have been transformed, and one wonders how so many people can make sufficient money with everybody selling the same things. Has demand itself increased so rapidly, or is the marketplace the only true locus where consumer demands can be met? Who regulates all of these people? Of course, inside the bazaar people rent spaces for a fee; they are legitimate sellers. Out on the street it is harder to tell. Policemen are so corrupt that their answers to such questions ordinarily cannot be taken at face value. They, too, find a way to thrive in the agora whose limits seem surpassed with each coming week. The new capitalism is growing by leaps and bounds.

The march of capitalism just outside the farms also does not recognize limits on either age or gender, regardless of the wishes of many men who would have women remain at home now that Communist officials no longer call the shots. Thus children and women of all ages staff sales tables and kiosks in the towns and villages to bring home much-needed cash.

As a place, the market must be all things to all people. It is the hub of thrift and fast enterprise. Villagers could not survive without it. The few products sold within the villages proper never provide the range of choices and the lower prices that render the goods in the town bazaars so much more available and affordable. The distinction between the two settings is a dramatic as the difference between a corner newsstand and the supermarket in a place where the corner newsstand was unheard of until quite recently—the mid-1990s.

If one pays 450 som ($0.70) for a pack of Bulgarian cigarettes at a kiosk in the village but only 380 som at the town bazaar, the difference does not necessarily have to do with convenience. Rather, the village-based seller buys a smaller quantity of cigarettes and travels farther into the hinterland with them. Because he had to pay more in all ways from the start, it only makes sense for him to recoup his "losses" through increased consumer prices. But, after all, this is exactly how the convenience mentality is born: "I would never ordinarily pay so much for these smokes, but what can I do? He's the only guy around now." It is always a "six of one, half a dozen of the other" kind of dilemma for the villager, at least ever since the pre-capitalistic consumer culture took root.

For most people, the mental and material expansion of the market provides a wider than ever consumer choice in real terms, but one that is not necessarily more satisfying than was true under Communism. Here the key issue is not price differentials or general affordability, but rather the sheer uselessness or unworthiness of the products, whether concerning socks, candies, tobacco, toys, soaps and detergents, or prepackaged foodstuffs.

THE MARKETPLACE ENCOUNTER AS
AN EXTENSION OF THE VILLAGE AND
ITS SOCIAL RELATIONS

In the area surrounding the marketplace, people walk livestock—the animals that they have tried to sell or just bought—through narrow, rutted paved streets. Everybody carries cloth or net bags; many of these are crudely fashioned sacks that transported sugar or rice to Central Asia from countries such as China and the United States. The sacks are practically bursting. People en route to the market always ask those on their way out how much they paid for selected items, such as a cow or a muskmelon (just as my traveling companion from Chapter 4 did).

One travels to the marketplace with a list of items to buy, but sees plenty of other unexpected goods; he then goes from one area to the next looking over all of the offerings. Maybe it is time to buy a new bicycle chain or a hoe if he can only bargain successfully for a price that meets his expectations.

All the while, there are endless tussles going on. One must jockey for space and squeeze and push through the most jammed areas. "*Gips*" is how people refer to such overcrowded areas and places, which means that the experience is akin to being as tightly wrapped as the gypsum powder that goes into making a bone cast. In these crushing circumstances, fisticuffs sometimes occur. Bystanders rarely break up such fights, mainly because they rarely have a clear notion about who wronged whom. But the fights usually do not turn terribly violent; people come to their senses. With a little distance from the madding crowd, it becomes easier to relax. Stealing or contradicting one's word about a set price and arguing about payments are frequently types of behavior that lead to disturbances.

Reprieves from frenzied shopping, as well as the constant negative reinforcement that most folk are too poor to afford all that they need, may be had in teahouses or outdoors at the kebab stands. Although they are mostly sites of repose for men, women may also enter these refreshment spaces when accompanied by male relatives or husbands. Here people have a chance to unburden themselves of packs and drink tea, vodka, and port wine, while eating bread, noodle soups, pilaf, or skewers of mutton and beef. The meat provides a kind of ecstasy-like pleasure to those who now eat it rarely. Women, unlike men, tend to eat rather quickly and then continue shopping or return home to resume housework and prepare meals. Men do not allow their female companions the time they themselves take for escaping it all with a bottle or two.

Because Sunday was the one true day off for all Soviet citizens, Uzbek men still treat it that way (unlike in most Muslim societies, where Friday is the main day of rest). They work as little as possible on Sundays, whether at home or in the wheat and cotton fields, or in the rice paddies. This practice helps explain why men cherish prolonging their Sunday marketing. After marketing, men often meet with friends, although men rarely formally plan to meet at the market. They wouldn't say, "See you Sunday at the market and we'll have tea." It is not necessary to formalize such meetings given the law of averages; chances of seeing friends at the bazaar are good. After all, men continue to do this shopping, and they really have only one chance per week to meet in so relaxed and informal a public space.

The cooperation shown within the larger community also carries over to the marketplace. Shoppers, overburdened by purchases, may call on the services of a not-so-encumbered friend to aid them in getting the items home. Sometimes doing so means "borrowing" a neighbor's child or asking a friend to relinquish his bicycle for a while. In the event that a shopper does not plan to return directly home from shopping, but rather needs to go visiting or take care of additional chores, he may ask a friend or neighbor to bring his new purchases back.

If the individual decides to visit others after shopping for lots of items, or goods that are heavy or unwieldy, two types of corresponding awkwardness may arise. The obvious one is the discomfort of walking or taking mass transportation while burdened with the goods. If a day's purchases involved livestock or fowl, visiting becomes that much more strained (hosts may think the dangling, crowing rooster was intended for them). Further awkwardness would arise if the buyer arrived at someone's house with purchases of fruits and vegetables, but did not offer them to the host. (Of course, people usually plan ahead for this sort of situation.) It would amount to a case of bad form not to do so—which explains why the friend or neighbor delivery option proves a welcome one.

Courtesy of Russell Zanca

F I G U R E 5.3 Men load sheep newly purchased at the bazaar into an excavator shovel for transport home.

Packing a live lamb or a feisty rooster into a car trunk or onto a bicycle is most likely not what a friend wishes to do, but all the same he would be disinclined to refuse the request. That kind of reaction would undermine a sense of community or neighborliness, and it would ensure that the refusing person would probably not receive help in similar situations from the rejected person—anti-reciprocity. Doing a favor for a person in need makes all-around good sense. The conditions of the marketplace and the harshness of marketing in this day and age turn mutual assistance into a kind of necessity, akin to the cooperation or help offered for neighbors' household projects. Max Weber talked about mutual cooperation among farming communities, regardless of the social situation, not so much as a matter of selflessness or doing tasks out of love for one's fellow man, but more as a matter of sensibility; one acts toward others as he hopes others will act toward him given a situation of need, either minor or major.

THE KIOSKS

Most Uzbek villagers display neither fear nor eagerness toward capitalism. Rather, they view its development with resignation, as if it were supposed to have happened, or as if it bears only a slight, more open distinction relative to the kinds of peasant bazaar marketing or illegal marketing activities that people practiced in the not-so-distant past. Few people have time to ponder its development. Why should they? To many, capitalism is little more than a survival strategy. These new activities provide supplementary income to other work, or provide most of the income, period, in the face of other jobs that seem superfluous because there is no steady income to be gained.

For youngsters and women selling laundry detergent, canned beef, vodkas and cognacs, and electronics, there seems an atmosphere of insouciance to it all. Even though it may qualify as "bread crumb capitalism," there is no reason why the activity cannot be both liberating and fun. After all, one sits outside prominently (the seller and the goods are both on display) and watches life go by, in addition to seeing fellow villagers' reactions to one's imported items. And, at the end of the day, it is the young seller who brings home real money.

At their tiny tables and in their decorated stalls (often painted to resemble soda pop cans or cigarette boxes, or just painted skillfully with the owner's name or the faces of pop and movie stars—Michael Jackson, Jet Li, Arnold Schwarzenegger), haggling does not rule the day. The seller sets the price, names it, looks away, and allows the prospective customer to examine the goods warily. It is ultimately the buyer's choice to buy from the seller or try his luck elsewhere. Sooner or later, people buy what many knowingly admit is junk because everyone needs something colorful, something out of the ordinary. And the more destitute people become, they more often they tend to buy the two products that seem never to be in short supply, or beyond their fiscal means—cigarettes and liquor.

Courtesy of Russell Zanca

FIGURE 5.4 A carefree school-girl helps to sell assorted goodies for her family after school in Boburkent to make a little extra money.

WISHFUL THINKING ABOUT THE COUNTRYSIDE

More than 40 years ago, it was possible for a patriotic Soviet social scientist to write the following about the Uzbek countryside and its rural intelligentsia:

> For the Soviet agricultural intelligentsia there is no reason to leave for the cities, as is characteristic for capitalist countries. Now in the villages there is a sphere of extra-curricular activities after work for a variety of specialists, in fact among the intelligentsia.
>
> The culture and daily life of the *kishlak* (village) is gradually becoming more like life in the city. (Mirkhsaidov 1964:4)

Such pronouncements, if they were ever really true then, do not seem accurate now. When speaking of an "agricultural intelligentsia," the author is not really talking about local poets, philosophers, or novelists. Instead, he speaks of school-teachers, doctors, those working in state administration, and so forth. Today these same types have and would leave the villages for matters far more pressing than the recent disappearance of rural science societies or the fact that few people use kolkhoz libraries very often.

To be fair, it is true that members of the rural intelligentsia lament the loss of what little cultural life thrived in the village at one time. To underscore this point, consider the following response to a question I asked of an older woman (OW)—not a member of the rural intelligentsia—during census work:

RZ: Well, are you satisfied or dissatisfied with the cultural life of the kolkhoz now?

OW: What cultural life? We used to have it with movies and such, but we have
        no culture at all now.

Today the matter for the intelligentsia, as they take up a more peasant-like
lifestyle, is how to earn a living in the absence of salaries. If some of these people
were sure that they could make better money selling fruit or driving a truck in a
city, many likely would make the temporary moves as labor migrants. But to
leave the *qishloq* (the village) presumes one will have a job along with finances
for housing and provisions. Presently, it just is not that common for people so
have such assurances and enough money on hand to take these laboring risks—or
at least many are unwilling to do so.

Teachers, of course, still teach and doctors continue practicing medicine. It is
just that much of the appeal, prestige, and incentives of their professions have
dwindled as these vocations have ceased providing living wages.

DOCTORS BECOMING PEASANTS

One medical specialist from Boburkent received the honor of becoming the
area chief in his field. He moved his operations from the unlit, battered village
clinic to a more prominent building in the center of the local district's business
area. I visited the dentist at his new workplace shortly after he attended a meeting to discuss changes in work regimes along with plans to redecorate and
revamp the medical center's rooms and offices. Because the dentist and staff
members were busy with other plans, I left with a couple of other men before
getting a chance to ask my questions. On the way out, I was struck by the lack
of equipment and supplies, to say nothing of the state of disrepair of the building itself.

A couple of days later I ran into the dentist along the main road outside a
small flour mill. He was en route to his shared hectare of cabbages and black-
eyed peas that he tends to with a local schoolteacher—two members of the intelligentsia. Both of these men were well into their forties and had been working
in their chosen professions for more than 15 years. The teacher had mentioned
previously that it would not matter much if the village had any sort of scientific
society at the time, because residents had no free time to think about relaxing in
that way, "unless," the schoolteacher joked, "we hold a session about making
money."

Returning to the encounter with the dentist, I asked straightaway about his
new job—specifically, about what he expected of the new place and how it
would function, whether he had big plans to change its town role, and if the
level of care and service would improve. His answers spelled anything but
hopefulness. Although he is now the facility's main dentist, his office was in
dire need of new materials and supplies, including surgical gowns, medications,
x-ray machines, lighting, and instruments. Medical professionals should have
received them from a branch of the Ministry of Health, but as of that time

nothing had arrived. The dentist also said that during the day of the meeting, staff members had argued over plans for cleaning out the interiors and repainting the office space, a responsibility that he must share with his co-workers and subordinates.

At the time of the interview—1995—the dentist received an official salary of approximately $26 per month, and his wife, a practicing nurse, received barely half that. The couple had two young children. Even given the precariousness of his situation, he worried more for the patients, who might not be able to afford his services and those of other medical professionals: "How can I continue treating them in that case?" It became clear that his mind was not trained on dentistry completely, because he soon changed the subject to farming. He wanted to discuss the cabbage crop, hoping for a bumper one at that. If all were to go well, he and his teacher-partner would receive approximately $20 for each ton of cabbage, with the possibility of delivering between 100 and 115 tons to clients.

Naturally, I wanted to know where he would sell all of these cabbages and how he would find the time to handle this task even with the help of a partner. The dentist spoke of trying to negotiate "contracts" with local institutions, such as a nearby hospital, and the local kindergarten. He declared the bazaar to be off of his local agenda because "I have no time to sit and argue with hundreds of people." The dentist also considered driving to Russia and "paying all of those bribes" (highway checkpoints throughout the former U.S.S.R. are notorious for bribes taken by and bribes paid to local highway law enforcement), but the roads would have become icy by the time the harvest would be packed up.

People throughout the former Soviet Union are well accustomed to bribery, especially when interaction consists of moving goods through channels that put people into contact with representatives of the state or government—customs officials, in this circumstance. What makes matters all the more complicated in the national configurations of post-Soviet life are the new national boundaries themselves, in addition to the various national currencies and their different strengths and weaknesses in the new settings (Humphrey 2002:127–146).

Like many other inhabitants, the dentist grumbled about the inability of the state's administration to provide necessities to anybody other than the kolkhozniks themselves. He had already asked once for a small wheat supplement, he reported, but had been turned down by the *rais*. At one point he described an issue in the office meeting the previous day when he became fed up with building maintenance and construction plans, interjecting, "Look guys, I have little time for this: I'm a peasant now, and I have to spend a lot of time tending to the crop I have on the kolkhoz."

Thus, in mulling over the remark by Mirkhsaidov—which began this section—about the "agricultural intelligentsia," it seems apparent that the kolkhozniks could not leave the villages today for reasons having nothing to do with a high culture. As mentioned earlier, rural Uzbeks choose to leave their natal villages only reluctantly, but this phenomenon of hearth loyalty has waned as marked increases in the suffering and speedy impoverishment cut across nearly all levels of rural society beginning in the mid-1990s and continuing into the present, regardless of gender, age, or education level or professional accomplishments.

RECONSIDERING FORMAL EDUCATION

As economic factors simultaneously keep villagers tethered to the badly supplied cotton kolkhozes via practically forcing many residents into farming and causing many to consider fleeing rural life, the choices for professional pursuits among youth have decreased. Furthermore, there is even a narrowing of possible employment for mature men and women already established in respectable fields because so many small enterprises and facilities from the Soviet system have either shut down or greatly reduced their operations and staff. These reductions have struck farm maintenance workshops, repair shops, health sector services, and small manufacturing enterprises, such as the local canning facility.

In an age when it becomes obvious that business acumen or wheeler-dealer sagacity proves more lucrative than, say, a doctorate in physics, it becomes easier to jump to the conclusion that rural people under-value education, especially technical and higher education, for the simple reason that such pursuits are not accorded the remuneration and prestige that come with a comfortable income and the status of making educated people. Throughout the late 1990s, the United Nations' *Human Development Reports* for Uzbekistan claimed that the overall value of education declined throughout the country for the reason outlined previously. These conclusions seem logical on their face, but seem less so when one does ethnographic research and talks to rural people about just such a matter.

Uzbek parents and villagers in general hold a nearly universal opinion that technical training and higher education still pave the way for a brighter future. Many parents continue to express their hopes that children will be able to study in cities, such as Andizhan and Tashkent, to say nothing of possibly studying abroad. The latter venture is seen as presenting the children with opportunities to see and experience the world, especially as their parents assume it will widen career options and make individual lives more exciting.

A middle-aged woman whose family is poor decried the end of the U.S.S.R. and specifically the situation in which her teenage son now finds himself. The boy works in a wholesale bazaar of the capital, selling some of the products with which he also works on the side. Although he earns the bulk of the income for the family, his mother wishes that he would finish high school and go on to study at a local institute or university. She sees no good coming from his slightly underhanded merchandising work:

> He's there in the bazaar with thousands of others like him [young men]. What is he learning?! To be a simple merchant. They are not good people. He needs to learn things so that one day he will have a job everyone can respect, and I'm telling you that selling those goods won't help him.

Paradoxically, this woman was well aware of the difficulties involved now in attempting to gain access to enrollment in higher education. First, the vast majority of students must pay at least part of their tuition. Then there is the extensive system of bribes that must be paid for admission and, later, for passing exams and courses, or even to speed reception of one's diploma. Owing to the fact that this woman's son is no gifted student, the deck is stacked against him. At any rate, if he were to apply to an institute, he would need to accumulate a sizable sum of money merely to complete his education. So for the time being, the boy would do well to keep his job.

Let's consider one more example of the importance that Uzbek villagers attach to education. A boy failed to make the grade for entrance into an agricultural institute in the provincial capital, Andizhan. He grew despondent after having traveled to the city only to find out the results of his scores. His parents did not seem to show any emotional response to this news once they learned the outcome. Because I traveled to and fro with the boy and vicariously suffered the hardship with him, I myself became frustrated with the lack of a reaction on the part of his mother (M) and father (F). Finally, I asked them whether the news upset them.

F: Well, he was never a particularly strong student.

M: It's his fault; he didn't pass because he is lazy.

RZ: So what's going to happen with him now?

M: God knows, maybe you can get him a good job [titters]). Take him back to America. [Ha! Ha!]

RZ: Well, he wouldn't get far there without English …

F: He'll work here with us for a while [meaning as a kolkhoz worker].

M: The army might be good for him. He'll learn something, and that would help him at least to get out of the village for a while.

Military service carries little prestige in Uzbekistan—as is true in countless countries where conscription whisks off country boys to fill the ranks. His mother's remark, "The army might be good for him," hardly serves a sterling endorsement. When a village boy gets a call-up into the military, it usually is clear that he did not study enough to have gained entrance to any institute of higher learning. To better oneself, to gain the pride of loved ones and neighbors, there remains no substitute for education.

Actually, Uzbeks admire higher education to such a degree that honorific titles are prefixed to given names. Examples of these prefixes include *khoja*, *qori*, *ishan*, *domla*, and *abdu*. All of these terms connote learnedness, authoritativeness, scholarliness, and professorial status. Originally, the terms dealt with lines of educated descent, such as *khoja*, or were related to familiarity with and knowledge in depth of the Qu'ran, such as *qori*. As the twenty-first century continued to find a vast number of Uzbekistan's 27 million people still experiencing deprivations in comparison to the late Soviet era, coupled with the loss of meaningful work (a job or profession for which one had studied or trained), it would be rare to meet a middle-aged adult who would equate a respectable career or a respectable job only with a high level of earned income. Uzbeks spent about three generations growing up under Soviet rule. That country, for all of its faults—from famines to exile to the repression of dissenting viewpoints and political executions—inculcated something akin to a religion of education and higher learning. Uzbekistan remains a country where a visiting anthropologist still can discuss sections from *Anna Karenina, The Count of Monte Cristo,* or *The Adventures of Huckleberry Finn* with the lowliest cotton picker on postsocialist plantations.

To be fair, there are also plenty of overconfident teenagers and young men who pose cynically as they scoff at the supposed need for anything beyond an elementary education. In this day and age, obtaining a formal education makes little sense to the youth because of the exorbitant fees incurred and lack of guaranteed, well-paid jobs after finishing. Such grievances are not far off the mark, but young people are not always inclined to think of themselves at age 50, and what they expect to have and have become by then.

Two kiosk sellers shy of age 20 confided in me that attending university is a "big waste of time." According to the youths, "the instructors are lousy, they don't care about teaching, and their *hands always are open* [waiting for bribes—RZ]." I agreed that the young men had legitimate concerns, but asked, "What will you become in the future with no degree?" One admitted that it was hard to say: "I could grow rich, or I could just be making enough to keep some money in my pocket. I know this job isn't the best, but I never liked studying anyway."

Even with the substantial economic and social organizational downturns that so many Uzbeks have experienced for the better part of 15 years, people still attach a high value to enlightenment. This perspective seems reasonable when people point to all of their successful relatives and the benefits that they received from pursuing the goals of the intelligentsia.

Courtesy of Russell Zanca

FIGURE 5.5 Young people in Uzbekistan are increasingly pursuing petty entrepreneurialism over education.

THIS IS NOT FARMING! WE'RE NOT FARMERS!

Uzbek agrarian workers became hired laborers on state land. This result occurred because of "complete collectivization," which began in earnest during 1930–1931 in Uzbekistan. The kolkhoznik status afforded a person benefits, but at the same time this type of worker had little say over what was raised or how much of it was to be produced. Furthermore, kolkhozniks did not get to decide how much of a harvest could be used for personal use or sales, or even how much they would be expected to produce individually. In effect, the collective experience resulted in a reduction in the rural person's status from one of peasant to indentured servant given that authorities oversaw these individuals' hours of forced work during the major harvest periods, at least for nearly 50 years from the mid-1930s to the mid-1980s. Hence many villagers today use the concept of "plantation" to describe what their lives are like under the Soviet and now Uzbek state systems. And, yes, they are making a comparison to what they know or heard obtained in the slave-holding southern United States prior to the American Civil War.

Moreover, the majority of Uzbeks, much like all of the other Soviet peoples, were forced to join the collective farms as they were whipped together by regional Communist Party and Soviet officials. To remain off to the side as an independent household meant that everything concerning supplies, including tools, seeds, fertilizers, and animals, became the individual's responsibility; his credit possibilities would diminish greatly in short order. It was also at this time that young *Komsomol* (Young Leninist League) radicals fanatically acted out the Party's slogan of "You're either with us or against us" in efforts to make their own mini-revolution; these ardent people wanted to prove their Communist-worthiness. This stance left little room for indecision. As the Soviet state itself became increasingly intolerant of any farming outside the collectives, demonstrating such individuality on a peasant's part became tantamount to cutting one's own throat, as there would be no support network to turn to in troubled times (Aminova 1969; Ibragimova 1963, 1969).

Although the original decision to collectivize agriculture had to do with ensuring grain supplies to the cities, and to the proletariat above all, the idea to collectivize nearly everyone and everything had reached such a fever pitch by 1929–1930 that the race to collectivize became a goal in and of itself for rural Communist Party officials, who wanted to prove their capabilities. Whether or not it was truly a matter of crucial importance to the state to requisition certain crops, the system began falling from the grasp of omniscient social scientists (this system's "prime movers") and flattened everything in its path. Historian Yuri Slezkine, who wrote about Soviet rule of circumpolar peoples, remarks about collectivization running amok: "Wheat, cotton, and walruses were to be procured in the same way" (1994:195–196). In many cases, exuberance turned from absurdity to cruelty as outsiders tried to root out and punish wealthier people among cultures where perceived differences in wealth did not seem to matter in the sense of resentment or antagonism. Some people were exiled—or suffered even worse fates—for these allegations.

Collectivization as a socioeconomic (not to mention political) reorganization of agriculture within the old Russian empire extended the guiding philosophy of liberating all the oppressed peoples from the "prisonhouse of nations," to quote a phrase used by Vladimir Lenin to describe the conditions for most of the non-Russian nationalities of the Russian empire. The architects of this collectivization process can be reduced to two camps, the fanatically paranoid and the woefully naive. The determination of the former group led them to construct the Soviet agricultural system in their own image. According to this perspective, the peasants—whether Russians, Georgians, or Uzbeks—had to be broken, had to learn that it was their lot to provision the cities before they provisioned themselves.

Sociologist Zygmunt Bauman shows us that in cultural and economic terms, similar movements designed to crush the spirits and control the wills of European peasants occurred after 1600. Originally, the lesson came from the clergy and the learned, only to be taken over later by the wealthy and the powerful. The end result by the middle of the eighteenth century was that peasant culture and peasant behavior were regulated and controlled by newly emerged, strong states. The traditions of self-managing and self-reproducing cultures were "laid in ruins." The peasantries and the impoverished became increasingly subordinate to and dependent upon the "administrative initiatives of trained professionals" (Bauman 1987:63–67). The means used in Enlightenment Europe were not the same as those used in the Soviet Union, but the end results shared some outcomes.

Given that increasingly fewer people remain alive who can explain what occurred during collectivization, many younger people today rely on what their grandparents told them not only about that period but also about the colonialist period. Although more anti-Bolshevik historical writings have been published about collectivization, most of the eyewitnesses to such events and times soon will be gone forever (Alimova 2006). During the 1990s and into the first decade of the new millennium, Uzbek and international scholars have intensively studied this formative period in Central Asian and greater Soviet history. Ideological appraisals of the past have swung from left to right, now defending the politics of the era, now condemning them completely. To say the search for truth about this period is contested would be a huge understatement. No matter what the ideological biases of scholars regarding the collectivization and Russian dominance over aspects of Central Asian culture, it is a positive thing to see the activities surrounding the scholarly investigation of this time (Zanca 2005; Kamp and Zanca 2007).

Many Uzbek villagers tend to characterize the pre-Soviet past in very positive terms, even romanticizing it to a degree. At times informants opined that before the Bolshevik Revolution of 1917, no one in the village had been poor, women always cooked with flaxseed oil (viewed much more favorably than cottonseed oil), and children did not suffer from many of today's illnesses.

When I occasionally challenged what I considered fanciful renditions of past events, informants sometimes conceded that not all could have been so perfect. Even so, they honestly believed that their forefathers enjoyed a more healthful lifestyle without all sorts of chemical pollutants such as are used in modern agriculture. Furthermore, people reasoned that even rich people took care of one another and looked after those who were impoverished. Although the Soviet system and its activists presumed a strong cultural bias against the rich on the part of villagers in Central Asia, this seems not to be a strongly held view among many villagers (at least not among the ones whom I met). Perhaps if affluent individuals were considered lazy and idle, benefiting from the wealth others had earned, resentment toward them in Russia and elsewhere in Eurasia would have been common, but even the Russian peasants respected those who worked hard and had some wealth to show for it (Fitzpatrick 1994). In Uzbekistan, people did not always hate others because they were rich, as long as people perceived that their economic success was used to aid others—the poor specifically—and that the wealthier landlords treated their own workers well.

In the name of liberation from feudal oppression, Bolshevik activists and Communist Party officials early in the twentieth century not only flouted local order, but also liquidated groups of people whom the rest of society likely respected or even admired. Few people whom I interviewed conceptualized the rooting out of *kulaks* (rich peasants) exactly as described here, but their statements about not seeing the pre-Soviet village as a place of hostile class relations probably is considerably more accurate than Soviet historical depictions of this era.

FROM CARETAKER STATE TO NEW THINKING ON SELF-RELIANCE

Notions of poverty often cause people discomfort: Poor people feel ashamed of their economic position and societal status, and those who are not poor feel ashamed of the fact that their society has produced such people, especially when an outsider is asking about them. Returning to discussions of poverty and gratuitous exploitation among peasants, some informants felt strongly that poor people are not always of society's making, but rather may be victims of their own artifice, whether past or present.

As cooperative and congenial as most families are on the Amir Temur collective, nearly 75 percent of the interviewees felt strongly about the necessity for self-reliance, which means that it is incumbent upon the most able-bodied of a given household to provide for the rest of its members. This notion of self-reliance arguably emerged in greater relief during the late 1980s and into the 1990s with the rapid institutionalization of market reforms in government and mass-media publications (usually, but not always, one and the same thing), along with television programs. These sources rhetorically emphasize the capable Uzbek peasant and espouse a legacy of individualistic commercial activity and a love for farming in the lush oases.

Agrarian cultures often "gild the lily" by idealizing the outcomes of ceaseless toil in an effort to ensure a life free from hunger and the misfortunes wrought by changeable climates. As Uzbekistan's slogan boards declaim, "*Barvaqt qilingan*

harakat, hosilga berar barakat" ("If you work all the time, you'll bestow great success to the harvest").

To be fair, the Soviet government never overtly promoted an ethic of sloth-
fulness, least of all on Uzbekistan's farms. Nevertheless, it was the socialist system
that allowed the slothful to prosper (Kornai 1992). Keep in mind that a good
chunk of resistance to collectivization was rooted in the Bolshevik elevation of
the "poor peasant" to the status of the worker's exalted ally. The people who
were not classified as poor understood that the Bolsheviks simply rewarded indolence (Fitzpatrick 1994). Today, if able-bodied people do not work hard, they
will not be subsidized or supported as they were until the early 1990s.

Moreover, as mentioned earlier, labor in nature was much more collectivis-
tic during the Soviet period than it is now, so the success rate (not to mention
the failure rate!) for individualistic activities has necessarily increased. In response
to this trend, increasing numbers of younger people have adopted a newer mind-
set of rugged individualism, even as they admit their hope that the farm administration might help them out with "even one sack of grain." Again, the
distinction between "making it on one's own" and exhibiting a solid work ethic
marks the divide between the post-Soviet era and the Soviet period.

One book that reflects the new thinking of the late glasnost–early independence period, *The Peasantry of Uzbekistan*, refers to the situation faced by people
on the new state farms until World War II as an "agro-gulag," equating the
state agricultural sector to the Soviet institution of penal labor camps forever
imprinted in Western minds thanks to the writings of Alexander Solzhenitsyn
(Golovanov 1992). I found this viewpoint extreme on first glance, but it has
come to make some sense historically and in light of the farm conditions I
observed.

ENDURING COLLECTIVISM

How is it possible to speak of the collectiveness of the farm in its moribund state
in the face of the disintegration of the largest socialist country?

To reiterate, in Uzbekistan the all-out effort to collectivize the villages
located in the country's primary cotton-growing areas began in earnest in the
winter of 1930. The Soviet state knew it could realize its dream (previously
shared by the tsarist system) of making the U.S.S.R. self-sufficient in cotton production and manufacturing once the FV cotton farms were collectivized—that is,
state controlled.

Along with everything else that it entailed, the collectivization of villages and
their resources meant that nearly all of the arable land, water resources, livestock,
and manpower became the provenance of the Soviet government. As the leading
administrative and authoritative political body of the country, the Communist
Party rapidly set to the task of ensuring that only Party members occupied key
positions, even within the remotest Uzbek hamlets. Once in place, the young
zealots' miniscule experience in administering peasants (Ibragimova 1969:43)

made it extremely difficult for any villager to make differences of opinion known should he want little part in a kolkhoz existence.

As mentioned earlier, the villager who held the highest status in the new collectives was the poor peasant who did not always enjoy the respect of neighbors, as they may have considered this individual to be lazy. Eventually, however, nearly all villagers saw the advantage in labeling themselves as poor if they could pull it off (the other two main classes were middle peasants and the rich). In this sense, the Soviet Communist class system differed greatly from the elaborate Chinese Communist one under the leadership of Mao Zedong, which consisted of 11 different peasant classes (Potter and Potter 1991). The qualifier "if they could pull it off" is important to acknowledge because the middle and rich classes under Soviet rule often were dispossessed or "de-kulakized," sometimes by being driven away from their homes and villages. The historian Ibragimova even discusses the creation of special collectives just for the kulaks, who later were taught the "values of humility and decency" (1963:256). Middle peasants may have been forced to hand over a horse or a couple of sheep, but they usually retained their homes and garden plots as long as they acted cooperatively. For the kulak, conversely, the matter was entirely different, and he was often disenfranchised right down to his home before being expelled from the village.

This legacy of collectivization and its implications for contemporary people in their kolkhoz villages struck me with full force during the summer and fall of 1996 as I carried out a census in Boburkent, surveying nearly 200 households. Most of the surveyed individuals were cooperative and exceeded my expectations for helpfulness. In certain families, however, my questions provoked suspicion. Two questions in particular among those that formed a part of the standard questioning fare during the census taking raised eyebrows: "How many hectares of cultivable land do you have with this homestead?" and "How many animals do you own and what kinds are they?"

Reacting to the question about land, many interviewees asked that I clarify the question so that we could clearly distinguish among their own household garden plots, recently given state plots (for raising wheat and rice since 1992), and the larger divisions (from 0.5 hectare to 3.0 hectare) set aside for peasants to farm kolkhoz cotton.

People are assigned cotton plots and required to maintain them throughout the growing and harvest periods. In short, the household or family becomes responsible for the planting, weeding, furrowing, and watering of a section of the cotton land. In turn, they are paid for this work. At harvest time, those family or household members must be assured placement with a cotton-picking brigade once harvesting starts. Ordinarily, a few families who live close by one another form part of a brigade—in essence, a team that works a sector of land. The spatial closeness of one's village community (*mahalla*) is often reflected in work areas in the fields. The initial harvesting phase generally coincides with the best sort and grade of cotton. Brigades typically work three to four hectares together.

In the 196 households that I surveyed, numerous members became tight-lipped when it came to providing precise information about the dimensions of the plots used for personal (household) consumption alone. Sometimes people would smile nervously and mutter a barely audible question to my assistant or to whoever else stood around watching the proceedings: "What's he need to know this for?" At other times people confronted me much more directly with tones of subtly disguised hostility: "Who wants to know about my land?" or "Why is knowing about my land important for your work?"

Concerning the question about domesticated animals, respondents often displayed nervousness when they had many by village standards, such as four sheep, two milking cows, a dozen chickens, or a few turkeys and ducks. Oftentimes interviewees attempted to conceal the truth until tripped up by a small child: "But Dad, we have three cows, not two." The father might then feign a sort of semiotic lapse, as if he could not discern the exact implication of the question as asked: "Oh, well, I didn't consider those calves as cows." (The word "*mol*" in Uzbek means any sort of "property" or "goods," but in villages commonly refers to cattle, and the Uzbek phrase for beef is "*mol gushti*.") At still other times a person might ask, "Who's going to see these results?" or "Hey, you don't need to write down that we have so many chickens." Sometimes I tried to lighten the atmosphere as I rattled off a list of the kinds of animals they might have. I would throw in elephant, chimpanzee, or lion just to try and convince people that this work seemed tedious to me, and that I did not show any great interest in just what kind or how many animals they had anyway.

If some villagers found my work questionable in 1993 when I first set foot in Boburkent, then that local wariness was only amplified by my asking the same kinds of questions years later that the early Soviets had once used to determine who needed state aid and who should "aid" others on the basis of ownership and possession. In retrospect, it was a line that I had to cross. I suspect that it will take much more time before certain villagers feel comfortable enough to answer such questions nonchalantly. Even given the receding Soviet system, the new Uzbek state retained so many dictatorial political aspects of the previous regime that there are really few grounds for people to abandon their fears of future dispossession and wealth "redistribution."

That village life continues to be essentially Soviet-style may be witnessed through both the political and institutional organizations of the villages. In this case the evidence appears to be irrefragable.

A typical collective farm village comprises a number of key links to the country at large and state power in particular. In the village, one finds a post office with telegraphic capabilities, a police station, an elementary school (classes through grade 11), a few shops, a barbershop, one or two mosques, a neighborhood committee office (*mahalla komitet*—a branch of state administration), a medical clinic that includes dental facilities, a garage, a teahouse, a butcher's stall, a number of repair kiosks (e.g., for repairing shoes), and flour and rice mills. Tied directly to farming, one also encounters primary enterprises such as a fruits and vegetables canning facility; a tractor garage staffed by mechanics and stocked with extremely limited supplies of fuel and spare parts; cotton storage facilities; a warehouse for fertilizers, pesticides, and defoliants; and a livestock yard where the hundreds of head of cooperative cattle for meat and dairy industries are stabled and tended.

The kolkhoz center that typically lies within the confines of a collective farm village. Most collective farms incorporate several villages, typically numbering from three to five, including the offices and representatives of state power.

STATE ADMINISTRATION OF THE KOLKHOZ

Even if we show that the kolkhoz looks as if it will not survive its old incarnation much longer, it has remained subject to the rule of the state and governed as an estate, with the Uzbek government acting as owner of the productive land.

The kolkhoz administrative building, along with its theatrical-looking "club," sit just back from the main paved road that links Amir Temur to larger population centers to the north and south. In addition to housing the farm's library, the club contains an auditorium where the formal side of holidays may be observed and where films are shown fortnightly or monthly. Entering the club gives one the feeling of a theater entrance. The spacious lobby often features wall portraits of international revolutionaries alongside bucolic depictions of Uzbeks happily laboring away in the fields under the burning sun; "Stalinist realism" is the label that best characterizes this artistic style. Like so much Soviet construction, the Amir Temur *klub* (official center for public speeches and entertainment) is crumbling, even though it was completed in 1964. It serves as one of the more

Courtesy of Russell Zanca

F I G U R E 5.6   An office of the rais in Boburkent. The position of rais represents a branch of regional government—something akin to sheriff and village mayor.

poignant symbols for the direction in which the old collective way of life is headed in the new millennium.

Near this politico-administrative complex stand statues—or *stood* statues would be more to the point. Until recently, one of the statues was of Lenin (now only a paint-chipped plinth remains), whereas the other is dedicated to the martyrs from World War II. Sometimes a monument built on behalf of the personage for whom the kolkhoz was named also appears in this area, and plans have been afoot for a while to erect a statue of Amir Temur himself. Off to the side or in front of the building and monuments, cultivations in the form of a rose garden and a small orchard with apple, peach, and almond trees grow.

On the kolkhoz, one individual enjoys preeminence: the *rais*. This person is endowed with the state's trust to ensure that the kolkhoz fulfills its agro-economic targets on the basis of its capabilities. The crop production and delivery plans are mapped out late in winter each year at the regional *hokimiiat* offices (*hokims* are the equivalent of American mayors or governors) by a team that also includes agronomists, brigade leaders, economists, and accountants. Later provincial authorities, and later still Tashkent authorities, decide whether to give their stamp of approval to the local plans.

The rais occupies a large office on the main floor of the administrative building. A secretary serves the rais within a waiting area and is responsible for screening those who would entreat the rais. Additionally, the secretary types all memos and reports as well as mans the telephones and telegraph. During peak harvest times, the administrative building is almost always open, and the rais often puts in 16-hour days. At these crucial times, the secretary's role is vital, because he has to take on all of the regular duties at doubled and tripled tempos owing to regional calls from the larger center offices to be kept abreast of the quantified harvest deliveries and harvest conditions, and owing to his need to regulate the many people clamoring to see the rais in efforts to provide him with production records, reports of problems, requests for extra hands or equipment, and requests for special permission to obtain more fuel for machinery, among other issues.

Next in leadership importance is the village councilman (*qishloq sovet*). In 1989, this position and office was renamed *oqsoqol* (village elder). The name change reflects the desire to enhance the air of the office with a sense of village tradition: Oqsoqols historically commanded village authority based on their seniority and the wisdom of life's experiences. The officer must see to the needs of the village on the whole; he must also keep the villagers' records, much like the function of a city hall. The oqsoqol handles matters directly affecting kolkhoz villagers, serving as a liaison between the village and kolkhoz administration and the concerns of villagers and the local hokimiiat in the region. If, for example, people from one street of a village think they need a new road or insist that drainage is poor (and neighbors simply working together cannot fix it), they then raise the issue with the oqsoqol in his office.

When the issue at hand pertains to villagers needing foodstuffs, such as a sack of wheat or a 40-liter canister of cooking oil (still subsidized by the state and often doled out as a form of payment for service to the kolkhoz), people may approach the oqsoqol about the matter. Naturally, this may become a very political act depending on the kolkhoz worker's sense of trust and/or personal relationship to the oqsoqol.

Despite the historical roots of his title, today's oqsoqol is not the kind of wizened warden of times past who would have achieved his authority because of his intelligence, judiciousness, and knowledge about issues of religion and traditions—at least this is the version of the oqsoqol as villagers describe it. In the Kokand Khanate, which included today's Namangan and Andizhan provinces from 1710 to 1876, the oqsoqol worked to collect taxes and regulate canal maintenance and water distribution. During the period of Russian colonialism, the status of oqsoqol again was instituted politically. Nevertheless, today's oqsoqols are less likely to have proved themselves as aged and profound than to have been Communist Party members of minor stature who long have enjoyed the perks of political positions on farms throughout most of their careers.

During my various stints of fieldwork, I came to know four different raises. All of them seemed as if they would have been more comfortable running a power plant or a factory rather than a farm where human interaction, human labor, and human needs are so intimately interconnected. For these raises, it could never be the kolkhozniks who were of primary concern but rather the production of the kolkhoz itself. A rais is trained (owing to his higher education in economics or agronomy, usually) to think in terms of kilograms, centners (100-kilogram units applied to the amount of a crop per hectare; for example, 33 centners of cotton/hectare = 3300 kilograms), and hectares; the very metric system itself is his obsession. He thinks in terms of how many kilos of wheat, of silk cocoons, and so on. How many centners of cotton per hectare? How many of the farm's hectares will be idled so that peasants can plant rice or double-crop wheat and rice?

Given his marching orders, the rais will cease to be the rais should he turn to regional bosses and say, "But we need better conditions in the kolkhoz field shelters, better foods, and more medicines for the clinic." The rais knows that if the kolkhoz meets the all-important targets for production, some benefits may accrue to the kolkhoz, including salary payments and bonuses on time, repair projects, and new services such as natural gas supplies. Conversely, he knows that conditions on the kolkhoz are sure to worsen if plan targets are not met by a significant margin—during the mid-1990s, Amir Temur routinely fell short of its mandated goals, making about 80 percent of state-set targets, especially in cotton. Thus the rais mainly sees the world in terms of statistics and numbers.

One might expect a modicum of accessibility to the rais, considering that he typically heads a farm employing 4500 of 7000 people. In reality, the rais generally demonstrates the old Soviet penchant for letting subordinates know just how powerful he is, no matter the overall rank of his position in the wider political spectrum. And it is with this air of self-importance and disregard for the hardships of commoners that the rais builds great resentment against himself—an act that may strike an outsider as one of masochism, given the total lack of anonymity or faceless bureaucracy in this setting.

The enduring attitude from the Soviet era in farm leadership attitude is that life is something one commands (Heller and Nekrich 1986). In speaking of unequal power relationships that deal with the carrying out of orders and fulfilling state procurement plans, the philosopher Jurgen Habermas writes about how the structural imbalance of power may be offset if the people in authority are "compensated for by collectively desired goals." For this to happen, collective society would have to be able to "examine the goals or either endorse or repudiate them." This appears to relate to what has been absent on kolkhozes—the general or public interest. In terms of interests and collective goals, Habermas says that fulfilling the general interest

> calls for a consensus among the members of a collectivity, no matter whether this normative consensus is secured in advance by tradition or has first to be brought about by democratic processes of bargaining and reaching an understanding. (1985[vol. 2]:271)

Habermas's concerns center on industrialized societies, but on the microcosmic level of Amir Temur his analysis seems apt. There a system is predicated, hypothetically, on collectivism, yet run by naked authority that disregards popular interests. Within the rais's own small circle of colleagues, which tend to range from agronomists to economists and accountants, there may be more dispersal of authority, as different levels of professional expertise may be needed to ensure plans are met as ordered. Peasants, in contrast, don't really factor into this collectivist agreement. Centralization merely became more localized with the collapse of the U.S.S.R. Furthermore, the disintegration of the farm itself has not significantly altered those authoritative and centralized arrangements (Hall 1996:76–77).

The rais literally embodies the historical antipathy between the power wielded by the state and the peasants' relative powerlessness. The rais lives among the people; indeed, he may have come from the kolkhoz that he now heads and been a child of a kolkhoz worker (from the late 1950s until early 1970s, a woman was the rais of Amir Temur, then known as *Engels*). Yet his position and the personal conduct flowing from it mark the rais as no longer being really of the people. To a lesser extent, many of the other local power brokers, including the economists and accountants, act similarly, usually depending on the number of years that they have served in such capacities.

Lest readers develop the mistaken impression that the kolkhoz is a seething cauldron of antagonism between the state's representatives and common residents, it is important to point out that this is not characteristic of daily interactions between such folk. Nevertheless, increasing numbers of people cannot see why status quo ante relations persist within the power structure, even though "privatization" and "de-collectivization" have been key watchwords of the new order since 1991.

On a hot August evening I dined with the rais after spending most of the day traveling together in his jeep—a job perk for professional and private use—visiting field after field of various crops as well as meeting with the agronomists and brigadiers (leaders of peasant work brigades) so that the rais could assign the best date to initiate the year's cotton harvest. Because this was the first time that we had really gotten together to talk, after months of having tried to arrange such a visit, the rais appointed a couple of his underlings to lay on a big spread. As a result we returned to a table replete with food and booze (including wine, champagne, cognac, and vodka); this was a feast. In the end, the rais himself drank heartily (I may have joined him had I not been treating myself to yet another round of giardia!), and he talked more openly than expected.

Although this official willingly admitted that his current job had been more or less forced on him by the regional authorities ("I had to take this job"), it was not the job he wanted because he had been working satisfactorily for years as an economist. When asked if he thought newly independent Uzbekistan was headed in the right direction, if de-collectivizing was the right path to take, and if privatizing the land would work well to everybody's advantage, the rais stated unequivocally that he thought the state's actions were justified. He felt the kolkhoz had outlived its usefulness, and that in time ordinary people would do much better once the state relinquished its monopoly over the land. In raising concerns about the plight of the average family and the fact that de-collectivization should be accompanied by substantial national growth to finance supplies and credit sources that so many of the country's impoverished peasants would need, he attempted to be reassuring.

The rais's answer seemed to parrot the official or government line about Uzbekistan "having great natural resources ... lots of gold and natural gas." Certainly, this is true, but this kind of response from officials already had become routine in my experience, and it did not appear to embody much of an action plan for improving the lot of the peasants. Of course, part of what enables such an official to maintain his position is showing no outward dissent.

On that evening we also dined with another villager. As we walked back toward his area of the village from the kolkhoz guesthouse, he muttered, "Now you see why these guys are so useless. Do you really think he [the rais] is interested in the peasants? I'm not saying he's a bad guy, but all of these people are old Communists with an old way of thinking."

In the communist past, it may be argued that a oneness of purpose found on collective farms was practiced only superficially in the utopian sense depicted by the philosopher Karl Mannheim, who referred to "ideologically determined conduct" (1985 [1936]:192–205). The true basis for fellowship might have been the historical collective pattern rather than Soviet collectivism, which effectively took peasants and herded them toward "unified" goals of production, education, and so on. Also, one could diverge from this line of reasoning by arguing for a kind of coercion hypothesis, stipulating that shared coercion—namely, people being forced to do things against their will by harsh state representatives—fostered collectivity. This occurred because everyone had to help guard against greater collective suffering.

Presently, the breakdown of kolkhoz unity is occurring incrementally at most levels as the old system necessarily fails. For individuals, the nature of coercive threats has softened considerably, along with the state's ability and desire to care for the general welfare. Individualism now stems more from a deep distrust of the state. This transformation is somewhat ironic: Uzbeks were supposed to have relied on the state for employment and basic welfare, but decades of corruption and hypocrisy wore away at the idea of reliance on officials or institutions; most recently, the system has proven incapable of making a positive difference in the lives of most householders. Furthermore, it is not as if the Uzbek people have a place where they might turn with good effect to argue, to complain, to make someone in a position of local power respond and change things. There are no mass media, local or national, interested in plebeian rancor or disagreement, or that show enough concern to create a forum for discussing real problems that relate not to run-of-the-mill corruption allegations but rather to the shortages, breakdowns, and wants of the villagers.

Thus political accountability in Uzbekistan does not occur from the bottom up, only sometimes from the top down, which is very closely related to the situation in the former Soviet system. The anthropologist Akhil Gupta urges us to be cautious about stereotyping or orientalizing corruption in the developing countries in rural areas versus the state. No doubt this approach is sensible, but we also must agree that villages in India, Uzbekistan, and Mexico are not the same (1995:387–395).

A new nation has taken shape in Uzbekistan. While certain media sources do discuss Soviet oppression and tyranny, the general idea is not to whip up the masses, not to give them a taste for investigating and bringing to light all the injustices committed by their former leaders. After all, many of the "new" are also "former"—and were not exactly seen readying Molotov cocktails to oust Soviet power in Uzbekistan. (There were no majority sentiments throughout the Central Asian republics to overthrow Soviet power.) The national leadership today favors conservative expressions, such as "Don't destroy an old house before you build another."

Do the villagers want the old system back and the new state to fail? Certainly not, but this has not blinded them to the old-wine-in-new-bottles reality that characterizes much of the relationship between state and peasantry. In the mass media, which are controlled completely by the state, there seems to be room for little else besides recalling past glories (a few nasty interludes of Stalinism notwithstanding), and a present that is good and bound just to keep getting better. Everything written and spoken promotes progress, not dreadfulness. William Roseberry, who was looking at a very different kind of state in Venezuela, noticed similar processes at work (1989:77). People are well aware that the emperor has no clothes, but rather than pointing this inconvenient fact out, they simply hope he gets dressed quickly.

THE *MAHALLA KOMITET* (NEIGHBORHOOD COMMITTEE)

The *mahalla komitet* (MK) regulates village affairs. Although it is a primary local institution with a head and a deputy, its real strength lies in its variety of committees; it has 11. The foremost are the poor families group, the women's group, the retirees group, the weddings and private parties council, and the holidays and kolkhoz celebration group. No village institution takes so direct a role in villagers' lives or mediates issues between village and the state's legal requirements as the MK does. In recent years, the MK has been busiest with helping the neediest families, dealing with land allocations (supplementary food plots), and providing additional funds and resources to help poorer families celebrate life-cycle events, especially weddings and circumcision parties.

During a sticky afternoon in late summer, I was invited to lunch by the oqsoqol's secretary. For lunch we loped over to the head of the MK in our torporous condition. This short, rotund man energetically prepared pilaf with quinces for us as he perspired profusely over his outdoor hearth. Once we finally sat down to eat, I broached the topic of the problems that most taxed his energy and emotions as the MK head. After sighing, the MK boss said that it was a matter of "a lot of shortages." What he apparently meant was that it was more than just the lack of things proper; it was also the fact that few people have the means to buy many of the products they need for daily life. Next question:

> RZ: Wouldn't you say poverty has become a greater problem in the village in recent years?
>
> MK's SECRETARY: Yeah that's right. [The man grimaced, and once again I felt as if I had put a damper on a pleasant occasion with my work; my questions succeeded in causing this reaction at social events more than I care to recall.]
>
> RZ: Okay, so what would you say the percentage of poor people in Boburkent is now?
>
> MK BOSS: It's around 20 percent.
>
> RZ: Do you know that for certain?
>
> MK BOSS: Of course, it's my job. I know what people earn and who gets paid, and also who it is we have to help. If the MK has to lend a hand to an older couple or provide funds for a *toi* [celebratory life-cycle party], it's usually a pretty good indication that they are poor.

During the meal, the bookkeeper and the boss exchanged furtive glances, and the former then produced a half-liter bottle of vodka. I apologized in advance, but told them that I was too ill to drink. The excuse worked poorly at first, but repeating my refusal helped win my case. They drank and I toasted with my tea.

Days later the secretary picked me up from the town's main road and drove me to Namangan. On the way there, he told me that he needed to see a doctor because of his diabetes. I questioned him about having drunk vodka during the meal with the MK boss given his medical condition. The secretary hesitated before answering, "I don't do that every day, you know. I know, I shouldn't really drink at all, but we bought the bottle because you were the guest; it's good to drink to a guest's health."

Revisiting the topic of the luncheon, the MK head told me on this occasion that his office spent considerable time asking his regional center contacts within Namangan for more funds to help younger families absorb costs for boys' circumcision parties. He noted that the regional government wants this issue to be a community-wide concern, and that the regional authorities claim to have little

money or inclination to maintain the old policies; villages now have to be account-
able unto themselves. Such celebrations are seen as wasteful. However, the MK head
countered the administrative position, saying that there are enough people cheating
the villages out of social funds at the *hokimiiat* solely to enrich themselves.

About a month later, this same MK head visited the family compound where
I resided to speak with the compound's oldest male member—the leading authority
in this setting—about a marital squabble concerning one of his sisters. At the time,
that particular sister had left her husband for her mother's house because of the
discord. Apparently, the husband had complained about the situation to the MK,
saying that his wife "was worthless and that he was not going to welcome her
back"; she had "stopped doing household chores." Everyone in the vicinity knew
the brother-in-law (*kuda*) to be slightly unbalanced and rash. Because the man had
also threatened bodily harm to his spouse, the MK head resolved to consult our
compound's head in this instance in an effort to settle the matter properly.

This act on the part of the MK head clearly demonstrated his unwillingness
to throw the weight of his own office around, in this instance subordinating his
own power and jurisdiction to a member of the fractious kin group caught up in
the dispute. His act of deferring to the household head balanced the interests and
concerns of local power with those of the community's residents. After two
more weeks elapsed, the anger cooled, and the wife and one of her daughters
returned to the impetuous husband.

Ordinarily, the MK itself has yet another subdivision that promotes "family
harmony" as its purview. Nevertheless, it soon became clear that its subcommittee
had become defunct; its lone member at the time was "busy with other matters."
The MK head explained to me that because he knew the family in question, he felt
confident about letting them deal with the trouble, but that every family has its
own characteristics. Mediation of disputes and intrafamilial disagreements, then, is
another priority of the MK. No other state-supported institution intervenes so directly in the personal and psychological dilemmas of individuals within the village.

To a significant degree, sociopolitical institutions of the village such as the
MK and the oqsoqol are not artificial add-ons of socialism. Thus one should
not expect them to disappear (at least not in the sense that there would not be
a continuation of offices that carry out similar duties), as may happen with the
more Soviet position of rais and the rest of the kolkhoz administration. The latter
roles are the direct descendants of collectivization and the attempt by Bolshevik
leaders of the 1920s and 1930s to ensure that only Communist Party members
held key political positions.

THE KOLKHOZNIK AS CONSUMER: *TIMOR EMPTOR!* (MAY THE BUYER BE AFRAID!)

Neither Soviet power nor Uzbekistani independence seem to be particularly
adept in meeting consumer demands in the villages. No proof of this claim can
be more exemplary than a tour of the village's remaining state or semi-private

shops. Someone used to living in a consumer-oriented society is left wondering why these local shops remain open at all. The goods that they continue to stock—including mineral water, vodka and sweet wine, toilet seats, bags of salt, canned vegetables and fruits, small bags of flour, an accidental hotplate or lamp, the odd can of paint, cakes of dark soap, and low-quality garments—hardly make them a useful addition to local commerce and merchandising.

Having interviewed shop workers and villagers, who seem to use the shops more for hanging out and chatting than for daily shopping needs, I found indifference and a level of dissatisfaction that had long ago reduced anger to resignation. Occasionally, people expressed a desire to buy a shop and stock it with desirable goods, but pointed to the insurmountable obstacles that render their hopes whimsical. People have no money to finance such buyouts, cannot routinely obtain credit, would not necessarily know how to afford a wide variety of stock, and know that few people could afford to pay for good-quality products. With (official) salaries hovering at slightly more than $10 per month, there is little reason to expect that store workers will attempt to change a problem they have dealt with for so long.

In complaining about the consumer goods available within the village, people told me that in the past, especially from the mid-1960s through the mid-1980s, one could buy sausages, canned fishes, and worthwhile household goods, including the all-important immersion heaters (a fast way to boil water for tea), light bulbs, candles, buckets, sickles, and a better variety of clothing. A schoolteacher in her late twenties who had quit working on account of caring for her two small children expressed a slight puzzlement when asked why she thought the local shops did so little to meet the needs of parents like her. She was not convinced that they were so bad, and told me she thought the shops had improved a bit of late. That remark agitated me, and I told her that I could not follow her reasoning. I listed what I considered the paltry inventories of the local shops: "They have no milk, no rice, … nothing good for your kids as far as I can tell." The former teacher smiled and said, "But we don't go to one of those stores when we need milk. Each family should have its own cow."

Each family does not own its own cow, although many do. A little more than half of the 196 households that I surveyed owned one or more head of cattle, but not all of these were milking cows.

The schoolteacher followed up her earlier remarks by saying that people consider the Noryn and Uchkapa marketplaces to be good sources of both specialty and general items. I told her that I knew most people did not look to the village shops for either staples or hard-to-find goods, but I wanted to know whether she wished to have the convenience and comfort of doing at least basic consumer shopping in her own village.

> There's no ease or comfort here. I imagine it must be really easy in America. You have everything there, and …

And so she talked, not really sharing my viewpoint.

Countryside people often try to impress upon outsiders the fact that their lifestyles are full of work and inconveniences. Although they understand perfectly well which sorts of changes would make it easier and of higher quality, they seem unwilling to take action, to petition people in authority, the people who are partly responsible for their welfare and village upkeep and that of the community, too. With their common understanding of the newly changing mechanisms of supply and distribution, most villagers would prefer to learn how the newly developing system operates and then work or participate within it, rather than go out on a limb to try to persuade their neighbors—or even leaders—to make further changes where they live to resume with decentralizing phenomena. For most kolkhoz workers, decentralization is a mixed bag, and it is a matter most are content to leave in the hands of the centralizers.

Part of the reason that outsiders—and Americans in particular (myself included)—are sometimes off the mark in promoting variants of liberal democracy in Uzbekistan has to do with what local people seek when looking to the political system. It is not necessarily the democracy of periodic elections that is coveted, but having a dependable patron. In the village context, this means the wider neighborhood and the society of the kolkhoz. Family interests, often fraught with bickering and lack of unanimity, almost always come before individually based ideas about success. Thus it is vital that the leadership, however untrustworthy it may be, sees a given family favorably, so that some of the former's patronage falls to the latter in a timely way. Individuals and their alternative successes and failures are not highlighted in the same way, with a few exceptions. The French anthropologist Olivier Roy (1999) has examined this issue more fully, specifically on collective farms in Tajikistan and elsewhere in Central Asia.

Few peasants place consumer advocacy atop their lists of contemporary socioeconomic priorities. Conversely, a focus on consumer advocacy could serve to underscore kolkhoz shortages for which both local and national authorities should be held to account. This change might empower kolkhoz workers in ways beyond their mere ability to buy various goods with greater convenience. In forcing the state to do something about basic, unfulfilled consumer needs on the part of villagers, the peasants would simultaneously force the state to rectify three generations' worth of neglect toward these people—negligence that seems to be affecting their very nutritional requirements (*Asian Development Bank Report*, 2001).

As peculiar as it may seem for the members of an agricultural community/village, fresh whole-milk products are not a part of the daily diets of most Uzbek people. It would be one thing if, similar to the situation with Japanese, Korean, and Chinese populations, milk products were simply not a part of the traditional Uzbek diet. Historically, however, Uzbeks have been a people of milk and meat, owing to no small degree to their ethnic origins as nomadic and semi-nomadic pastoralist people. Furthermore, circumstantial historical and archeological evidence proves that milk and milk products have long been part of the diets of other sedentarized Ferghana Valley peoples for the better part of two millennia (Bernshtam 1951:10–11). The very idea that one goes without milk on Amir Temur if one does not own a milking cow indicates that the farming people have been a low priority in the eyes of the state. What magnifies this bad situation is the existence of hundreds of cows within the kolkhoz of nearly 6000 people.

One of schoolchildren's great delights came in the form of an infrequently procured can of condensed milk, canned milk imported from countries such as Lithuania and Slovakia. Apparently, the kolkhoz continues to send the milk that it produces to the regional and provincial centers. The nutritional needs of peasants—the nation's primary producers of nutrition ipso facto—remain a secondary issue for those who govern the nation.

Inquiry into this problem usually met with empathy and the kind of tacit recognition that made this anthropologist feel that it at least made sense to raise the issue (i.e., that other people also found it a matter of genuine concern). Naturally, those partly responsible for kolkhoz functions have many reasons and excuses as to why the situation exists:

- There are not enough vaccines for the cattle.
- It is too expensive to buy more feed.
- If we do not sell these products as ordered (by the state), we will not receive any money to pay our staff.
- We do not have well-trained staff to look after the health of the cattle anymore because those people have to make money from other sources.

SO LONG, AGRO-WELFARE

Talon (ration coupons) once enabled almost all villagers to purchase fixed amounts of butter, sugar, powdered milk, flour, and tea during lean periods. By 1996, however, the Uzbek government had dramatically reduced the scope of rationing, restricting it society's most vulnerable, such as the disabled, the elderly, and parents with young children. Price controls and the rationing of staples ceased because the government judged them to be incompatible with independence as the country began filing down its Communist shackles and lurched toward a free-market economy.

When the new state assumed power (and not exactly in the wake of a vacuum, given that roughly one-third of the old Communists—from the Communist Party of Uzbekistan—continued to fill ruling positions), the representatives did work hard to legitimate the notion of an independent and nationalist Uzbekistan. The majority of Uzbeks reveled in the notion that the republic had broken from the Soviet Union. While not everyone yearned to break free from their Soviet chains, few Uzbeks shed many tears in the wake of the Soviet Union's passing. Although approval and nostalgia/reminiscence for the Soviet period do exist today (especially for the time covering the mid-1950s until the mid-1980s, as discussed earlier in this chapter), few people lament the demise of the repression, forced cotton picking, and the prohibitions on travel and movement since the 1930s that once characterized Soviet life for the agrarian residents (Nove 1986; Heller and Nekrich 1986; Fitzpatrick 1994).

Combining negative factors that feed back on one another, the Uzbek state policies seem to continue eroding a long-troubled relationship between the state and the peasantry. Max Weber pointed out this kind of antagonism as typical when he discussed the peasant's basic inability to gain economic mastery over his own life, especially when the state seizes his vital resource—land—for the "polity" on behalf of the "community" (1968:363–365). Generally, Uzbek villagers cannot anticipate the kinds of extreme changes characteristic of this most recent period. If prescience characterized these rural people, then they would enable themselves to take control of their own flagging positions. However, wage arrears, the lack of freedom to trade and market their own goods and wares independently, the lack of a stable currency, the constant inflationary cycles, and a lack of credit and investment opportunities for the farming communities combine to prevent villagers from becoming economically competent, let alone skillful. Realistically, the one arena where the most savvy villagers can claim and exercise economic competence resides in the marketplaces and bazaars. There a person may engage in the age-old art of haggling for the goods and services he may wish to sell or buy. As Clifford Geertz indicated decades ago in his Moroccan ethnography, the marketplace functions as a realm outside of mainstream economies where village economic knowledge is privileged above the nation's (Eickelman 1981:188).

As economic persons inhabiting the world beyond marketplaces—often the case—villagers lack the seasoned elements to take advantage of other fiscal worlds. At almost every turn, their capacity to secure biological and cultural necessities is stymied. Clearly, one cannot blame the state entirely for the declining fortunes of most individuals. Nevertheless, when a rural person reflects upon recent economic events and compares them to his own economic actions and exchanges only some 20 or so years ago, it sometimes seems that Soviet power's policies strike the villager as more rational and predictable (to say nothing of being more just in a strict economic sense).

CONCLUSION

From marketplaces to new shops and new economic responsibilities for professionals, the activities of many kolkhoz residents have changed rapidly since the collapse of the socialist system. Where new opportunities have arisen, many people feel they have had to sacrifice the predictability and stability of the old order. In this chapter, we examined the changing face of Uzbek socioeconomic lifestyles with the decline of state support for kolkhozes. The villagers continue to adapt to their environment as working people, even when they consider the work demeaning because of their training or the professional status that they already have. They try to make money in agriculture in untried ways, and their consumption and shopping practices change depending on the nature of where and from whom they go to obtain daily goods and services. It is an economic world of daily life embodying both collapse and flux.

QUESTIONS

1. Rural marketplaces played a vital role in kolkhoz life even during the Soviet period. How and why has their role increased in importance in the post–Soviet period?

2. Which kinds of goods and services would you expect to find at a "peasant bazaar"?

3. Why is it so difficult for people to make a living in agriculture on the rural farms today?

6

Uzbekistan's Cotton, Home Economics, and the Larger World

In the life of a villager, political and economic specificities of cotton work aside, almost all field and home labor stems from a shared goal: maximize one's household food security and monetary income. People did not just abandon the socialist type of labor because they thought it a flop, but because after 1991 only the form of socialism remained without the benefits, so the kolkhozes became unsustainable as guaranteed sources of sustenance and income. Moreover, the increasing amount of physical work and sex-ratio imbalance of field laborers occurred once men increasingly abandoned their jobs connected to cotton as they seized any new job opportunities or those they might will into existence, such as the untold number of individuals becoming "salesmen," "traders," and "businessmen." Some of these people work within the state sector, but most work outside it in these capacities. While these professional statuses would have garnered contempt during the Soviet period because of their associations with capitalism, today they are seen to be the only sensible work one can access.

The anthropologist Eric Wolf (1966) wrote about peasants' basic need, which is to guarantee their own "subsistence fund"—the basic necessities for day-to-day living. The kolkhoz order in the post-Soviet conditions could not enable peasants to maintain such a subsistence fund. Even so, the leadership tried to keep cracking the whip, reasoning that peasants would keep following orders just as they had when conditions were slightly more comfortable. Yet, having abnegated those standards of welfare disbursement and support, people simply could not live in some autarkic manner.

After 2000, Uzbeks began leaving Uzbekistan in myriad numbers to find work across borders as labor migrants. This phenomenon has become such a significant trend that it is estimated today that somewhere on the order of 15 percent of the entire population of Uzbekistan works outside the country for at least part of the year—seasonal labor migration.

While it is true that Uzbek kolkhozniks were not paid as well as their European counterparts within the Soviet Union (Gleason 1992:75), people whom I interviewed demonstrated that they clearly understood what was happening to their living standards and way of life. A number of villagers also felt sure that farm administrators themselves cheated the kolkhozniks. Bearing this in mind, it struck me that we needed to understand from the kolkhoznik's perspective what wage differentials from the Soviet and post-Soviet periods meant, if, for example, we compare the monthly 85–110 rubles a farm peasant would have earned in 1985 to the 2500 Uzbek som (post-1994 currency) he might have taken in during the mid-1990s. According to Abdullo S.:

> At the time I didn't think that was much of a salary either [85–110 rubles]. But, God, when I think about the fact that I could buy most things I needed and wanted and still might have something left over at the end of the month, and then I realize what I can buy today, there's no question but that it was much better then. Of course, I was a bachelor then, but I feel I'd be doing pretty badly on my current salary if I were still a bachelor.

Taking this man's thoughts into account, it is also necessary to recognize that the lion's share of the typical peasant's income was not always derived from cotton work or the important raising of silk worms, but from a combination of incomes that featured the private marketing of household produce, animals, and other home-industry products (Rumer 1989:127).

DOMESTIC SERFDOM: MOTHER-IN-LAW/
DAUGHTER-IN-LAW RELATIONS

In the Uzbek home, women oppress women. This statement is exemplified by the relationship between the mother-in-law (*qainona*) and the daughter-in-law (*kelin;* literally, "the one who came"). Around a given household, the qainona in effect becomes the head activist on behalf of patriarchal domination as she herself reproduces the treatment to which she once was subject. Recent anthropological literature on China, for example, shows us that rural Chinese brides also endure "abusive mothers-in-law" in ways similar to brides in Uzbekistan. In fact, peoples in many regions of the globe exhibit this complex, including those in countries of South Asia and in the Middle East. Ann Anagnost (1991:324) suggests that this behavior arises in China in part because brides lack economic power or any professional role outside the new home (Anagnost's residence pattern tends to be patrilocal or virilocal). Pertaining to the Uzbek case, brides begin to reassert some autonomy and make individual decisions only after they have given birth. Because the role of the mother is believed to be more important in the upbringing and socialization of the child, a woman's status increases with motherhood. In terms of adult social life, this may be an even more important rite of passage than marriage itself because of the wife's new and permanent place in the patrilineage; the baby now ties her to the patrilineage in a consanguineous sense.

Soviet anthropological literature seems not to have treated this special affinal relationship (mother-in-law to daughter-in-law) in any systematic fashion. It also has not explored the connection of this relationship to the poor nutritional and ill health effects for young women that result from it. In fact, Soviet social science, as practiced by Uzbek women, has yielded works that touch on the issues of women's oppression in the FV more as matters affected by politics, economy, and religion than by sociocultural practices and the psychology of household life (Bikjanova 1959; Alimova 1991). Even the late Soviet ethnographic work of Tashbaeva and Savurov, which looks at both the innovative and the traditional in contemporary Uzbek family life, casts the antagonistic qainona–kelin relationship as a product of backwardness or conservatism. These authors see it as a cultural phenomenon, and suggest that the only thing needed to cure it would be more Soviet agitation and propaganda, all the while taking little recognition of its embeddedness and ubiquity (Tashbaeva and Savurov 1989:29–52).

My research brought me into contact with this relationship almost daily. Naturally, all mothers-in-law are not alike, and there are many who treat their daughters-in-law fairly and kindly. As a rule, however, mothers-in-law exhibit nearly the opposite behavior. Of all the fears a young woman carries with her into marriage, that of her new mother-in-law stands out. Adumbrating the initiatory period of this relationship, which may last as long as a decade, the kelin becomes the virtual servant of the household. She takes on extreme work burdens, and her activities, methods, and behavior entail constant qainona scrutiny; the elder ever is on the lookout to find fault, or so it seems to the kelin. Uzbek families expect the bride to give birth within the first year after marriage. While birth invariably boosts the kelin's status, the kelin's work burdens and chores become heavy again only a couple of months after birth, despite her added responsibilities of nursing and newborn care, though here grandmothers do provide much help. Qainonas help out because grandchildren are an intense source of joy and love, but the kelins' increased needs for rest and good nutrition usually go unmet. Clinically speaking, postpartum care for mothers in rural villages simply cannot compare to the world encountered by educated, middle-class Western women. Furthermore, young women face the pressure to have more children.

If a woman has three to four children by age 30 (a common pattern in Boburkent), she may also expect to develop chronic fatigue, anemia (partly responsible for the chronic fatigue), and other mineral and vitamin deficiencies that render her more susceptible to illnesses. Unfortunately, it is not at all clear to what extent, if any, the growing poverty and accompanying decline in various foodstuffs for individuals, especially animal products, have affected women's health. This problem, much like others that pertain to environmental and

Courtesy of Russell Zanca

FIGURE 6.1 A light-hearted moment shows a grandmother and qainona supervising sewing.

ecological issues relating to human demographics and public health, has not been thoroughly examined. The lack of data from empirical inquiry often leads to hyperbole and rumors concerning the negative results for the local population. Moreover, in an atmosphere where people have long been denied access to statistical or quantitative data about factors having a direct impact on their own lives, rumors tend to spread fast and find ready acceptance as gospel truth.

Is a woman's qainona directly responsible for these health-related problems? Certainly not. At the same time, the qainona plays a reinforcing role in the social organization of the village whereby the concerns and needs of young women are routinely neglected. Until the time such relationships within rural families are addressed and linked to those elements of social organization that promote the domination and inequality between these senior and junior in-laws, it is unlikely that judicial measures or political campaigns will have much effect. Essentially, the patrilineage turns this relationship into an initiation in perpetuity that is broken by the qainona's eventual mellowing. For numerous rural women, this phase occurs only after the harsh treatment has taken a toll on their mental and physical well-being.

WOMEN MAKE THE BEST COTTON PICKERS

Hurmatlli Hamshaharlar!
Pakhta iighim-terimda faol ishtiroq etailik.
[Esteemed Citizens!

Participate actively in our cotton picking and collecting.]

—An exhortatory slogan sign strung up across many a road throughout the towns and villages of Uzbekistan once the cotton harvest approaches in late summer

As discussed in Chapter 3, cotton harvesting in the FV commences in early September and usually ends by mid-November. Inclement weather, however, may extend the picking at least another month. As a matter of fact, in the late Soviet period peasants had to pick cotton even when it was wet or partially frozen because centrally planned targets had to be fulfilled. This practice was in keeping with the Soviet system's fetishizing of bigger and bigger production quotas, no matter how poor the overall quality; producing more was perceived as being equivalent to the state and the population becoming ever wealthier and more successful. Kolkhozes themselves received payments and profits according to the overall metric tonnage collected, so at the local level an administrative "devotion" to picking lousy cotton was driven by a logic only economists determined. In reality, this damaged cotton had limited industrial and commercial use.

Kolkhozniks make up most of the pickers. These peasants are assigned to specific brigades. The Amir Temur kolkhoz comprised 11 brigades during my research trips. Once the harvests is under way, supplementary brigades of schoolchildren, along with their supervising teachers, also contribute middling value to the picking. Better than 70 percent of the pickers are women, and an additional 20 percent are schoolchildren (aged ten and older). The children might miss five to six weeks of school during the peak period. Few adults expect the schoolchildren, especially the boys, to do much picking, so 30 to 40 kilograms of cotton picked per day suffices. Seasoned women, to the contrary, are expected to pick anywhere from 90 to 130 kilograms per day. Heroic cotton pickers routinely appear on television and print news, including the regional papers (e.g., *Labor's Advocate* and *The Namangan Truth*). Such women often pick as much as 150 to 190 kilograms per day, and record breakers have exceeded 200 kilograms on a single day. Even Soviet anthropologists held up these women who "overfulfilled" plan targets as models (Bikjanova 1959:55–57).

Most men who pick tend to be older—50 and older. Many retired men, who were lifelong kolkhozniks, also reserve the right to pick if they request it. Today, however, young men with little education or training will do almost anything except pick cotton, because picking is seen as demeaning and even unmanly. This does not mean exactly that men (and women, for that matter) consider the work to be effeminate, for cotton picking is intensive and backbreaking. Rather, for the younger men, it is more a case of their own declarations of will: They will not pick, and that is all there is to it. The lack of whole-hearted village labor support during these harvests helps explain why schoolchildren, soldiers, and urban university students have had to pick up the slack historically. What was once packaged as a patriotic commitment to help the economy and an exercise in socialist mass participation could not overcome the fact that farm residents consider the job as just above worthless. Ideological spin-doctoring to the contrary, these harvests necessitate *corvee* labor (Swain 1985).

The kolkhoz administration, of course, plays the role of feudal lord in manipulating these relations. Other cotton brigade positions include those devoted to pesticide control, defoliation, cotton weighing, ginning, tractor driving, irrigating, and managing. Although I visited and worked on several different brigades, I never remember seeing a single woman occupy any brigade leadership position. This being said, fairness demands that I point out that women of the kolkhoz have occasionally occupied very prominent positions of authority within the administration, including that of *rais*.

Male brigade members, especially adult men, may be seen whiling away their time restfully (at times playing chess, checkers, backgammon, and card games) unlike their toiling female counterparts. This helps explain why, conversely, most boys, including adolescents, work so hard around the house and in the fields: They often are supervised by their mothers, or told to help their mothers by their fathers.

The renowned American country musician and singer, Johnny Cash, spent much of his youth as a cotton picker. He claimed that he developed his love for singing while picking cotton because it relieved him from the tedium and the pain of the task at hand. Learning this fact about the late, great Johnny Cash when I returned from Uzbekistan reminded me of what a male informant gleefully mentioned about how he got out of the cotton fields as an adolescent. This guy also loved singing and realized his voice was very good because whenever he began singing in the morning, other children would stop working to listen to him; he was providing an impromptu concert. Before long, his teacher found other work for the young man while the rest of the children continued picking.

Uzbek women also related that they used to sing in the fields frequently, but stated that members of the younger generation no longer knew those songs from their youth. No one ever forbid singing, but it stopped being fashionable. Nevertheless, today one occasionally hears women signing folk songs, and children "perform" pop songs they have heard on radio or television as they dance around singing into a hoe handle or plant stalk entertaining one another. Despite these exceptions, relatively few people pass the time singing. Rather, they chat with one another as they go up the rows of plants collecting the cotton wool from bolls, or shout across the rows to friends or acquaintances in the distance.

Cotton fields are also the site of more joking and laughter than one might think probable on first encounter. This anthropologist himself became a source of mirth when first working with a brigade, declaring *"Belim oghiapti-ku!"* ("Man, my back hurts!") after working for only 30 minutes. "Your back would hurt a lot more if you had any cotton in that sack," one bemused woman said. At this remark everyone began giggling, and all that day the question that got repeated concerned how much did I enjoy picking cotton and would I consider living with them forever in Uzbekistan to pick cotton. In the end, diversions seem more necessary than frivolous when one realizes just how arduous and dull picking really is.

The fields form a big social site for boys and girls who have potential interest in each other. The fields, much like a schoolyard or village square, are fertile romantic terrain. Boys astutely analyze the human topography of these fields, deciding exactly where the objects of their amorous longings are working. None of this activity, of course, is lost on the girls, who view their own objects with less directness or boldness. The twentieth-century Uzbek novelist Oibek captured this passion of "boy meets girl in the cotton fields" in his celebrated novel of 1938, *Qutlogh Qon* (*Holy Blood*). What ensues is the delicate and cautious practice of flirting, a style of flirtation that many of us would recognize only by being coached. As long as the boys and girls keep up the illusion of picking (no blatant loafing), adults do not bother them very much.

Boys often espy girls whom they consider comely from their own row—that is, from the position where they happen to be picking. If the boy is truly smitten, especially if he is seeing a girl for the first time, he may stop picking altogether, or fake picking by bending down and springing up as often as possible while he steals glances at her. He may get the attention of nearby friends with a "psst" here and there, followed by a tilting of his head in the direction of the girl. This happened to me on more than one occasion, being "pssted" at, and all I could do was smile, nod my head, and continue with my novice picking.

THE COTTON PICKER'S DAY

After women have fixed the family breakfast (taken usually between 6:30 A.M. and 7:00 A.M.), they gather up those items necessary for a day picking cotton under the merciless sun, where temperatures, even in early October, often exceed 90 degrees Fahrenheit. The most important items are a beverage tankard (filled preferably with cooled tea), a couple of loaves of bread (especially if a woman takes a child or two with her), and one or more apron sacks for packing the picked cotton while moving along the rows. Apron sacks are worn around the waist and cause increasing stress on the lower back. This is owed to constant bending and the rapidly increasing weight the worker carries as she fills her sack. Once a person gathers about 25 kilograms of cotton, she unties the apron sack, lays it out across a furrow, and continues picking while depositing new batches of cotton into the opened, spread-out sack. A fully bundled-up sack may hold 35 to 40 kilograms maximum after the picker compacts the load by stomping it. Then a relative or friend helps knot up the sack into a bulky bundle. The picker then places this burden atop her head and periodically walks from the depths of the fields to the border where small weigh-in stations are located. Additionally, a woman might bring a hoe to the fields for nearby vegetable plot work, or she may tow the family cow or bull (sometimes two head of cattle) on her way to the field, depositing or parking the animal in a clover field for all-day grazing.

Given the location of village households in relation to the farm's cotton fields, kolkhozniks walk anywhere from 1.5 to 3 kilometers to reach their work destinations. Sandy or loess trails lead to the fields. Many boys and men bike to the fields, but it would be a matter of impropriety for women to do so; sometimes a husband or son will drive a woman as she sits on the bike's back part.

Attire for the fields is loose, threadbare clothing—work clothes. Women typically wear Uzbek pants (*lozim*) under tattered housedresses or over jogging/track pants (appropriate for girls). They wear kerchiefs or large scarves (*rumol*) to protect their heads from the sun. Over bare feet galoshes are worn; they are ideal for durability, foul weather protection, comfort, and ease of movement. Those men who do work in the fields use their shirts to shield their heads, working bare-chested or in tank tops.

Picking starts by 8:00 A.M. It makes little sense to begin much earlier, because dewy cotton makes the picking harder. The first couple of hours are trying enough because the bolls stay damp. After 10 A.M., one is challenged by the rising sun and heat, though picking the wool becomes easier. Because the kolkhozniks are paid by the kilogram of cotton picked, and then given more or less (value added or subtracted) depending on the cotton's sort or grade, picking as much cotton as possible is the ultimate goal for the duration of time in the field.

Seasoned pickers try to gather 50 kilograms or so by lunch, which begins at noon or slightly after. Pickers, then, after packing between 12 to 15k kilograms per hour into their sacks (which means they pick methodically and rapidly, breaking from the trance-like state of picking only long enough to give themselves momentary relief from backaches), look around, exhale, wipe away perspiration, wave away insects, swap a word with friends, and little else.

Before the pickers break for lunch, they typically have the bundles weighed and tabulated by the *brigadir* (brigade leader) and his assistants. The picked cotton is then handed to boys or men who dump it and spread it out on a huge wheeled container with mesh grating that will be pulled by tractor later to the ginning and baling facilities. Each container holds upward of 1000 kilograms of cotton.

A certain amount of anxiety creeps in before the weighing because pickers want to make sure that their loads receive proper recording and family name inscription in the brigadir's ledger. Because women occasionally go elsewhere after picking to busy themselves with other chores or attend important social events, they must assign another friend or child (their own) the weigh-in task to make sure that the amount receives proper registration. Table 6.1 provides an example of what the tabulations look like in the ledger.

Lunch happens at the communal shelter, which contains little wings for men and women. At one time, the shelter reportedly featured recreational space with a ping-pong table and cots for napping. During my fieldwork, however, it consisted of only empty, dilapidated rooms within a decrepit wooden frame. When the weather is good, men spend little time in the shelter, preferring the comfort of their raised wooden platforms (*suri*), which they make more comfortable with padded quilts for sitting and lying down. Men sit in the shade of huge willow trees. Women arrange themselves on the ground near the canal and within the relatively cool darkness of the rooms themselves. Their appearance contrasts to the men's because they appear physically drained from the picking. Men relax with their lunch and dog-eared, erotic playing cards and worn-away board games and chess sets. Women do not sit at tables or on the suris.

Each day people eat a communal lunch. Villagers are assigned rotating duties to prepare lunches for their brigades; a man or a woman may be the cook for a week. Lunch invariably should be a soup or a stew-like soup made from

TABLE 6.1   Individual Cotton Pickers with Total Weight and Income Figures for Cotton

Name	Amount of Cotton Picked (kg)	Sort/Type*	Payment (Uzbek som)
Akhmedova (F**)	38	2	76
Sabirova	43	2	86
Ghulomova	47	2	94
Abdujaparova	48	2	96

*The sort specifies the quality of the cotton. On a given day, in a particular field, it would be uncommon to have more than one sort; hence the medium 2 here. Still, kolkhozniks are not necessarily paid based on the quality of the cotton they pick. The data here are modeled on the 1996 harvest, when kolkhozniks on average were paid 2 som/kg. At the time, this amount equaled approximately $0.05/kg based on the official exchange rate or, more realistically, slightly more than a penny at the black-market rate. The quality of the cotton picked better determines how the kolkhoz itself will be paid by the state; quality and quantity must be added to determine the payment calculation.

**Whenever a person's surname ends with an "a," it denotes female sex.

whatever is available, including corn, pumpkins and squashes, macaroni, eggplants, carrots, and black-eyed peas. It is essential that kolkhozniks bring their own bowls, cups, and utensils, or else they will have to wait for others to eat and finish and then use theirs. Naturally, the ravenous brigade members vocalize their displeasure with the wateriness of the soups. Tea accompanies every meal and break, and the people drink it from big bowls along with icy canal water to slake their thirst.

Parents sometimes have lunch served by their children. Even teenage boys will bring food to their mothers from the communal cauldron, especially when their mother cannot but help to wear their fatigue or exhaustion. At lunchtime people willingly share the food that they brought from home among fellow brigade members. The equality of poverty seems to coincide with a collectivist ethos in work as well. After eating and resting and napping for an hour or so, the pickers walk back to the field site when the sun's full power has started to subside.

TARNISHED "GOLD": COTTON EARNINGS AND THE INDIVIDUAL

Kolkhozniks spend anywhere from 10 to 12 hours each day picking cotton during the peak harvest period, depending on factors such as crop quality and the volume of cotton wool exposed for picking per hectare. For example, 38 to 40 centners of cotton per hectare is considered excellent, but on Amir Temur averages rarely exceed 35 centners—that is, 3500 kilograms per hectare. To be sure, if a woman can pick 130 kilograms per day without straining herself too badly, she will do so, owing to the relatively high earnings she takes from it. Most pickers consider the 2 som per kilogram pay rate laughable in bitterest terms, but they also know that making an all-out effort to earn 230 to 250 som per day is better than slowing down one's work and earning far less.

The best picking comes during the first three to four weeks of the harvest; this period marks the first of three rounds of picking. It yields the highest quality and heaviest hauls for pickers. From early September through early October, peasant women can be seen returning from the fields as late as 8 o'clock in the evening, their skin tanned and leathery, their eyes reddened and sagging uncontrollably.

During poor harvest years, the gung-ho approach of the early days is often replaced by a devil-may-care attitude because the energy expended to pick perhaps 70 kilograms or less of low-grade cotton strikes people as barely worthwhile. At this stage of the game, it is clearly a case of too much work for too little money. With low yields also auguring poor-quality cotton, pickers and brigade leaders understand the bad repercussions for the kolkhoz itself from the poor harvest: Little money will be allocated for infrastructure, welfare, and new construction. Therefore, people prefer to deal with domestic matters for family well-being. As a result, they focus on storing and canning foods, and they engage in petty commodity production—mostly produce from their home garden plots.

Table 6.2 is adapted from newspaper and television illustrations of state cotton planning at the provincial level that I observed during the mid-late 1990s. Fulfilling these plans will determine the extent to which individual kolkhozes are later either rewarded or punished by the administrative system in terms of resource allocations.

This information provides media viewers with an awareness of how well their own region is faring, even if they are skeptical about the veracity of the data. They have some idea as to whether their province has a real chance to achieve state production targets based on common knowledge of crop profile, grade, and other factors. Most people know fairly well a month into the harvest if it will turn out to be poor, adequate, or excellent. Television and newspaper reports help them gauge their own efforts. Combining both types of knowledge, people decide on the nature and degree of their participation.

T A B L E   6.2   **Uzbekistan's Provincial Percentages of One Day's Cotton Collection in Fulfilling the Overall Plan**

Province	Tons Picked	Percentage of Plan	Total Plan (tons)	Total Percentage to Date
Navoii	2036	0.9	404,000	27.4
Bukhara	2312	1.1	397,000	29.1
Tashkent	1580	0.7	325,000	11.5
Andijan	2754	1.4	506,000	37.2
Namangan	2012	0.9	448,000	31.8

Courtesy of Russell Zanca

FIGURE 6.2 Cotton workers at break.

INSULT TO INJURY

For the farm itself to receive adequate or better inputs and investment, the state requires the kolkhoz to fulfill at least 75 percent of its plan target. If the farm falls short, especially in cotton and wheat production, then it can look forward to increasing fiscal hardship. In this way, the state—namely, relevant ministries, such as labor and agriculture—metes out punishment to the peasantry owing to shortcomings in productivity that are almost always caused by forces far beyond the control of farm labor power and individuals' efforts; acts of nature do not always take the blame in bad harvest years, either. What seems like lunacy takes on the form of kolkhoz abuse, which has been noted as a practice of some countries, especially poor ones, with a majority of rural inhabitants and an urban-focused state. In this type of system, "inefficiency is used to deny credit" (Bartlett 1980:13). If viewed systematically, it would be one of negative feedback: The kolkhoz does not receive adequate inputs in terms of fertilizers, tools, and other resources from the state, yet is expected to produce an amount and quality more or less dictated by the state. As the farm often fails to meet these targets, it is given even less support for the following year. Visually, if we modeled the conditions of the kolkhoz, they would be seen as falling steadily along a vertical axis.

The days of villagers making Herculean efforts or going the proverbial extra yard have ceased based upon three generations of experience with the old system. What is more, the types of bonuses and special prizes formerly awarded to "Heroes of Socialist Labor" are far and few between in comparison to the Soviet period. Skepticism often accompanied those badges of honor anyway. One older "hero" related that when he was given a medal and certificate, he frustrated the goodwill of presenting officials by telling them, "I'm honored, but I don't need the medal. What I need is extra money." The officials' response was predictable: "Keep your smart comments to yourself, Comrade; you could get into trouble for talking this way."

At harvest time, part of the antagonism vented by peasants toward officials is the drive by some to gain positions on brigades for the first round of picking. Kolkhozniks themselves do not make these requests, but other farm residents who wish to get in on brigade work may do so—perhaps mothers with young children, the unemployed (mainly youth from 16 to 30 years old), or those who have jobs but no money owing to deferred salaries. Naturally, interpersonal hostilities can come into play here because we are dealing with neighbors and co-villagers. The claim of the administrators, and their justification for not allowing inclusion of more pickers, is that no more room remains, that no more slots are available, and that if more people are added the bona fide brigade members will become angry.

This specific issue of a labor glut or excess laborers is one of the few persisting remnants of the former U.S.S.R., which used to claim that it not only had no unemployment, but also could not find enough people to fill all available jobs. In this instance, one may plausibly credit the labor glut to the FV's high population density (highest among all rural areas of the former U.S.S.R.) as well as the restrictions on access to arable land relative to population size in Uzbekistan's provinces of Ferghana, Andijan, and Namangan. Conversely, the state could pass a moratorium on child labor at harvest time, but this issue is not as simple as it appears. By 1993, faced with the decreasing lack of mechanization (owing to prices for fuel, spare parts, and other factors), more and more hands were needed. Manual picking skyrocketed as a proportion of all cotton picked. Therefore, at harvest time in the best cotton-growing regions, such as the FV, child labor maximizes the potential yield. Moreover, many of those who clamor to join picking brigades weigh their options carefully, which means that they often wait until relatively late in the game to declare their interest. The state cannot necessarily depend on this additional labor source, a literally opportunist one. One political scientist, Gregory Gleason (1992:66–98), has argued that the Soviet failure to mechanize Uzbek cotton farming—a negligence blamed on authorities in Moscow and Tashkent—resulted in the simultaneous needs for increasing the human factor in cotton labor and preventing the migration trends characteristic of rural societies that have dramatically transformed the technological basis of agriculture elsewhere.

For many pickers, attitudes about the virtue and necessity of the yearly cotton harvest reflect the nationalistic or, at least, statist discourse bespeaking universal wealth and welfare for the well-being and strengthening of the nation. Of course, pickers do not speak as if reading aloud from a newspaper editorial, but they have absorbed and personalized certain official themes that link the Soviet legacy to the construction or erection of independence. Thus people speak about the potential for the harvest to keep the country peaceful and stable, to guarantee its citizens a modicum of income, and to enable their own industries to develop better, even when many of them know that the yearly harvests have been at least as much of a scourge and source of impoverishment as they have bestowed benefits. One could argue that many people engage in a kind of wishful thinking. They think that if good harvests and new foreign markets soon are found, then perhaps the state will acquire the money and resources to spread around as it did until recently.

Both residents and farm officials told me that they did not know how much money the state received from each ton of cotton sold internationally, which, by implication, meant that they had little to no idea of the prices obtained on the international market for cotton. That kolkhozniks and other common villagers simply guessed at prices came as no shock, but to think that local bureaucrats also admitted ignorance strikes one as dumfounding.

Kolkhozniks argue that the state representatives would not care to know all of those prices anyway because they care little about the villagers—why would they even make an effort to know? Besides, how did they get their positions of authority and power? Was it on account of their spending time asking tough and probing questions of authorities located even higher up in the state hierarchy? Villagers view such men (rarely women) as timeservers, people who know how to do little else than follow commands and leap when ordered. As for these same people, who appear at once as defenders of and apologists for the state-dominated cotton harvest, they manifest little confusion about their lack of knowledge concerning the main source of their livelihoods for the past 80-odd years: "Our president is an old Communist, so even if he has good ideas or smarts, there is no way he'll be able to change the system immediately." The presidential efforts are seen as being geared foremost toward stabilizing personal power and the foundations of the new state that he helped to create. History shows this view to be correct. This has been the price paid by a leadership interested only in its own sense of the proper pace for economic reforms and political control. The leadership evinces little inclination to involve the population at large in decision making, let alone give them a means to access information in any structurally new way, including expansive Internet access.

That the pace of reforms has been slothful in developing should not come as a big surprise. However, the favoring of "big government" or statist policies in former Soviet territories and countries would not necessarily be bad if strong centralization were accompanied by active, vibrant participation in the workplace and at the community level. The fact is this rarely turns out to be the case in Third World (in the present case, post–Second World—that is, postsocialist world) settings, where historical patterns of the overbearing state also have been associated with human rights violations, massive corruption, and the suppression of voices and activities from the grassroots level (Cohen 1994). Villagers in this situation are so accustomed to deception, so used to being lied to, that they do not get easily upset or irritated because they cannot, for example, buy four hectares of land, or because new rounds of shortages do not overly worry the state's leaders. Teilman characterizes these issues as a lack of "brokerage," indicating that go-getters or gamblers in such powerless, rural settings are exceptional:

> In many new nations the access to the state's political and economic institutions is, for the general public, very restricted. This is the result of a small elite-class controlling the national political institutions and, by virtue of that control, the major economic resources. (1991:103)

Clearly, this situation has nothing to do with local indolence or stupidity, at least not in most instances. Even so, this outsider reasonably may argue for villagers to do more on their own behalf, to better unify themselves and put more pressure on the local authorities. This judgment in metaphorical terms appears as "batting from the dugout." Given that they have little recent history of spontaneous political gatherings (save for the Andijan uprising of 2005, discussed later in this chapter), no true right of free association through which to air grievances, and the legacy of a severely control-oriented state behind them, what could motivate villagers to risk dangerous uncertainty in their own fates? Right now, their main business consists of indefatigable attempts to fulfill their subsistence needs and maintain (or reproduce) the sociocultural life as people long have known it.

Whenever political discussions with villagers became personal, especially on the question of apathy and my perception of Uzbek unwillingness to take direct action, people had a way of deflating my concerns. Sometimes, either consciously or unconsciously, they imitated the stereotypical images of themselves constructed mainly during the Soviet period. Anthropologists and political scientists might consider these notions of self-imagining as hegemonic because they show a kind of satisfaction with the order that exists. For example, one informant said, "But, come on, you now that we Uzbeks are like sheep. We respect age and authority too much sometimes for our own good." Stating things in this manner shows that the informant is fully aware that he does not have to accept this position, or certainly that he thinks beyond it. Nevertheless, cultural conventions and patterns often have a way of exercising a kind of centripetal force toward our individual thoughts and activities. On the one hand, such an informant went on to agree that taking political action against people in authority could make sense in a number of circumstances. On the other hand, the answer bespeaks an important division between the anthropologist and the person whom the anthropologist studies and scrutinizes: The informant's answer serves to silence the outsider, a person who may be perceived as both meddlesome and unaware of some of the complexities of internal sociopolitical dynamics. Students of Uzbek history know well enough that Uzbeks have proved themselves to be less sheep-like and more tiger-like time and again since their recognized formation as an ethno-national people within Central Asia.

In 1996, Vladimir Zhirinovskii, then leader of the Russian Liberal-Democratic Party, joked that President Islom Karimov of Uzbekistan was the richest man in the former U.S.S.R. because he owned "22 million sheep." This insensitive characterization of Uzbeks found some resonance as people internalized it, as quoted in the previous paragraph. Not everyone uses this metaphor simply to deflect criticism or agitation: There are people who honestly think too many of their co-ethnics live with a herd mentality. At the same time, it would be irresponsible not to consider the influence of Uzbeks' recent political experiences. Too many years of Stalinist and general Soviet brutality and oppression have made a cautious lot of the Uzbek peasantry, people on the whole who have endured even worse than what the present offers. Similar to other impoverished peoples the world over, Uzbek do not simply organize and rebel because they have limited prospects, a declining quality of life, and a lack of faith in local and national leaders.

Part of the argument made in this book is that while millions of Uzbeks more or less are stuck on what are de facto cotton plantations in the wake of socialism and the imposition of a very authoritarian regime, the residents do seek to detach themselves from state control. They seek this freedom as they attempt to exploit new laboring ventures that the collapsed system cannot pretend it doesn't support, such as entrepreneurialism, and the individual's right to support his family. Although individualistic pursuits may bring peasants into conflict with authorities, it is rare that people intend to act confrontationally. If this is resistance, it is not really the kind that people undertake consciously to fight against the authorities. The slow collapse of the old system through the mid- to late 1990s continued to provide nearly sufficient niches in the Uzbek economy to enable people to avoid—rather than challenge—the exponents and representatives of the new system insofar as kolkhozniks and other village residents can seize initiatives. What we have seen in the new millennium, conversely, is the state charging hard to take back greater control over independent economic activities.

Most Westerners never question the notion that it is much better to work for oneself than for the state, at least in terms of a person having the potential to make more money for himself. This is an ethos to which we grow accustomed from an early age, and a position that was brought home to most Americans with great force during the Cold War period. Nevertheless, there can be an element of misguidance to this kind of axiom when one sees it from various post-Soviet perspectives. Obviously, most people prefer to work for themselves if the incomes are good and they have the free time and health to enjoy all of the benefits. What observers of post-Soviet conditions may think of as "nostalgia" for the socialist past, however, is not necessarily rooted in some collective wish on the part of the masses to idle about and be coddled by the nanny state (although, truthfully, some people do support that kind of system in the villages). Rather, looking to their recent past, some of the favorable feelings result from a common belief that Soviet society—late Soviet society—was a better and richer place when the peasants served as the cogs of the old agro-juggernaut that was the Uzbek Soviet socialist cotton economy.

In their own way, Uzbek residents do assert themselves, despite our Western inclination to perceive their rural actions as conformist. Actually, it is easy to see the entire socialist Eurasian landscape and human activities in this way because the postsocialist countries there seem remarkably uniform across thousands of miles of steppe, mountains, valleys, and tundra. Theirs is a sameness in schools in public transportation, in food products, in clothing, an in behaviors. Of course, this is why ethnographic experience and observation prove indispensable; they allow us to dig beneath the surface and see just how nonconformist individuals can be, and how their thoughts and activities are more varied than we understand them to be when observing only from a distance.

Each time a kolkhoznik fails to show up for brigade work, voices his anger at the rais for insufficient supplements to his salary for grain or cooking oil, or gripes about the lack of selection at nearby stores, then that person acts independently.

Historians of Russia who write social history have noted this phenomenon of late, especially based on their painstaking analysis of archival documents during the 1930s (Fitzpatrick 1994). Moreover, on a different plane, were scholars to explain that all of the underground or self-published literature from Soviet dissidents (from the 1930s to the 1980s) came about because just a tiny number of Soviet citizens broke from the typically non-independent thinking and acting society, then scholars would wind up being hard pressed to explain each case as a mere aberration. That form of literary presentation, known as *samizdat*, dealt with more than dissident political opinions: Samizdat writings included history retrieved by intellectuals and republished in just a number of typewritten copies so that people would not lose the history of their own culture's thoughts, achievements, and subjugation (Sinyavsky 1990:233–234). And if those writings did not reflect mass thinking, or did not at least garner mass reading interest, then one has to explain why they were so widely distributed—relatively speaking—when the state took so many pains to prevent their dissemination.

Conformism and village life tend to go hand-in-hand. Being a conformist has less to do with exercising one's will and more to do with thinking through one's next step with the knowledge that predominates from the midst of the social world in which one happens to reside. Far from being a matter of determinism, careful consideration of the possible consequences of one's proposed course of action must be filtered through the normative values and opportunities of the local world—a part of what Bourdieu (1990) described as the *habitus*.

Applying this notion to Boburkent, we may consider the case of quitting one's kolkhoz job. For example, a given individual decides to quit, and takes whatever funds he has available for, say, a chewing gum venture, risky as it may seem to relatives and friends. At times villagers quit the kolkhoz job when a new work opportunity emerges, even if it is temporary. I recall talking to the brother of a young family man who seemed to have disappeared from the village. I asked Davronjon what happened.

D: My brother is doing some electrical repair and phone line work in Q. because they're reconstructing the system there.

RZ: But what about his job here? [He did similar work in Boburkent.]

D: He left it.

RZ: Just like that?

D: Yeah. What's the good of staying on here? Do you have any idea how long he went with no salary, no supplies, no anything?

RZ: No. How long?

D: Months.

RZ: So they're really paying him in Q.?

D: I think so. After all, that's why he left. You know he has kids.

RZ: But how do they have money to pay him?

D: I don't know; might be money for the workers because the *hokimiiat* [governor's office] was ordered to do this project.

RZ: Well, did he leave for good? Is the job permanent?

D: Nah, I don't think so. It's just a temporary thing.

The choice Davronjon's brother made was a relatively safe one, for it is doubtful he will face repercussions from the farm administration. Unfortunately, the kind of opportunity he opted for is not open to many; he lucked out. Receiving a real salary—a timely one—is an anomaly for villagers, as noted earlier. If Davronjon is correct, it brings us back to the mysteries of everyday labor and the state's financial institutions, mysteries this author is hard pressed to solve. What seems somewhat true from informants' remarks is that funds are appropriated for particular small-scale projects that either the regional or provincial government administration deems necessary, yet very few labor sectors benefit from such slap-dash, last-minute projects, and certainly no more than a fraction of villagers do.

A far more reckless course of action in terms of willful protest or resistance might be the option of trying to organize friends, neighbors, and co-workers into an independent, anti-authoritarian movement; such a move would be considered foolish as well as dangerous. Here execution of one's will in an atypical, anomalous, or innovative manner cannot but mesh with or keep within the boundaries of the quotidian. It would not make sense. In dealing with a context that is atypical, nonconformism perhaps strikes an outsider as noteworthy for its plainness or inconsequentiality.

Even though it appears likely that the plantation-like patterns of living and working in the kolkhozes will continue to a significant degree until the organization of the Uzbek state and its politics change, peasants and other village residents still seek to overcome restrictions on their movements, such as new customs regimes, or residence patterns, mainly out of need but also because their modern history is not one of isolation. People from these farming villages constitute part of a translocal and transnational economy, and a part of the farming population will sever its ties to the agrarian cycle if only for part of each year. In typical developing-world fashion, the past decade or so has seen steady movement of residents to the outskirts of urban areas, which in turn increases the populations of cities, such as Andijan, Namangan, and the capital. In most cases, villagers have made a rural proletariat of themselves, with few of them finding satisfying work on any permanent basis. If they succeed in opening and maintaining their own businesses, however, then the rules may change positively.

Curiously, as much as the Soviet period and its policies favored the development of rural people and areas into an agrarian proletariat, they (willingly or unwillingly) helped the Uzbek people maintain their peasant-like structure. The state did take better care of rural citizens and at times provided them with ample opportunities to leave their villages for good in ways practically unheard of before 1917. What happened in the best sense is that technological, intellectual, and, perhaps, the health–nutritional horizons of this population expanded and deepened from the 1920s until the late 1980s. The Soviets ascribed a new status to these people, just as they had to tens of millions of Russian peasants—namely, kolkhoznik (the term used steadily throughout this book). But even now

Russians continue to designate farming people as the *krest'ianstvo* (peasantry), just as the Uzbeks speak of *dehqonchilik* (a term of Persian origin, meaning "people who work the land"—that is, peasantry). Of course, getting bogged down in terminology does not always lead to clarity, but it is still crucial to realize that this terminology shows historical continuity with little alteration of the fundamental concept and reference point behind such words.

Diversity and sophistication should be used to characterize the FV Uzbek peasantry stemming from the Soviet Enlightenment project. In part, the level of education in Uzbek villages did result from the Bolshevik goals spearheaded by Lenin and other, later policies of Soviet education, specifically formulated with rural populations in mind (Lenin 1978; Laird and Francisco 1980:150–152; Kerblay 1983; Humphrey 1988:53–70). These policies promoted upward and outward mobility, including affirmative action (Martin 2001). The elaborate network of telephone lines, print media, visual media, and roads and transportation (no matter how poorly some of these systems and the media function) are surprising in a country that remains agricultural, impoverished, and isolated in terms of international trade and relations (and concretely isolated in the sense of direct people-to-people contacts with other countries). This may explain in part why when it comes to criticizing the Soviet Union, the majority of Uzbek people interviewed stop short of throwing out the baby with the bathwater. It also helps to explain why men generally need little time to adapt themselves to work assignments in towns or cities, regardless of their attraction to living in cities. Through military service and higher education, as well as extensive transportation links, almost all men have experience with urban living. Furthermore, almost all village families have at least some relatives living in cities.

During the last years of Soviet power, many people began to assert the symbols of their nations over homogenized Soviet symbols, and clothing was one such manifestation of national identity. Many people became increasingly aware that ethnic or national consciousness may be reflected in their way of attiring the body.

AFFIRMING VILLAGE IDENTITY: YOU ARE
WHAT YOU WEAR

While en route to catch a train to Namangan, I asked my friend Suraiyo where I could buy the distinctly corduroy, paisley-like patterned men's robe (*chopan*) that was then so popular in Namangan, and how much I should expect to pay for one. After she told me about the best bazaar for these robes, along with what she thought average prices should be, she expressed her curiosity at the popularity of these robes.

S: I don't suppose you've seen too many of that particular type in the village.

RZ: No, hardly any of that type at all. Is it distinctly "Namangan"?

S: Yes, I think so. But men always wear chopans in the village, especially to keep warm when doing work outdoors. They mostly wear their old black ones for that.

RZ: Yeah, why is that?

S: I think because it's the most common. You know, up until recently all these elaborate chopans were not so common. Young men especially hardly wore them at all until a few years ago.

RZ: So what made them so fashionable again?

S: Well, here specifically I think it resulted from a lot of people starting to reject Soviet- or European-style dress. They wanted to show that Uzbek clothes are good, too. Of course, it's cheaper to buy a chopan than a coat and the manufacturing is all done here. I think a lot of people are buying them out of necessity, too. Some of them probably would buy a better-quality import winter jacket or coat if they could afford it.

The chopan is a robe, but not in the American sense of something one wears strictly around the house over pajamas. Chopans are thick, padded with cotton, and usually fit easily over a sweater or sports jacket. The sleeves are tailored extra long and wide for the cold weather, so that a person may stand about or walk clasping the wrists by opposite hands, thereby sealing off the sleeves—a great warming tactic in a place where few people wear gloves.

As with many other items of Uzbek material culture, Russian and Soviet ethnographers have researched chopans well. They have written extensively about the garment's origins, styles based on ethnic or tribal geography, analysis of style patterns, types of fabrics used, and the historic production centers. Additionally, they have described to what purposes the robes have been and continue to be worn (Sukhareva 1979; Sadykova et al., 1986; Zakharova et al., 1986). Such studies succeed in presenting culture as a series of museum exhibits; each ethnic or national group in the U.S.S.R. is be packaged neatly and differentiated from the others. Such scholarly writings, as painstakingly researched as many are, accomplished just this feat.

Beneficial as many of these books and articles have proved to students of Central Asia, they do not do a good job of explaining why such material culture should or could be used to express separatism. It is likely that the Soviet-calculated presentation of Central Asian peoples by politicians, ideologists, and even social scientists has contributed to the popular potential for making material items represent resurgent pride in one's own ethnicity.

Because my fieldwork stays in the mid-1990s coincided with a renewed popularity in wearing chopans, especially in the FV, it must also be said that this seeming defining article of Uzbek sartorial culture had been a kind of recent invention. In the countryside, it did not seem so easy to discern such a cultural happening, perhaps because much of any nation's countryside seems more old-fashioned to visiting urbanites. Moreover, the chopan has always been a normal part of men's attire within the villages during the cold months (November through April). The profusion of shell styles, such as the corduroy paisley mentioned previously, is not so common, however. Men traditionally wear black or blue silk or satin varieties, with the blue featuring prominently during funerals and funerary events; that is, these items are considered appropriate mourning attire.

When I asked villagers if they thought wearing chopans was becoming popular fashion, they confirmed the hunch and told me the proof was to be found in the number of people making and selling them in marketplaces; this kind of marketing was less pronounced a decade earlier. In fact, manufacture of chopans has become a fledgling cottage industry in Uzbekistan. Today many young men are less interested in appearing "modern," developed," or "hip" in the Russian sense, as would most surely have characterized youth styles for town and country Central Asians in the 1960s, 1970s, and 1980s. (This assertion is based on my rifling through hundreds of photos from informants' scrapbooks and photo albums from these decades.)

The concept of national distinctiveness goes hand-in-hand with national independence. For example, once Iran proclaimed it had abandoned the Western orbit after its revolution in 1979, neckties fell out of favor in that country, and a distinctly Iranian collarless shirt came into vogue. Some Russians have even taken to wearing chopans, especially in Tashkent's more Russo-centric districts. Wearing the chopan might signify an end to aping the dictates of Soviet/Russian attire, or an end to pretending that all cultures are becoming as one (a Russian one!).

Rather than seeing chopan wearing as something akin to Uzbek "retro" style or as a nostalgic act, it might be seen as another element of common ethnic affirmation and assertion. Moreover, it is relatively certain that if the garment were made from gold thread, silk, and inlaid pearls, it would not make the comeback it has, no matter how hard young Uzbek men would wish to celebrate their ethnic heritage. The fact that chopans are most often created by weaving simple materials and do not heavily tax the consumer also helps explain their comeback.

IDENTITY AND PLANTATION

In considering their identity, along with objectifying certain qualities as part of "a" or "the" national identity, Uzbeks often refer to what most regard as a key virtue—namely, their field labor. If there is some quintessence of a modern plantation peasant, then one may see it in the early mornings and toward dusk. The person's body, her very physical configuration, reveals qualities that figure as identity markers: Cut-up, gnarled, and overworked hands descend from a solid frame, now wiry and veiny, now brawny or bulky. People dress in filthy tatters. Looking exhausted, the person still with determination strides with hoe handle resting on a shoulder, face darkened and crevassed by endless sunny days, temporarily heedless of pains, thirst, and the hint of hunger. People make connections as they remark on their personhood, labor, and field sites:

- "All we Uzbeks know is hoeing."
- "For us, it all back and forth to the [cotton] fields."

- "An Uzbek woman has little time for anything besides her chores—watching kids, cooking, grazing the cow, picking cotton, cleaning up…"

Through such comments, rural people imply the strength of their work ethic, their unflagging willingness to do whatever it takes to make their lands productive and their households maintained. *Mekhnatkash* is a word used self-referentially and generally in Uzbekistan to describe Uzbek farming people; it means "labor loving" or "workaholic."

Self-representation to the contrary, it does not matter so much how capable and strong-willed the Boburkenters think they are individually and collectively, because they have put their faith in the god Technology for at least the last two generations. We see this when some people cannot equate being productive or developed without having technology available for everything. In most cases they are correct, but many people seem so enthralled by technology that they also think it impossible, for example, to make high-quality wines or good-quality furniture without sophisticated machinery. This is the legacy of Soviet industrialization married to the ingrained ideological desire to overtake the west in achievements and advances.

New American tractors were introduced into Uzbekistan only in the mid-1990s. Several informants wanted me to tell them how long it might be before one appeared in the fields of the Amir Temur (1997). One man who had seen a John Deere combine harvester in Andijan remarked that it made wheat harvesting very easy and required much less time in comparison to the sickle or Soviet harvester. He offered the following assessment:

> Whoa! That tractor was something to see. Beautifully colored, did a fast, smooth job of it! They say they're pretty durable and easy to handle, too. We certainly could use them here; they'd improve things a lot. Now I understand America's wealth. Building that kind of technology only boosts productivity.

Certainly, a good deal of what he said is commonsensical because better tractors would improve the situation for their farms, especially given the crucial importance of timing once a crop has matured. Technology can serve as a boon with the proper conditions. Here, regrettably, too many kolkhozniks have been blinded by the glare of the stainless steel of implements for too long. Many people appear to ignore the fact that better technological inputs cannot simply improve agricultural yields or do so in the most timely fashion.

While villagers expend long hours in nurturing their crops almost every day of the growing season, from April through October, their efforts too often seem tantamount to spinning one's wheels. Lots of sweat and motion do not necessarily advance or improve living conditions. New machinery cannot make soils richer, and it cannot prevent local managers and officials from stealing unspecified amounts from the various harvests. In short, Uzbekistan faces a systemic crisis in agriculture that will not be rectified solely by introducing new tractors.

Among the intricacies of the national labor ministry's salary grades for kolkhozniks is the stipulation that those who must work by hand (provided for in the past when farm machinery could not navigate fields due to inclement weather) are to be paid a higher salary than if most of the picking had been performed by machine. Today, of course, this stipulation is more irrelevant than ever. The average person is not paid according to any fixed schedule anyway. It almost seems that the state goes out of its way to drive people from its fields in pursuit of villagers' own basic needs that the former itself cannot provide.

Although this untoward consequence hinders the state's ability to monopolize the agricultural economy, it simply marks another signpost on the way toward making unhappy factotums out of most of the villagers. What results is a diversification in rural livelihoods—lifestyles, too—brought about by the government's market reforms. Diversification could prove beneficial in the long run, but for now it results from the languishing collective farm situation itself. Entrepreneurial activity remains the domain of only a few brave souls, as investment assets offer little return in this economy. Diversifying activities mostly constitute a scrambling type that involves the race for two basic consumer goods: (1) household-centered commodities, such as produce, other foodstuffs, and crafts; and (2) commodities bought as resale items from larger markets—that is, imported, mass-manufactured goods.

This attempt to transform the kolkhoz into a model of capitalistic self-sufficiency has become fundamental in a way similar to the all-out drive for collectivization in the first place. Nevertheless, it would be irresponsible to suggest that the levels of societal disruptiveness, violence, and the misery of hunger and starvation associated with these sea changes compare; they do not.

Psychologically, however, a way of life to which people were mostly reconciled has been quickly pulled away. The great numbers of working-age residents and retirees (ages 35 to 75) in Uzbekistan certainly understand the changes put forth and proposed, yet many of them continue to look to the state to organize projects and create conditions (from building plants, to constructing factories, to bringing in foreign capital, to supplying farm inputs) that will enable them to regain their old living standards. As alluded to several times earlier, this expectation is not based on faith or implicit trust placed in the personalities and organs of state power; rather, it reflects the fact that people have grown accustomed to the state playing the absolute hegemon where national economic initiatives or new policies are at issue. Even when state leaders communicate to people that they should act as they see fit and speak their own minds, it still feels as if the people are waiting for the state to tell them how to do it and what to say. This inertia lies at the heart of my position in reference to psychological intractability.

At street level, whether we peek into a state shop or stroll through a local bazaar, most people see the state receding from public life. Villagers know in the broadest sense that it is time to make it on their own, but it remains difficult for people to shake the feeling that because no unknown force caused them to lose so much, the new leadership itself is culpable and really must do more on behalf of the economy's reeling agricultural sector. After all, most of the country's population is involved in agriculture, the peasants feed Uzbekistan, and they bring in most of the country's precious foreign capital via cotton production.

To a Westerner, the inventory from a village store appears to demonstrate the antithesis of what one would believe such a consumer place represents to a rural community, such as modernization. It should bring about the arrival of the developed world in underdeveloped regions, just as it really did in the 1930s in Uzbek villages; such shops were part of the socialist alternative to capitalist development in the Third World, although the overall ends were similar. Village stores, according to villagers themselves, were much better stocked, with a greater quantity and variety of goods, until 1991 (a time when an inflationary cycle was coming to an end).

Reveling in its old, indefatigable role as inspirational guru on behalf of the masses, the Uzbek leadership focuses only on the good and the getting better—pure, Soviet style. But in the end, all of this powdering of blemishes (economic weaknesses and failures) ultimately winds up undermining support for the Uzbek leaders. Because people are so used to Soviet propaganda, common first reactions to many news items that emphasize improving national conditions include denial of their validity. Because so little changes substantially, skepticism proves to render a truer picture of reality than simply a negative take on reality. An even more important fact here is that villagers and the state tacitly agree about the subject of kolkhoz work: The state demands high qualities and high yields of cotton and wheat, but admits it cannot guarantee a living wage in exchange for productivity. The state leaders also realize that peasant farmers wish the de-collectivization of agriculture was carefully managed and subsidized, as contradictory as the last point seems. Because it is not, however, both parties seek out and to a limited degree allow money-making affairs that do not coincide with state demands.

F I G U R E   6.3   New entrepreneurs in a well-stocked shop of Boburkent. Most items are imported, pricy, and not necessities.

In the end, the peasants feel the squeeze. They understand that they are last in line to receive a part of the state's largesse or its attention on the road to becoming capitalist. Over time, people actually do want less and less state interference when they attempt to pursue independent strategies. Unfortunately, not being interfered with proves a taxing chore in itself, given that the authorities view the accumulation of even the smallest amount of capital in villagers' hands with asperity.

When it comes to laws regulating private trade, interest rates on loans, rules for establishing businesses, and the sale of real estate, the state alters the playing field quite often. Thus making money independently and legally requires even greater finesse, payoffs, and bribes than would seem possible. To many informants, the state's *raison d'etre* consists of little other than fining and penalizing. The fact that most small-scale contracts between an individual and a local business or institution, such as a hospital, remain verbal does little to promote the establishment of legally binding agreements. Villagers no sooner agree that this should be the case before they remind an outsider that legal documents or provisions also enable another government office to readily intrude on the process, thereby ensuring that a third authoritative party will want its own cut. As one man told me in reference to real estate sales and the nefarious role of the notary public, "I don't need to give money to someone who wouldn't do much for me anyway if a problem with my business partner arose." The implication here is that one has to pay the notary a lot just to substantiate the act of making a deal legal.

As for as business agreements go, this begs the question: What recourse does a subordinate villager have if a deal goes awry—for example, if a client reneges on a deal or cheats? When asked about this possibility, one informant said, "I'm not worried about that. We are the kind of people who honor our agreements. Don't you see there's no place to hide from me or run? We all know each other here." Verbal agreements apparently are articles of faith. This informant thinks it has to work out well because it should. Possibly, location does work in favor of villagers: Familiarity and the relative confinement of villages militate against unethical high jinks. Negative reciprocity in this setting would be riskier than the fact of simple oral agreements.

When writing about rural life, anthropologists have to be cautious about inadvertently caricaturing notions of honor and family, although Uzbeks themselves often invoke such ethnically defining traits. By the same token, one should not disparage the terms as orientalizing devices cavalierly imposed on village life. In daily life, they serve as core, guiding values. However, honor can become a value of convenience, and family bonds may fray easily over issues as far removed as social behavior and marriage arrangements. Naturally, it is easy to oversimplify the complexity of family life and a person's abstract desire to be honorable.

Discussing interfamilial commitments, one embittered man asked me rhetorically:

> Would you put your trust in some relative who's never going to come through for you or in a real friend who always helps you? Look, people in your family ... there are all kinds, but a friend will be there; friends care about each other.

Honoring agreements or commitments becomes an increasingly elusive state of mind depending on how an individual perceives who it is promising to do what. Therefore, a given person has an intuitive sense of how likely another will be to keep his or her word, based either on that person's reputation or his own dealings with that person in the pas—unless, of course, the given individual judges character badly, a problem that anyone may suffer. Robert Canfield (2007:45–57), drawing on his experiences among the Hazara of Afghanistan, notes that we are all capable of misunderstanding the cultural conventions that we have been taught, especially when we act within cultural norms. This point may be more surprising and less obvious than it would appear, for villagers are not wont to refuse requests (at least not outright), but always answer with "*Hop*" or "*Bopti*," ("Sure" or "Okay"), something all Uzbeks know to be an ambiguous affirmation in response to a request.

Here I am not necessarily talking about honor in the sense of machismo or manliness, or of political leadership and face, as many other anthropologists working in the Middle East, North Africa, or the Caucasus have described (Bourdieu 1977; Abu-Lughod 1986; Stewart 1994; Grant and Yalcin-Heckmann 2007). Rather, I am considering both sexes when I speak of honor. Honor here connotes both notions of commitment and the giving of one's word. It is the implied honorableness in the phrase, "I'll come by for you at 7:30 tomorrow morning and drive you to the border." Or it may be the honor of carrying out someone request for an item, if the person who would be honorable promises to bring back the requested thing.

Ideally, villagers believe in the importance of honoring one's word or conducting oneself honorably because they view it as a ballast of their mores. Still, for many, there also exists a counterweight to this concept, a sort of relativism that may be derived from the inability, impermissibility, or unwillingness among authorities and the powerful to act honorably. This concept permeates much of their daily lives. It has helped to establish a world that quite often is haphazard or incidental, and the result assumes a quality of forces beyond one's own control in the face of many events, big and small, that ordinarily would bring about anger and frustration. It allows for the diffusion of strained feelings, as the offended party will give the offender the benefit of the doubt. For example, the villager may suggest, "Could have been out of his hands or beyond his control"—and the offender is off the hook. Dishonor, in a way, has become an acceptable form of conduct, if it turns out that these consequences were the result either of a forbidding state or "our busted system" ("*tuzimiz chatoq*"). The latter Uzbek phrase (an oft-heard invocation) may refer to problems with transportation, the post office, or communications among others. It implies a post-Soviet disorder.

The following list highlights several hypothetical (reality-based) instances of acceptable dishonor based on village happenings and problems associated with faulty infrastructure and unhelpful authority:

- "I tried to call and tell you that I couldn't come, but the phone's not working."

- "It's too bad you had to come all this way, but the *hokimiiat* will not permit us to copy that map for you."
- "Of course, I would have driven you, but we can't find any gasoline."
- "I know we were supposed to go hunting today, but the police have my guns, and I can't get them back unless I pay a fee; I don't have money just now."

Clearly, each explanation comes with its own reasonable excuse. Who is really to blame? In time, one begins to tease out a locus for honor that removes it from its known place and situates it in the very act of making the declaration. That is, the honor itself now lies in the sentiment. One ultimately judges the speaker silently and notes the experience for future reference. All one can say to maintain propriety and an atmosphere of friendliness is, "It was good of you to offer."

Given the travails of the post-Soviet period, the tendency to dishonorably rely on "forces beyond my control" has grown. This makes the *dishonoree* none the happier, but it is considered very bad form to show rancor or to call the dishonorable person's bluff. Things work out more peacefully this way. Over time, people develop a keener sense of separating out the respectable from the disreputable, and, eventually, they will deal as little as possible with the latter type.

CONCLUSION

While today's collective farm workers live a hybridized peasant existence on agricultural units that the Uzbek state treats as neglected plantations, the farms' residents themselves have to take whatever initiatives exist while still maintaining their relationship to farming, and especially the all-important cotton planting and harvesting seasons. In an ironic twist, as farm-derived incomes and mechanization decline, the state needs more hands in the cotton fields than it has in several decades. For the residents of kolkhozes, however, they often cannot submit to these coercive demands and still survive. Instead, they seek wages and employment in three main arenas: (1) the local, regional, and urban marketplaces; (2) relocation to the country's cities to engage in all manner of work; and (3) in pursuit of serious remuneration, migration abroad. Villagers almost never seek confrontational strategies in their interpersonal working relations or with their immediate authorities. Nevertheless, the collapse of the socialist system more than 15 years ago clearly left the Uzbek people with an economic predicament that makes it practically impossible to survive only on what the farm provides.

Increasing globalization, religious activism, and violent repression continue to harshly affect the Uzbek rural population. The process of labor migration from Uzbekistan, alternative approaches to religion, and the Andijan riot and killings of 2005 imply that Uzbekistan is poised to experience increasing hardships and even more turmoil. In response, many citizens are choosing to get away from their country rather than challenge the overwhelming forces of an implacable authoritarian state. In this climate, labor migration in the short term allows both citizens and state authorities a way out of antagonism and clashing positions.

QUESTIONS

1. Which options for work and income attract villagers given the poor rewards for cotton farming?
2. Since the demise of the Soviet Union, which manifestations of Uzbek identity have emerged more strongly in terms of clothing, activities, and other cultural aspects?

Conclusion

To conclude this book, I focus on the increasing globalization, religious activism, and repression that are currently affecting the rural Uzbek population. The process of labor migration, alternative approaches to religion, and the Andijan riot and killings of 2005 show that Uzbekistan seems poised for increasing hardships and turmoil. Many citizens are choosing simply to get away rather than challenge the overwhelming forces of authoritarian rule. In this climate, migration in the short term allows both citizens and state authorities a way out of antagonism and clashing positions.

ANDIJAN VIOLENCE: CONTINUING DETERIORATION OR WATERSHED?

If Uzbeks planned direct actions, from protests to strikes, or even mere public voicing of complaints and grievances to improve basic conditions, such planning now has become mostly contemplation as it became clearer recently that the state will tolerate little dissent. People understood this during the late 1990s and into the early 2000s, but nothing served notice quite like the Andijan violence of 2005. Before providing an overview of that event, it seems reasonable to assert that since the events in Andijan, most rural Uzbeks have decided that challenging the state might best be achieved by ignoring deep-seated outrage and antagonism and, instead, seeking better conditions by leaving Uzbekistan. The other action-oriented strategies reside in religious lifestyles and religious political extremism, including Islamist terrorism, but the latter is not popular and has swept up perhaps a few thousand people in this country. For Uzbekistan, the Andijan riot proved a watershed event in the sense that it marked an end to the supposition that the first post-Soviet regime was simply a slow reformer but committed to market principles and pluralism. Rather, it became a new animal—a nonwelfare, neo-Stalinist state. If the leadership chose to emulate a single role model, it was as much China as Russia, but certainly not the United States or Germany.

Investigative journalists and scholars rightly paid attention to the immediate events that led up to the demonstrations and subsequent killings in Andijan that transpired in May 2005. However, the level of dissatisfaction and frustration that brought tens of thousands of urban residents out into the streets of Uzbekistan's easternmost city (population 300,000) had been building for years. And if the Andijan riot had not happened when it did, it is likely that this kind of terrible event would have happened elsewhere, as so many millions of people sympathized with their Ferghana Valley countrymen. Curiously, what led to the final explosion that resulted in the deaths of at least hundreds of citizens (estimates ranged from fewer than 200 to more than 1000 casualties) encapsulates the major issues/crises of contemporary life: poverty, state oppression, terrorism, entrepreneurialism, and Islam.

Now for the immediate background: During the spring of 2005, a legal trial in Andijan involving a number of businessmen and their associates took place. The charges were an odd mix of allegations, including corruption, illegal business practices, and Islamic extremism or terrorism. The accused supposedly constituted part of a movement known as Akromiya, named after the group's founder, Akrom Yuldashev. On the basis of circumstantial evidence, the Uzbek government argued that members of Akromiya used their business networks and earnings to recruit people first toward a fundamentalist-style Islam and then toward a religious view of the world that would cause members to be willing to take extreme actions to overthrow the government by committing themselves to *jihad* by force. Members of the so-called Akromiya denied these charges. As had happened so often in Uzbekistan in the past when treasonous allegation was at issue, the accused were found guilty.

While this trial garnered about as much press attention within Uzbekistan and abroad as anything taking place in Central Asia does, more trouble was brewing in the heart of the city. Some of these public outpourings of anger were, indeed, connected to the trial of the "Akromists," more than 20 of whom had been sent to the main city prison. While all hell broke loose after the accused were found guilty, the trouble related to the wishes of thousands of protesters who wanted to see President Karimov and tell him about their problems relating to continuing impoverishment and the lack of opportunities combined with police abuse and corruption. Crowds congregated in Bobur Square (named after a famous Central Asian leader of the sixteenth century who was born in Andijan, and who went on to found the Mughal Dynasty of India). The evening before the violence occurred, many in the crowd took heart because they heard that the president was on his way to Andijan, but his arrival never came to pass.

During the morning of May 13, elite Interior Ministry troops arrived in armored personnel carriers near Bobur Square. Rather than warning the crowds to disperse, they opened fire on the protesters, injuring and killing indiscriminately, according to numerous eyewitnesses. But the plot thickened even further: A riot also occurred that day in the main prison, with members of "Akromiya" being freed and guards taken hostage. Armed protesters also were present in Bobur Square. During the shooting, these armed protesters took civil servants hostage amid the din of slogans, such as "God is Great!" and "Freedom!" Some protesters urged others to leave the square, while some urged them to stay.

Hours after the smoke had cleared, it became clear that hundreds lay dead. Thousands sought to escape the wrath of the security forces, fleeing on foot some 30 miles to the northeast, to Uzbekistan's less oppressive neighbor, Kyrgyzstan. Indeed, their flight did not stop until some of those who had been on the square arrived as far to the west as Romania and the United States.

How many were killed in Bobur Square and the ensuing panic? 200? 500? 1300? Estimates vary. Known as an undemocratic regime, the government was roundly condemned among most Western powers, including the United States, and has been treated more or less as a pariah state since this event. Nevertheless, all the facts are not in, and they may not be in for years.

The Uzbek government wanted nothing to do with international investigations after the shootings, and it would not allow any to be undertaken, claiming such activities would be a violation of Uzbek sovereignty. So is there a likely answer to the questions of what really happened and why the government killed perhaps hundreds of people? Definitively, no, but with conjecture, yes. I propose a credible scenario: The Uzbek authorities probably would have preferred not to kill protesters, but determined that extremists either were among them or led them. Therefore, they decided kill as many as necessary to make sure the extremists died. Outsiders, this author included, consider that this kind of approach mutually reinforces the state's harshness and paranoia when dealing with dissenters, all the while leading more and more people to consider the necessity of violence to achieve a new solution.

THE TERRORS OF INDEPENDENCE

During the 1990s, the Uzbek leadership talked a lot about its status quo, something it labeled "Peace and Stability." People in Boburkent, whether very supportive of the government or not, would point to this national condition when I asked them about their attitude toward national leaders. A person might say, "Well, if you compare us to Tajikistan [a southern neighbor and country that endured civil war from 1991 to 1997], at least we have peace and stability," or "It's obvious the economy is not good, but fortunately there's no war and the country's stable." All of this began changing in the late 1990s.

What began happening with greater frequency in the late 1990s was terrorism. Islamist terror—a term that has to be qualified because of the manipulations by security forces—probably stems from unresolved issues concerning religious freedom and, more pointedly, from the state's intolerance of devoutness since the early 1990s. Summarily, President Karimov never seems to have intended tolerating Islam in public life, but has become so wedded to a secular model that he has treated devout Muslims with contempt and politicized Muslims as

Courtesy of Russell Zanca

FIGURE C.1   A local mullo outside a rural home.

enemies. Various incidents from the early 1990s involving the president and organized activists in the Ferghana Valley attest to this internecine rivalry. By 1997, acts of terror were being perpetrated in the Ferghana Valley that involved the killing of law enforcement personnel. Such crimes probably stemmed as much from rural disgust with corruption and injustice as they did from a desire to take the country in a more religious direction. Nevertheless, they set the stage for bigger, nation-wide acts of terror.

In February 1999, powerful explosions rocked Tashkent, killing tens of people, and supposedly aimed at assassinating Karimov. A group that has come to be known as the Islamic Movement of Uzbekistan (I.M.U.) has been blamed for these and other attacks, and many of those who stood trial in Tashkent for the bombings have been executed. However, skeptics both within and outside of Uzbekistan raised doubts about the parties whom the government blamed for these attacks, and some conspiracy-minded critics claim the government itself was responsible for setting off the bombs. Again, given the Uzbek authorities' unwillingness to allow independent investigations into these and subsequent acts, it is difficult to imagine that we soon will have definitive answers to these lingering questions. At the same time, it is unreasonable to pretend Uzbekistan has no problem with terrorists seeking to overthrow the regime. It does. One result of this and other acts through 2004, culminating in the Andijan events, is that Uzbekistan is not a country of peace and stability.

While terrorism has undermined the state's smooth sailing mantra, it has also provided it with the pretext to clamp down on any and all dissenting forces. Thus, since 1999, the Uzbek regime has waged an unrelenting campaign to eliminate all forms of opposition, mainly in the name of stamping out terror. Islamism (roughly defined as the use of Islam to advance the cause of a theocratic government based on a particular orthodoxy), visibly in the guise of organizations such as the I.M.U., probably does not possess sufficient popularity to overthrow Uzbekistan's non-democratically elected government, generally because Uzbeks do not have a strong tradition of Islamism.

In 2001, the United States cultivated better relations with the Uzbek government because, in addition to Uzbekistan's problems with terror, the United States saw Uzbekistan as a willing ally in its war in Afghanistan, Uzbekistan's southern neighbor. U.S. authorities apparently turned a blind eye to Uzbekistan's disquieting human rights record in the name of combating terrorism. Many observers noted that the Karimov regime used this relationship to arrest and repress thousands of citizens, mostly by claiming that the practicing Muslims picked up by the government forces were involved in terrorism, if not outright members of terrorist organizations. Observers of Uzbekistan, this author included, think that in addition to immorality these policies have only furthered a self-fulfilling prophecy—viz., the creation of more would-be Islamists by repressing people on specious grounds or, even worse, by planting evidence (including narcotics and firearms). Such measures are the complete antithesis of a "peace and stability" outlook; in fact, they reflect the emergence of a "police state" approach toward governance.

Of course, from the current regime's perspective, its governance is successful. After all, Karimov remains the president, virtually no dissent is tolerated, and it even appears—at least in the short term—that the Andijan violence resulted in a cowered population, one unwilling to take the risks associated with change-inducing, large-scale activity (Tavernise 2008).

Islamists exist, and their numbers could continue to grow. Even so, there are currently no serious indications that devout activists, dedicated to either violent or nonviolent regime change, pose a major challenge to the state. Economically, the Uzbek government has also succeeded in limiting entrepreneurialism and the emergence of an independent middle class both by heavily regulating the economic activities in rural areas and by controlling banking transactions and accounts. In essence, the government's tight control over the domestic cotton industry is more or less mirrored by what goes on across the country.

This approach toward economic control, which affects seemingly very low-level economic activities, including rural livestock sales or the renting of land and property, also reaches foreign investors. Even determined businesspeople from countries such as Turkey and the United States have left Uzbekistan because of the onerous imposition of regulations, currency conversion restrictions, and taxation rates. All of these measures seem to fly in the face of an approach designed to enrich Uzbekistan and allow for expanded growth throughout the country. In reality, the state guides itself not by any Western-inspired free market development scheme, but rather by other authoritarian models available much closer to home—to wit, Russia and China. Eurasia's great hegemons support the ways in which Uzbekistan cracks down on dissent and controls its economy because they follow practices laid down originally under Communist politics—a past they all understand and share.

Courtesy of Russell Zanca

FIGURE C.2 Religious men in Namangan at a social event.

THE EMPTYING OF UZBEKISTAN OWING
TO LABOR MIGRATION

Essentially, the current regime's thwarting of freedoms, bolstered by its willing-ness to imprison, torture, and execute those who supposedly contravene the so-cial order, leaves urban and rural people alike with few choices other than enduring current conditions as they do everything possible to make their living quietly. The one significant choice of the post-Soviet era that Uzbeks have been making with greater frequency since 2000 is the one to work abroad, ostensibly to make money and support families in Uzbekistan while also trying to engineer a better life for individuals who take the risk to leave and work elsewhere. Actu-ally, Uzbekistan's experiences with labor migration are not unique among Eurasian countries, but the circumstances for each country, such as neighbors Kyrgyzstan and Tajikistan, are. The argument here takes the view that the com-bination of economic fetters and the snuffing out of freedom of conscience—be it political or religious—practically force millions of people to leave at least temporarily.

Labor migration began in the 1990s, often involving young people who trav-eled to Russia or Turkey and brought back goods to sell; the literature refers to this process as "shuttle trade." The far more dangerous and harmful type of early labor migration from Uzbekistan involved mainly young women who either knowingly or unknowingly worked abroad (in a much wider range of countries) as prostitutes. Of course, these labor ventures also operated on an intra-Uzbek level as a rural–urban phenomenon. At first, there was more of an ethnic component to these movements, especially prostitution, which involved many more non-Uzbeks, especially Russian, Ukrainian, and other non-Central Asian settler populations. Eventually, however, the ethnic imbalance changed as many young Uzbek women, even from rural areas, adopted these strategies.

Before engaging in a discussion of labor migration and its particular saliency to the life of villagers throughout rural Uzbekistan, readers should understand that these processes affecting millions are characteristic of those that have been and are now taking place in many countries of the non-Western world. Despite the government's authoritarianism and harsh dictatorship, Uzbekistan has moved into the contemporary capitalist world. Economic dislocation and migration appear to be inevitable results of the disbanding of the erstwhile command-administrative system and economy that existed for nearly 70 years under Communism. In the future, more scholarly investigation will look to compare the experiences of people in the postsocialist countries, especially those considered underdeveloped, such as Uzbekistan and Tajikistan (as opposed to, say, Hungary and Poland) to citizens of nonsocialist countries of Africa and Asia. Efforts will look at such phenomena as the general education of migrants, intentions of migration, demographic factors of the people migrating, types of jobs and professions available to migrants, the importance and amounts of remittances (monies sent back to the country of origin), the duration of migration in individuals' lives, and the rights of migrants in countries of destination, among many other factors.

Were it not the case that millions of Uzbeks work abroad, one has to wonder if massive political rebellion, acts of Islamist terrorism, or even increased acts of nonviolent resistance to the state would not be commonplace. While the answer is impossible to know (especially because we cannot know definitively what drives anti-state violence even now), it is curious that the Uzbek state allows so many people, especially its youth, to try to make ends meet and support families by working abroad. This fact is curious because the leadership tries to control virtually all channels of information both within Uzbekistan and from outside the country, whether in the form of mass media or the Internet. The state does so by curtailing any independent reporting and blocking news websites in addition to restricting internet access. Still, with so many people coming and going, rural people have a much better sense of what is going on in the world than they would have had during most of the Soviet era.

In recent years, anthropologists have devoted much intellectual energy to globalization. The globalization trend implies many things, but chiefly it signifies a world that is in rapid, almost uncontrollable flux because of capitalist economics that inadvertently cause massive movements of humanity from earth's poorest countries to the wealthiest nations. Labor migration has become an important subject within general globalization studies. One aspect of this subject is transnationalism—a term that implies a newer model of immigration. Transnationalism may include well educated, highly skilled people who move between countries such as India, Germany, and the United States with frequency and smoothness (and sometimes with plenty of cash), as well as the uneducated and unskilled who move from Uzbekistan to Kazakhstan to Russia or from Senegal to France. The main idea is that labor migrants today move rapidly, and maybe have no intention of living abroad for longer than some specified period. Furthermore, international restrictions on immigration and acquiring citizenship differ today compared to the rules that applied just a few generations ago in the wealthiest countries. Although labor migrants from Eurasia may make a new life for themselves in whatever working conditions they enter into, under the transnationalist understanding they are likely to look at migration as a temporary measure to improve not only their own lives, but also—and maybe more importantly—the lives of the family members whom they have left behind. This makes labor migration rather different from patterns noted as recently as 25 years ago, when most people migrated as families to make a new life for themselves and their children in their newly adopted countries.

The conditions of labor migration throughout Eurasia almost seem ideal because people leave countries with high unemployment and seek work in countries where employment opportunities abound. This trend partly explains why Uzbek choose Kazakhstan and Russia as targets for emigration. Also, both Kazakhstan and Russia have experienced the kinds of boom times that remain unimaginable in Uzbekistan. Actually, labor migrants moved about in the Soviet period as well. However, a major difference between then and now is that migration was regulated legally and migrants generally were well paid for their efforts, especially those who decided to accept industrial jobs, railway work, and other positions key to the basic economy. Even those people who, in the 1970s and 1980s, temporarily moved north to sell produce made out well and recall their experiences favorably. Today, however, what appears to be a normal process, in principle, turns out to be highly risky, unregulated and even dangerous for the millions of men and women opting to move. Uzbek labor migrants face at least three major risks in the post-Soviet era:

- Gross exploitation and vulnerability as illegal migrants in agriculture, industry, and prostitution
- Virtual enslavement if documents are confiscated
- Xenophobia and racism that can lead to violent attacks and murder by organized groups

Generally, villagers tend to stick to migration patterns that reflect their know-how; that is, they tend to migrate for the purposes of agricultural work, whether in the vast cotton and wheat fields of southern Kazakhstan, or in Russia's potato and cabbage farms. When the mainly young men who choose to immigrate hop on buses and trains to get to their destinations, they often encounter ordeals if they do not participate in a well-developed network of fellow migrants who have gone before. Given that moving among newly independent countries now entails border crossings, the would-be migrants are subject to illegal payouts to border guards and rail police once they cross into, say, Kazakhstan from Uzbekistan. Even worse, the security personnel sometimes seize a person's passport and other vital documents, and they may even forcibly throw the

Uzbek citizens off the bus or train. However, these are not random acts of senseless abuse.

Suppose a youth travels from Boburkent to Qyzylorda (Kazakhstan) because he knows that the tobacco harvest will soon begin, but his documents are confiscated and he is kicked off a train in what he considers the middle of nowhere. Unbeknownst to him is the arrangement between local landowners and the security personnel. The latter are bribed or paid off to help ensure a steady supply of what has become virtual slave labor. The landowner tells the Uzbek that he will get his documents back, along with good wages, if he just works for his enterprise. What choice does the young man have? Whom can he rely on? He has no protection and no established network of countrymen who will help him. This scenario is not restricted to agricultural areas of southern Kazakhstan, but also affects young migrants throughout rural areas and cities in Eurasia. Migrants are vulnerable partly because they are so desperate for work, and partly because there are few enforceable legal controls or agreements among the Eurasian countries designed to aid migrants and protect their rights—not to be enslaved, for example.

Lest the reader consider that slavery in this sense is permanent or something akin to the U.S. model of slavery that applied in the eighteenth and nineteenth centuries, it should be noted that this practice really is something different— though terrible nonetheless for those who fall victim to it. Basically, people are deprived of the freedom to move and they receive no wages. At the end of some fixed period (say, six months or one year), the landowner, plant owner, or businessman usually just casts the person off, perhaps giving back the documents, and, in the best of worlds, some remuneration for this grossly exploited labor. This emerging postsocialist phenomenon it is widespread, but it is not a pervasive practice everywhere. Most writings about Eurasian migrant slavery appear on Internet sites and in journalistic accounts. The scholarship necessary to examine this issue surely will be risky but should be a part of our focus in the social sciences. Again, while not much research has been undertaken specifically with regard to this modern slavery, there is a growing literature devoted to Eurasian labor migration.

If there are success stories among labor migrants, they probably involve those Uzbeks who have specifically chosen to migrate to established Uzbek communities—that is, places where Uzbeks do not simply farm but also work as professionals and own their own businesses. Examples of such places include Moscow, Ivanovo (east of Moscow), and Astrakhan in southern Russia near the Volga River. Although nothing is easy about establishing oneself and working in such environments, Uzbeks eventually are able to accumulate wages and remit substantial monies back home. For migrants in Russia who steadily earn money and support relatives in Uzbekistan, there is still one colossal risk, however.

Xenophobia and racism exist in Russia just as they do in many parts of the world where people feel their communities, towns, and cities are populated by people who may be newcomers, and by people whom the majority and dominant population fear and despise. The worst manifestations of this trend in Russia occur when organized gangs of skinheads or nationalists attack and either injure or murder the "foreigners." I put "foreigners" in quotes here for two reasons: (1) Uzbeks, for example, were not necessarily foreigners before 1991 in Russia or anywhere else in the former Soviet Union, and (2) the marauding gangs have mistakenly murdered Russian citizens because they "looked different." While scholars debate the degree to which feelings of ethnic distinction and separateness are wholly modern political constructions or something much more deeply rooted in human self-awareness of cultural differences (Brubaker 2003; Hale 2008), it is probably safe to say that interethnic tensions increase when people of different ethnicities do not socialize, when they (Russians, in the present case) strongly perceive that newcomers are taking things (jobs, resources) that belong to the majority population, and when states do not intervene strongly to try to prevent such behavior. No matter how synergistic one might think this migration should prove to both countries (owing to the Uzbek surfeit of labor and the Russian shortage of labor), the relations are anything but harmonious and represent the third major risk to Uzbek individuals' well-being in this discussion of labor migration.

Before ending this discussion and summing up this book, it is necessary to discuss a final serious aspect of labor migration—namely, the significant depopulation of Uzbekistan. While figures and statistics related to labor migration vary widely, estimates suggest that between 10 percent and 25 percent of Uzbekistan's population has left the country for employment elsewhere. It seems clear that Uzbekistan could not sustain its economy without vast numbers of its people working abroad. If we err on the conservative side, this means that approximately 3 million people have left or live outside of Uzbekistan at any one time, even as they retain their Uzbek citizenship. Obviously, the remittances that these millions of immigrants send to their Uzbek-bound families becomes part of a lifeline for millions of others, so it's nearly impossible to conceive that any adult citizen of Uzbekistan is not directly or indirectly part of the migration picture. Migration from the Caucasus, Central Asia, and Eastern Europe to Russia has been so great, in fact, that by 2006 Russia became the second leading destination for migrants, after the United States.

In the absence of reliable data, anthropologists appreciate anecdotal evidence that they are able to scrutinize based on previous experiences. In 2008, I talked to a colleague, Dr. Marianne Kamp, who had just visited Tashkent. I asked her about her travels and findings, the fortunes of mutual friends, and so on, and then I asked about the general political and social climate. In a nutshell, Kamp was amazed by how "empty" the city seemed, especially when she decided to visit an ordinarily crowded open-air market on a Sunday morning. The Chorsu Bazaar sits in Tashkent's old city, and has long served as an intense hub of commerce on Sunday mornings. Typically, throngs have packed in so tightly that one simply pushes and jostles one's way through the paths to visit various stalls or areas of merchandise. Kamp claimed it was not crowded at all during her Sunday visit; neither, she said, was the city metro, ordinarily a mob scene on the weekends, too. These experiences related to marketing and public transportation in Tashkent, taken with others, convinced her that labor migration was having a substantial impact on depopulation.

INTERDEPENDENCE AND RESEARCH NEEDS

In the Uzbek countryside, people experience a different cost of living. While they may eat well from their garden patches, of their own produce and animals, they are dependent on the outside world for all sorts of basic necessities. We know that the exodus from the countryside is large and will remain so for the foreseeable future. The question that looms concerns the sustainability of rural economies and lifestyles. Who will continue farming? Beyond this, we must ask all of the detailed questions connected to the national economy's backbone (cotton)—how much wealth it might generate, who constitutes the labor force, which kinds of coercive actions the state will take to ensure a satisfying harvest, and so on. For anthropologists interested in Eurasia and rural life, these farming communities will continue to play a role in research that connects people to an international system in ways barely known less than 20 years ago.

More than four decades ago, Eric Wolf began writing a kind of anthropology that confronted most anthropologists with what they themselves knew and had been exposed to, but which they still did not write directly: Peasants and most other seemingly isolated peoples from the non-Western world were much more connected to a global system than anthropologists had traditionally suggested. That global system is capitalism. It is in Wolf's sense of connectedness that I have tried to write this book, all the while maintaining that the village way of life that I happened upon just after the breakup of the U.S.S.R. remained relatively unknown to Western audiences. As it turns out, this way of life was rapidly changing. Given the changes discussed throughout the book—be it in

Courtesy of Russell Zanca

FIGURE C.3 Boys in the mid-1990s. What does their future hold in light of the loss of the kolkhoz system? Will they leave Uzbekistan?

wedding practices, cotton fields labor, or onerous political restrictions and violence—I would argue that there is an odd simultaneity of villagers being pulled back toward an earlier type of lean peasant existence, even as they seek out all sorts of opportunities and experiences beyond agriculture.

Surely, it is senseless to sugarcoat the abuses and poverty of the Communist era in Uzbekistan. Communist rule came to an end nearly 20 years ago, and for its seven decades included many periods of incomparable hardship and human cruelty. Nevertheless, when it expired, Uzbek villagers knew a patterned regularity and standard of living unparalleled by their twentieth–century standards. If Soviet Communism integrated the rural Central Asian Uzbeks into Western modernization, albeit in a unique and hybridized socialist model, the direction in which the free market is moving them remains a work in progress.

The end of Communism in east–central Europe and Eurasia (the former Soviet space) allowed a new generation of scholars from the social sciences and humanities to initiate long-term research in institutions, cities, and villages in ways that really had not been possible for almost the whole of the twentieth century. Anthropologists especially have benefited from these opportunities, and my hope is that this book serves as both a contribution to the anthropology of Eurasia and an inspiration to students to undertake their own fieldwork projects in Eurasia before long.

Bibliography

Alimova, D. A., Editor. 1991. *Zhenskii Vopros v Srednei Azii: Istoriia Izucheniia I Sovremennye Problemy.* Tashkent: Izdatel'stvo FAN Akademii Nauk Republiki Uzbekistan.

Alimova, D. A., Editor. 2006. *Tragediia Sredneaziatskogo Kishlaka: Kollektivizatsiia, Raskulachivanie, Ssylka, 1929–1955* (3 vols.). Tashkent: Shark.

Aminova, R. Kh. 1969. *Agrarnye Preobrazovaniia v Uzbekistane Nakkanune Sploshnoi Kollektivizatsii (1925–1929).* Tashkent: Izdatel'stvo FAN Uzbekskoi SSR.

Arnott, Margaret Louise. 1975. The Beads of Mani. In *Gastronomy: The Anthropology of Food and Food Habits*, Ed. Margaret L. Arnott. Pp. 297–304. The Hague: Mouton Publishers.

Arsen'eva, K. K. and F. F. Petrushevskago, Editors. 1900. Sarty. In *Enttsiklopedicheskii Slovar* (56). Pp. 449–451. Sankt Peterburg: Brokgauz-Efron Publishers.

Asian Development Bank. 2001. Women in the Republic of Uzbekistan: Country Briefing Paper. http://www.adb.org/Documents/ Books/Country_Briefing_Papers/ Women_in_Uzbekistan/

Balfet, Helene. 1975. Bread in Some Regions of the Mediterranean Area: A Contribution to the Studies on Eating Habits. In *Gastronomy: The Anthropology of Food and Food Habits*, Ed. Margaret L. Arnott. Pp. 305–314. The Hague: Mouton Publishers.

Bartlett, Peggy F. 1980. *Agricultural Decision Making: Anthropological Contributions to Rural Devlopment.* New York: Academic Press.

Bauman, Zygmunt. 1987. *Legislators and Interpreters: On Modernity, Postmodernity, and Intellectuals.* Ithaca, NY: Cornell University Press.

Bernshtam, A. N. 1951. *Drevnaia Fergana.* Tashkent: Izdatel'stvo Akademii Nauk UzSSR.

Bikjanova, M. 1959. *Sem'ia na Kolkhozakh Uzbekistana.* Tashkent: Izdatel'stvo Akademii Nauka UzSSR.

Bobokulov, Inomjon. 2006. Central Asia: Is There an Alternative to Regional Integration? *Central Asian Survey* 25(1–2): 75–91.

Bourdieu, Pierre. 1977. *Outline of a Theory of Practice.* Translated by Richard Nice. Cambridge, UK: Cambridge University Press.

Bourdieu, Pierre. 1990 *The Logic of Practice*. Palo Alto, CA: Stanford University Press.

Brower, Daniel. 2003. *Turkestan and the Fate of the Russian Empire*. London and New York: Routledge Curzon.

Cohen, Ronald. 1994. Growth Is Development, Distribution Is Politics. In *Research in Economic Anthropology* (Vol. 15), Ed. Barry L. Issac. Pp. 15–38. Greenwich, CT: JAI Press.

Counihan, Carole. 1997. Bread as World: Food Habits and Social Relations in Modernizing Sardinia. In *Food and Culture: A Reader*, Eds. Carole Counihan and Penny Van Esterik. Pp. 283–295. London and New York: Routledge.

Crankshaw, Edward. 1959. *Khrushchev's Russia*. Baltimore: Penguin Books.

Dadabaev, Timur. 2004. Post-Soviet Realities of Society in Uzbekistan. *Central Asian Survey*, 23(2): 141–166.

Eickelman, Dale F. 1981. *The Middle East: An Anthropological Approach*. Englewood Cliffs, NJ: Prentice-Hall.

Findley, Carter Vaughn. 2005. *The Turks in World History*. New York: Oxford University Press.

Fitzpatrick, Sheila. 1994. *Stalin's Peasants: Resistance and Survival in the Russian Village after Collectivization*. New York/Oxford, UK: Oxford University Press.

Fridman, L. A. 1994. Economic Crisis as a Factor of Building Up of Socio-political and Ethnonational Tensions in the Countries of Central Asia and Transcaucasia. In *Central Asia and Transcaucasia: Ethnicity and Conflict*, Ed. V. V. Naumkin. Pp. 31–69. Westport, CT: Greenwood Press.

Gleason, Gregory. 1992. Marketization and Migration: The Politics of Cotton in Central Asia. *Journal of Soviet Nationalities* 2(1): 66–95.

Golovanov, A. A. 1992. *Krest'ianstvo Uzbekistana: Evolutsiia Sotsial'nogo Polozheniia 1917–1937 gg*. Tashkent: Izdate'stvo FAN Akademii Nauk Respubliki Uzbekistana.

Gramsci, Antonio. 1988. *An Antonio Gramsci Reader: Selected Writings 1916–1935*, Ed. David Forgacs. New York: Schoken Books.

Gupta, Akhil. 1995. Blurred Boundaries: The Discourse of Corruption, the Culture of Politics, and the Imagined State. *American Ethnologist* 22: 375–402.

Habermas, Jurgen. 1985. *The Theory of Communicative Action, Volume 2: Lifeworld and System: A Critique of Functionalist Reason*. Boston: Beacon Press.

Hall, R. H. 1996. *Organisations. Structures, Processes, and Outcomes*. New York: Simon and Schuster.

Haugen, Arne. 2003. *The Establishment of National Republics in Soviet Central Asia*. Basingstroke, UK: Palgrave MacMillan.

Heller, Mikhail, and Alexander M. Nekrich. 1986. *Utopia in Power: The History of the Soviet Union from 1917 to the Present*. New York: Summit Books.

Herzfeld, Michael. 1985. *The Poetics of Manhood: Contest and Identity in a Cretan Mountain Village*. Princeton, NJ: Princeton University Press.

Horsman, Stuart. 2003. Independent Uzbekistan: Ten Years of Gradualism or Stagnation? In *Oil, Transition and Security in Central Asia*, Ed. Sally N. Cummings. Pp. 47–58. London/New York: Routledge Curzon.

Humphrey, Caroline. 1998. *Marx Went Away—But Karl Stayed Behind* (Updated Edition of *Karl Marx Collective: Economy, Society and Religion in a Siberian Collective Farm*). Ann Arbor, MI: University of Michigan Press.

Humphrey, Caroline. 2002. *The Unmaking of Soviet Life: Everyday Economies after Socialism*. Ithaca, NY/London: Cornell University Press.

Humphrey, Caroline. 2004. *Rural Society in the Soviet Union*. Boston: Unwin Hyman.

Ibragimova, A. Iu.1963. Sotsialisticheskoe Pereustroistvo Sel'skogo Khoziastva Uzbekistana. In *Ocherki Istorii Kollektivizatsii Sel'skogo Khoziastvo v Soiuznikh Respublikakh*, Ed. V. P. Danilov. Pp. 224–257. Moskva: Izdatel'stvo Akademii Nauk.

Ibragimova, A. Iu. 1969. *Pobeda Leninskogo Kooperativnogo Plana v Uzbekistane (1929–1933)*. Tashkent: Izdatel'stvo FAN Uzbekskoi SSR.

Ilkhamov, Alisher. 2004. Archaeology of Uzbek Identity. *Central Asian Survey* 23(3–4): 289–326.

Kamp, Marianne. 2006. *The New Woman in Uzbekistan: Islam, Modernity, and Unveiling under Communism*. Seattle/London: University of Washington Press.

Kamp, Marianne, and Russell Zanca. 2007. *Writing the History of Collectivization in Uzbekistan: Oral Narratives*. Working paper for the National Council for Eurasian and East European Research.

Keller, Shoshana. 2007. Story, Time, and Dependent Nationhood in the Uzbek History Curriculum. *Slavic Review* 66(2): 257–277.

Kenez, Peter. 2005. *A History of the Soviet Union from the Beginning to the End* (2nd ed.). Cambridge, UK: Cambridge University Press. (Kenez's remarks on collectivization are also valuable. Also look at his sections on "Really Existing Socialism" and the Soviet collapse.)

Kerblay, Basile. *Modern Soviet Society*. Translated by Rupert Sawyer. New York: Pantheon Books.

Khalid, Adeeb. 2006. Between Empire and Revolution: New Work on Soviet Central Asia. *Kritika: Explorations in Russian and Eurasian History* 7(4): 865–884.

Kleinbach, Russell, Mehrigiul Ablezova, and Medina Aitieva. 2004. Kidnapping for Marriage (*Ala Kachuu*) in a Kyrgyz Village. *Central Asian Survey* 24(2): 191–202.

Kornai, Janos. 1992. *The Socialist System: Political Economy of Communism*. Princeton, NJ: Princeton University Press.

Laird, Roy D., and Ronald A. Francisco. 1980. Observations of Rural Life in Soviet Russia. In *Contemporary Soviet Society: Sociological Perspectives*, Eds. Jerry G. Pankhurst and Michael Paul Sacks. Pp. 140–155. New York: Praeger.

Lane, David. 1971. *The End of Inequality? Stratification under State Socialism*. Middlesex: Penguin Books.

Lenin, Vladmir I. 1978. *On Culture and Cultural Revolution*. Moscow: Progress Publishers.

Lubin, Nancy, and William Feirman. 1994. Uzbeks. In *Encyclopedia of World Cultures, Volume VI: Russia and Eurasia/China*, Eds. Paul Freidrich and Norma Diamond. Pp. 395–399. Boston: G. K. Hall.

Mannheim, Karl. 1985 [1936]. *Ideology and Utopia: An Introduction to the Sociology of Knowledge*. New York: Harcourt Brace Jovanovich.

Martin, Terry. 2001. *The Affirmative Action Empire: Nations and Nationalism in the Soviet Union, 1923–1939*. Ithaca, NY: Cornell University Press.

Megoran, Nick. 2007. On Researching "Ethnic Conflict": Epistemology, Politics, and a Central Asian Boundary Dispute. *Europe–Asia Studies* 59(2): 253–277.

Mintz, Sidney. 1986. *Sweetness and Power: The Place of Sugar in*

Modern History. New York: Penguin Books.

Mirzoyev, Bobur. 2007. Pop Songs as a Formidable Ideological Weapon. http://enews.ferghana.ru/article.php?id=2090&print=1

Montanari, Massimo. 1993. *Food Is Culture*. New York: Columbia University Press.

Northrop, Douglas. 2005. *Veiled Empire: Gender and Power in Stalinist Central Asia*. Ithaca, NY/London: Cornell University Press.

Nove, Alec. 1986[1969]. *An Economic History of the U.S.S.R.* Middlesex: Penguin Books.

Olcott, Martha Brill, and Bakhtiar Babajanov. 2003. The Terrorist Notebooks. *Foreign Policy* March/April: 30–40.

Peletz, Michael. 1988. *A Share of the Harvest: Kinship, Property, and Social History Among the Malays of Rembau*. Berkeley, CA/London: University of California Press.

Pelkmans, Mathijs. 1994. *Defending the Border: Identity, Religion, and Modernity in the Republic of Georgia*. Ithaca, NY/London: Cornell University Press.

Petrova-Averkieva, Yu. 1980. Historicism in Soviet Ethnographic Science. In *Soviet and Western Anthropology*, Ed. Ernest Gellner. Pp. 19–29. New York: Columbia University Press.

Pipes, Richard. 1974. *Russia under the Old Regime*. New York: Charles Scribner's Sons.

Pomfret, Richard. 2006. *The Central Asian Economies Since Independence*. Princeton, NJ/Oxford, UK: Princeton University Press.

Potter, Sulamith Heins, and Jack M. Potter. 1990. *China's Peasants: The Anthropology of a Revolution*. Cambridge, UK: Cambridge University Press.

Razakov, Talant. 1995. *Osh Koogalan (Osh Events): Based on KGB Archives*. Bishkek: Renassans.

Richardson, Tanya. 2005. Walking Streets, Talking History: The Making of Odessa. *Ethnology* 1: 13–34.

Roseberry, William. 1989. *Anthropologies and Histories: Essays in Culture, History and Political Economy*. New Brunswick, NJ: Rutgers University Press.

Roy, Olivier. 1986. *Islam and Resistance in Afghanistan*. Cambridge, UK: Cambridge University Press.

Roy, Olivier. 1999. *The New Central Asia: The Creation of Nations*. New York: New York University Press.

Rumer, Boris. 1989. *Soviet Central Asia: "A Tragic Experiment."* Boston: Unwin Hyman.

Sahadeo, Jeff. 2007. *Russian Colonial Society in Tashkent, 1865–1923*. Bloomington, IN/Indianapolis: Indiana University Press.

Severin, Barbara. 1996. Differences in Food Production and Food Consumption among the Former Republics of the Soviet Union. In *The Fomer Soviet Union in Transition*, Eds. Richard F. Kaufman and John P. Hardt. Pp. 514–540. Armonk, NY: M. E. Sharpe.

Sinyavsky, Andrei. 1990. *Soviet Civilization: A Cultural History*. Translated by Joanne Turnbull. New York: Arcade (Little, Brown).

Slezkine, Yuri. 1994. Arctic Mirrors: Russia and the Small Peoples of the North. Ithaca, NY/London: Cornell University Press.

Sukhareva, O. A., and Bikjanova, M.A. 1955. Proshloe i Nastoiashchee Seleniia Aikyran: Opyt Etnograficheskogo Izucheniia Kolkhoza Imeni Stalina Chartakskogo Raiona Namanganskoi Oblasti. Tashkent: Izdatel'stvo Akademii Nauk Uzbekskoi SSR.

Swain, Nigel. 1985. *Collective Farms Which Work?* Cambridge, UK: Cambridge University Press.

Tashbaeva, T. Kh., and M. D. Savurov. 1989. Novoe i Traditsionnoe v Bytu Sel'skoi Sem'I Uzbekov. Tashkent: Izdatel'stvo FAN Uzbekskoi SSR.

Tavernise, Sabrina. 2008. After '05 Uzbek Uprising Issues Linger for the West. *New York Times*, May 29. http://www.nytimes.com/2008/05/29/world/asia/29uzbek.html

Teilman, H. J. 1991. Innovation as a Social Process: The Making of Ideological "New Combinations." In *The Social Dynamics of Economic Integration: Studies in Economic Anthropology*, Eds. J. P. M. van den Breemer and H. T. van der Pas. Pp. 97–113. Leiden: DSWO Press.

Turner, Jack. 2004. *Spice: the History of a Temptation*. New York: Alfred A. Knopf.

United Nations Human Development Report. 1997. *Country Report: Uzbekistan 1996*. Geneva: UNESCO.

Valiev, A. Kh. 1958. *Polozhenie Osedlogo Dekhkanstva v Ferganskoi Doline v Poslednom Chetverte XIX I Nachalo XX Vekov* [dissertation]. Tashkent.

Van Atta, Don. 1993. *The "Farmer Threat": The Political Economy of Agrarian Reform in Post-Soviet Russia*. Boulder, CO: Westview Press.

Weber, Max. 1968. *Economy and Society: An Outline of Interpretive Sociology* (2 vols.). Berkeley, CA: University of California Press.

Weinthal, Erika. 2002. *State Making and Environmental Cooperation: Linking Domestic and International Politics in Central Asia*. Cambridge, MA/London: MIT Press.

Werner, Cynthia. 2003. The Rise of Non-consensual Bride Kidnapping in Post-Soviet Kazakhstan. In *The Transformation of Central Asia: States and Societies from Soviet Rule to Independence*, Ed. Pauline Jones Luong. Pp. 59–88. Ithaca, NY/London: Cornell University Press.

Williams, W. W. 1996. From Asia's Good Earth: Rice, Society, and Science. *Hemispheres*. December: 80–88.

Wolf, Eric. 1966. *Peasants*. Englewood Cliffs, NJ: Prentice-Hall.

Zanca, Russell. 2005. Dilemmas of Representation: Stalinist Collectivization in Uzbekistan and an Ethnographic Past in the Present. *Journal of the Society for the Anthropology of Europe* 5: 8–14.

Index

Page numbers followed by *f* indicate figures; and those followed by *t* indicate tables.

hokim, 52

homes, 24, 57, 58. *See also* Houses

honor and family, caricaturing
    notions of, 182

honoring agreements or
    commitments, 183

hospitality, price of, 119–121

host-guest relationships, 119

house doors, 25

house/compound layout in Boburkent, 25*f*

households
    extended family, 56*f*
    Kolkhoz family, 24–26

houses, 25

Human Development Reports for Uzbekistan,
    United Nations', 137

humanists, bureaucratic helmsman and
    wealth-distributing, 87

Humphrey, Caroline, 28

identity
    national, 178
    and plantation, 178–184

ideologies, official changing of, 46

independence day, 82–84

Indian movies, 79–85
    independence day, 82–84
    New Year's Day (Navruz), 81–82
    weddings, 84–85

*Instruction on Organizational Measures
    in Ferghana Valley Province*
    (Von Kaufman), 54

intelligentsia, agricultural, 136

irrigation, massive and often wasteful
    use of, 64

irrigation administrators, corruption
    and, 52

jealousy and American scholars, 9

Jews, Bukharan, 2

jobs and professions, villagers had wide range
    of, 17

joking and laughter, cotton fields
    site of, 164

Karimov, Islom, 172

kiosks, 16, 17, 62, 133

Kipchaks, 38, 39

kitchen or hearth area, 26

Kokand Khanate (Kokand Kingdom)
    society and land during, 50–53
    taxation levied on subjects of, 51*t*

kolkhoz (collective farm) as plantation,
    64–89
    cotton in social life, 64–66

entertain us, 79

Indian movies, 79–85

mud collective and talk of better days,
    68–70

poverty, cotton, and path to past, 85–89

price of picking cotton, 70–72

speaking of things better left unsaid, 67–68

talk of transition undermined by
    Communist ethos, 72–77

women as full-time cotton peasants,
    77–79

kolkhoz job, quitting one's, 174

Kolkhoz system remains state fiefdom, 30

kolkhoz town center, commercial
    life of, 15

kolkhoz unity, breakdown of, 150

kolkhoz villages, contemporary Uzbek, 37

kolkhozchi women, 78–79

kolkhozes (collective farms), 1
    administration plays role of feudal
        lord, 164
    agricultural targets for, 169
    family households, 24–26
    Klub, 82*f*
    leadership and co-villagers, 64
    library, 59
    living arrangements and households,
        24–26
    road to, 13–15
    selfish state relationship to, 26–30
    state administration of, 146–151

kolkhozes (collective farms), historical
    connections and today's, 32–63
    contesting history, 58–63
    paradoxes of colonialist observers, 46–49
    pre-Russian imperial Uzbek villages,
        50–53
    Russian imperial approach to landlessness
        and peasantry, 53–55
    savages ignoble and noble yesterday and
        today, 46–49
    social relations and structure past and
        present, 55–58
    society and land during Kokand
        Khanate, 50–53
    Soviet-constructed past reflecting on
        continuity, 40–46

kolkhozes (collective farms), surviving
    on, 127–158
    bazaar as microcosm of post-Soviet life,
        127–130
    caretaker state and thinking on
        self-reliance, 142–143
    doctors becoming peasants, 135–136
    enduring collectivism, 143–146